Temptations
of
Power

TEMPTATIONS
OF
POWER

ISLAMISTS AND ILLIBERAL DEMOCRACY IN A NEW MIDDLE EAST

by

SHADI HAMID

OXFORD
UNIVERSITY PRESS

OXFORD
UNIVERSITY PRESS

Oxford University Press is a department of the University of Oxford.
It furthers the University's objective of excellence in research, scholarship,
and education by publishing worldwide.

Oxford   New York
Auckland   Cape Town   Dar es Salaam   Hong Kong   Karachi
Kuala Lumpur   Madrid   Melbourne   Mexico City   Nairobi
New Delhi   Shanghai   Taipei   Toronto

With offices in
Argentina   Austria   Brazil   Chile   Czech Republic   France   Greece
Guatemala   Hungary   Italy   Japan   Poland   Portugal   Singapore
South Korea   Switzerland   Thailand   Turkey   Ukraine   Vietnam

Oxford is a registered trade mark of Oxford University Press
in the UK and certain other countries.

Published in the United States of America by
Oxford University Press
198 Madison Avenue, New York, NY 10016

Library of Congress Cataloging-in-Publication Data
Hamid, Shadi, 1983–
Temptations of power : Islamists and illiberal democracy in a new Middle East / by Shadi Hamid.
p.   cm.
Summary: "Shadi Hamid draws from years of research to offer an in-depth look at the past, present,
and future of Islamist political parties across the Arab world"— Provided by publisher.
ISBN 978–0–19–931405–8 (hardback)
1. Islam and politics. 2. Islamic fundamentalism. 3. Middle East—Politics and government—21st
century. 4. Democracy—Middle East—History—21st century. 5. Revolutions—Middle
East—History—21st century. I. Title.
BP173.7H3555 2014
324.2'1820956—dc23

2013035230

1   3   5   7   9   8   6   4   2

Printed in the United States of America
on acid-free paper

CONTENTS

———————

ACKNOWLEDGMENTS

IN ONE WAY OR another, this book has been in the making for nearly a decade. I began my field research on Islamist movements in 2004–5 during my time in Jordan as a Fulbright fellow. Since then, countless friends and colleagues have helped me along the way. It is bittersweet to finally conclude such a long and fascinating course of inquiry. Over this period, a lot has happened, including several revolutions.

My parents and brother sometimes had to put up with my reclusive writing-induced behavior, and they did so with love, understanding, and unceasing support. Words cannot do justice, so I won't even try. Throughout the book's long gestation, they sometimes wondered what exactly it was I was doing. Hopefully, now, they will have a better idea.

Writing on a deadline is a difficult thing, especially when you're trying to piece together so many disparate parts. At Brookings, I was fortunate enough to have the constant support and encouragement of Martin Indyk, Tamara Wittes, and Kenneth Pollack. They believed in this project when it was an idea and little else. The Brookings Institution in general, and the Brookings Doha Center in particular, turned out to be an ideal place to think, research, and write (and rewrite). Many thanks are owed to Salman Shaikh, director of the Brookings Doha Center, and deputy director Ibrahim Sharqieh for nurturing such a supportive environment.

Michael O'Hanlon, Andrew Exum, and Steven Brooke generously reviewed the full manuscript and offered extremely helpful comments and suggestions, challenging me to further refine my ideas. Like few others, Steven saw my views evolve over many years, during which we had countless discussions about the Muslim Brotherhood and its evolution.

The people who put up with me the most were probably my research assistants, in particular Courtney Freer and Samuel Plumbly. I am immensely grateful not just for their research support, but also for their friendship and enthusiasm for the project. Sam read draft after draft of chapter after chapter and probably ended up absorbing most of the book's content by osmosis. He was usually the first person to read anything I wrote and his feedback was invaluable every step of the way. I would also like to thank Elizabeth Zumwalt Harmon, whose comments and suggestions greatly improved the initial book proposal and chapter outline, and Meredith Wheeler, who read through many chapter drafts and offered additional research support during the final months of writing. Sam Heller and Andrew Leber were also extremely helpful during the various stages of the writing process.

The earlier chapters draw on my PhD dissertation, most of which I wrote during fellowships at the American Center for Oriental Research in Amman, Jordan (ACOR) and Stanford University's Center on Democracy, Development, and the Rule of Law (CDDRL). At Stanford, I benefited from the insights of Michael McFaul and Larry Diamond as well as the brilliant young scholars Stephane Lacroix and Avital Livni. Whenever I doubted myself on a particular point, my first instinct was to run it by Stephane, whose deep, encyclopedic knowledge of Islamist movements is something to behold. Avital introduced me to the literature on niche parties and was a constant source of good advice.

Many thanks are also owed to Laurence Whitehead and Michael Willis, both of whom supervised my doctoral work at Oxford University and served as sources of guidance and inspiration. I am grateful to the Marshall Scholarship for supporting my course of study at Oxford. It was during my time at Oxford that I began grappling with many of the ideas that would inform this book.

There are so many people in Egypt, Jordan, and Tunisia who were generous with their time and attention that I cannot begin to list them all. Without them, none of this would be possible. Special thanks are owed to Bochra Zaafarani, Zied Mhirsi, and their team at *Tunisia Live* for facilitating contacts and generally helping me navigate post-revolutionary Tunisia.

I would also like to thank the friends, scholars, and teachers who have, in so many different ways, influenced my research and writing, including Stephen McInerney, Monica Marks, Peter Mandaville, Ibrahim El-Houdaiby, Andrew March, Nathan Brown, Emad Shahin, Samer Shehata, Daniel Brumberg, John Voll, Khalil al-Anani, Omar Ashour, Asma Ghribi, Seth Anziska, Marc Grinberg, Michael Signer, James Piscatori, Thomas Carothers, and Eugene Rogan.

Portions of Chapter 5 draw on materials previously published as "Arab Islamist Parties: Losing on Purpose?" *Journal of Democracy* 22 (January 2011): pp. 68–80.

My editor at Oxford University Press, David McBride, was incredibly patient and supportive every step of the way. Thanks are also due to Sarah Rosenthal, who helped move the book through production. They, and so many others, helped make it a painless process.

1

Islamists in Transition

EGYPT'S MUSLIM BROTHERHOOD WAS the Middle East's oldest, most influential Islamist movement. Yet its headquarters were in a nondescript apartment building, taking up two floors by the Nile in the district of Manial al-Rhoda. When I first began interviewing Brotherhood officials in the summer of 2005, their offices were modest and dingy, befitting an opposition group with a long history—almost eight decades—of near-constant repression.

In the years that followed, I continued to meet the Brotherhood's leaders at their headquarters. They eventually renovated the two floors, a sign perhaps of their growing importance. In late 2005, the group, despite widespread fraud, won an unprecedented 88 seats in parliament, a five-fold increase from their previous share. For both better and worse, they were now the leaders of Egypt's opposition. And they had a national platform in the glare of an increasingly angry, frustrated public that was turning against President Hosni Mubarak and his ruling National Democratic Party. The Brotherhood's parliamentarians enjoyed the trappings of district offices all across Egypt, in cities, towns, and far-flung villages. When I visited some of those offices, I was struck by how removed they seemed from Egypt's otherwise depressing realities. I would walk inside and see things one usually doesn't associate with stifling autocracies. There were volunteers, bustling in and out as if on a mission. There were campaign posters, and other signs of political life.

One day in July 2006, I went to the office of Hazem Farouq, a relatively young and jovial Brotherhood figure. A first-time member of parliament, he approached his job with the gusto of the newly converted. He had what seemed like a permanent smile. I followed him outside his office to a nearby mosque in Shubra al-Kheima. He prayed side by side with his constituents and then welcomed about two dozen of them afterward for an impromptu discussion. He seemed to be enjoying it, and they did too: they were not used to politicians actually talking to them. But that was then.

On May 8, 2010, I met with Mohamed Morsi for the first time, when relatively few Egyptians had even heard of him. By then, the promise of parliamentary opposition had given way to some of the worst anti-Islamist repression since the so-called *mihna* (ordeal) of the 1960s. Just after the new parliament was seated in early 2006, the arrests began. Over the course of the next year, more than one thousand Brotherhood members were detained, including 30 of the group's top financiers, among them a man named Khairat al-Shater. The crackdown came to a head in March 2007, when 34 constitutional amendments were passed. Amnesty International assailed the amendments, which were meant to permanently enshrine the ruling party's hold on power, calling them the "greatest erosion of human rights in 26 years."[1]

That was the context. But Mohamed Morsi didn't sound defeated, at least not yet. Like other Brotherhood leaders, he had reconciled himself to the grim reality and lowered his ambitions accordingly. In our conversation, he even objected to using the word "opposition" to describe the Brotherhood. "The word 'opposition' has the connotation of seeking power," Morsi told me. "But, at this moment, we are not seeking power because [that] requires preparation, and society is not prepared."[2] The Brotherhood, being a religious movement more than a political party, had the benefit of a long time horizon. They could wait.

I was back in Egypt in November 2010 to observe the parliamentary elections, arguably the most fraudulent in the country's history. I went from polling station to polling station, talking to Brotherhood activists. The election was being stolen in broad daylight. Brotherhood "whips" ran me through the violations, one by one. But they weren't angry. They were surprisingly calm. Egypt's Islamists would live to fight another day.

Little did they know that the day would come in less than two months, when Egypt's uprising broke out on January 25, 2011. Eighteen days later, Mubarak had fallen. On March 4, the revolution's first prime minister, Essam Sharaf, addressed a raucous crowd in Tahrir Square. Standing by his side was senior Brotherhood figure Mohamed al-Beltagy. Less than two years after that, the Brotherhood had won the presidency and, with President Mohamed Morsi's ouster of top military officials in August 2012, handed a major blow to the old regime. It was a remarkable reversal of fortune for the Brotherhood, but one that brought with it a new set of threats and challenges. In Tahrir Square, when Morsi's victory was announced, the crowds erupted into a loud, continuous roar. They may not have particularly cared for Morsi himself, but they believed in what he seemed to stand for—the Islamic "project," a revolution against the old order, or whatever else it might be. Or perhaps they just felt sheer relief that his opponent, Ahmed Shafiq, Mubarak's last prime minister, had been defeated by the thinnest of margins.

No one could have guessed in November 2010 that Morsi would soon become president. And few would have guessed, when he became president, that the Brotherhood would just as quickly suffer a terrible defeat, on July 3, 2013, at the hands of a motley crew of youth activists, liberals, old regime elements, and, of course, the military. As devastating as the military coup and the subsequent crackdown were, there was also, at least initially, a sense of relief. They had returned to a purer, more natural state: the state of opposition, something they had grown used to over the course of more than 80 difficult years. Tens of thousands of Brotherhood members and supporters gathered by Cairo's Rabaa Adawiya mosque in a massive sit-in to protest the coup and call for Morsi's reinstatement. More than a protest, it was an alternative city with kitchens, pharmacies, food stalls, sleeping quarters, and, of course, a "media center." The military-appointed government said it would disperse the sit-in by force if necessary. There had already been two massacres—with over 140 killed. Yet when I entered the sit-in for the first time and met the Brotherhood's Essam al-Erian, he was wearing a T-shirt and sweatpants. Despite the specter of bloodshed, he looked more calm and comfortable than I ever remembered seeing him. Another senior Brotherhood official, Gehad al-Haddad—who had given up a successful business career in England to return to Egypt—told me he was "very much at peace."[3] They were ready to die, they said.

Their newfound clarity, however, could not obscure a simple fact, and one that became clearer with time. In those heady months of 2011 and 2012, the prospect of power was all too tempting. And it was a temptation that Brotherhood leaders proved unable to resist, despite insisting that they knew better.

This book focuses on the two distinct phases in the Islamist narrative—one defined by the experience of repression and the other by the democratic openings made possible by the Arab revolutions. The care and caution that had characterized Islamist groups for decades was pushed to the side in the wake of the uprisings of 2011. There was little time for preparation. With striking speed, they widened their ambitions. There was a time when Islamists used to lose elections on purpose.[4] Now they seemed intent on making the most of a moment they feared would pass them by. In power, in both Egypt and Tunisia, they struggled to reconcile vague, overarching ideas with the more mundane demands of everyday politics and governance.

Is there a discernible logic to the seemingly sudden shifts in Islamist behavior? As we will see, state repression, through either its presence or relative absence, is critical to understanding the evolution of Islamist groups both before and after the Arab Spring. In addressing the two phases of Islamist evolution—first in opposition and then in the halls of power—I look at how Islamists' experiences under autocracy shaped their behavior, instilling in them an almost obsessive commitment to gradualism.

Throughout much of the academic literature—as well as in media coverage, popular writing, and, more recently, policymaking circles—there has been an almost built-in assumption that good things go together, that more democracy makes for more "moderate" Islamists. Similarly, when political opportunities close, the risk of Islamist radicalization increases.

These assumptions, while intuitive, largely miss the mark. One of the main arguments I make in this book is that repression can "force" the moderation of Islamist parties—and often did, particularly during the 1990s and 2000s. Under repression, Islamists put aside and postponed their dream of an "Islamic state," which they had little use for when their fundamental liberties were being denied. In such a context, Islamists democratized their internal organizational structures, opened new channels of cooperation with secular parties, and moderated their policies—on sharia law, democracy, political pluralism, and minority and women's rights—in the hope of forestalling repression or at least mitigating its negative effects.

As we will see, moderation, at times, represents a very conscious choice on the part of the groups in question. Other times, it is the natural endpoint of an uneven, sometimes counterintuitive process of political learning. This was most striking in the case of the Wasat ("center") party, which broke off from the Brotherhood in 1996. Its application for legal status was denied, not just once but several times. With each setback, Wasat chose to respond by further distancing itself from its Islamist origins and highlighting its democratic *bona fides*. In the face of repression, the party became even more moderate than it already was. Put differently, trying to not get thrown in prison has a way of concentrating the mind and clarifying your priorities.

While embracing the democratic process may not seem like a particularly groundbreaking shift, for mainstream Islamist groups it was. There is no particular reason why Islamic government should be democratic, and for much of the 20th century, most works of Islamic political theory had little use for free elections or political pluralism. In 1969's *Preachers Not Judges*, one of the key works expounding on the Brotherhood's understanding of the Islamic state, General Guide[5] Hassan al-Houdaiby stays well within the bounds of orthodoxy. Drawing heavily on the writing of medieval scholars, he calls for the revival of the caliphate. As Houdaiby sees it, the job of the executive is simply to implement the preexisting corpus of Islamic law. The leader, the *imam al-haqq*, rather than being elected through an open vote, must meet prerequisites of Islamic education and fitness of character. As Barbara Zollner notes, "[Houdaiby] does not even consider the possibility of an Islamic state without the leadership of the imam al-haqq."[6] What Islamists, in time, would become reflects a striking departure from Houdaiby's thinking.

While repression circumscribes Islamist ambition and compels a degree of moderation, the advent of democracy has its own profound impact. The opening of democratic space fundamentally alters the political landscape of countries in transition, creating conducive conditions for the "Islamization" of public discourse. With the introduction of an empowered and socially conservative electorate, the calculations of politicians change in important ways. In the past, leaders were largely insulated from the wrath of voters. But, as societies open up, politicians seeking reelection, whether Islamist or secular, must pay heed to popular sentiment. For liberals, it requires sometimes embracing illiberal ways of speaking about religion and its place in public life, particularly when campaigning in rural parts of the country. For Islamist groups, there is considerable pressure from their own rank-and-file to stay faithful to the cause. Given high levels of political fragmentation and polarization during transitions, they cannot afford to alienate their most committed supporters. Beyond the "base," many Egyptians and Tunisians vote for Islamists precisely because of their Islamism, hoping to see them enact conservative social legislation or use the state to promote a particular conception of religion.

In understanding Islamist behavior, the very fact of repression is critical. Any organization accustomed to authoritarianism is bound to face uncertainty and confusion when that same authoritarianism is, with little notice, removed. This is particularly the case with Islamist groups, which became conditioned to repression over the course of decades. If, as discussed above, repression was pushing Islamists along a more moderate path, then democratization would compel them to ask the questions they had long kept submerged. For the first time in decades, Islamist parties in post-revolution Egypt and Tunisia had to contend with the fundamental matters of state and government. They had survived. They had gained power. Now the question dogging them for years remained: what did they hope to do with that power? Islamists were Islamists for a reason. They weren't liberals in disguise. If there was a demand for Islamism—and, in countries as varied as Egypt and Tunisia, there most certainly was—then someone would need to supply it. This is where the comparisons with socialists and Christian Democrats, who eventually gave up their greater ideological ambitions, tend to fall short. Islamist parties were not necessarily going to follow the same path.

In his controversial 1989 essay, "The End of History," Francis Fukuyama had perhaps gotten ahead of himself, proclaiming the triumph of liberal democracy over other ideologies. In another sense, however, Fukuyama was quite prescient. In the essay's final paragraph, he wistfully writes that "the end of history will be a very sad time. The struggle for recognition, the willingness to risk one's life for a purely abstract goal, the worldwide ideological struggle that called forth daring, courage, imagination, and idealism, will be replaced by economic calculation, the endless solving of technical problems, environmental concerns, and the satisfaction of sophisticated consumer demands." This was what the future held in a world where the only real battles left were those fought within the strict confines of liberal democracy. But he went on: "I have the most ambivalent feelings for the civilization that has been created in Europe since 1945 . . . Perhaps this very prospect of centuries of boredom at the end of history will serve to get history started once again."[7]

Just as Fukuyama's declarations were premature in 1989, to say that history is beginning again would be similarly misguided. But something new is, in fact, happening. The rise of Islamists—in Tunisia, Libya, Syria, and, until 2013, Egypt—reintroduced a difficult debate about what "we" and "they" hold dear. What if enough Arabs, working through the democratic process, decide that they would rather not accept gender equality, international human rights norms, or the kinds of civil liberties that the citizens of Western democracies take for granted? Unlike other illiberal democracies, in say Hugo Chávez's Venezuela or Viktor Orbán's Hungary, Islamist illiberalism would not primarily be a function of the struggle for power and the universal desire to exert hegemony over one's opponents. Their illiberalism would be deeply felt, the product of a different worldview and a different, if somewhat submerged, political tradition.

As we will find, Islamist groups, in all their diversity and internal contradictions, have struggled to define what it is exactly that they want. They have no models to emulate (mainstream Islamists do not consider Saudi Arabia, Afghanistan, Sudan, or Iran to be anything close to models). With only a few exceptions, they had little experience in government. They had spent several decades in opposition, repressed and excluded to various degrees, all with a single-minded focus on survival. That didn't leave much time for thinking about the nature of the nation-state or working out an intellectual framework for governance. When they did have time—for example when Tunisia's Rachid Ghannouchi was living in exile in London—they tried to reconcile Islamism and democracy with mixed results. Ghannouchi, the longtime leader of the Ennahda party, was a moderate's moderate, but even his intellectual framework diverged significantly from the liberal democratic tradition, as imagined and practiced in the West. He probably never thought he would have an opportunity to put his ideas into practice. But his chance finally came, after spending more than two decades in exile, wondering if he would ever set foot in his country again.

The Politicization of Political Islam

Few topics have attracted more attention and interest than the role of Islamist movements after the Arab uprisings. Hundreds of conferences have been convened and thousands of lectures given, with the goal of making sense of a complex phenomenon. In an era of media wars and polarized politics, Arab political discourse has taken on an existential, combative tone, with the microscope on each and every move Islamist groups make (or don't make). In Western discourse, the focus is understandably on what Islamists are doing now, more so than how their actions and decisions fit within a broader narrative. This book takes a conscious step back, away from the day-to-day controversies that, while interesting in their own right, tell us little about the long-term trends in Islamist and Arab politics.

This book tries to understand why Islamists make certain tactical and strategic choices rather than others, and how they perceive their own actions. This latter point is important. I take seriously the notion that to truly understand Islamist movements, you have to do something very simple: talk to them, get to know them, and try, in the process, to understand their fears and aspirations. These are, after all, not just "rational actors" or mere "ideologues," depending on your perspective; they are real people who are shaped by their experiences and those of the movements to which they have pledged allegiance.

I focus my attention on *mainstream* Islamist movements, most of which are descendants or affiliates of the Egyptian Muslim Brotherhood. In contrast to militant and radical Islamist groups which, with a small ideologically committed vanguard, aim to surgically seize the state, these mass movements were, at least until the Arab uprisings of

2011, more interested in winning hearts and minds than in winning political office.

The Muslim Brotherhood, founded in 1928 by a schoolteacher named Hassan al-Banna, was originally concerned with preaching, education, and recruiting new members in a hostile environment. According to its bylaws, the Brotherhood aimed "to raise a generation of Muslims who would understand Islam correctly and act according to its teachings." Until 1934, the bylaws forbade direct political action.[8] Yet over time— more than eight decades to be exact—Islamists came to terms with not just politics but parliaments, and then not just parliaments but power. In parallel, a small but vocal minority of Islamists, such as former Brotherhood leader Abdel Moneim Abul Futouh, would pledge allegiance to Banna's core aims of religious education, or *da'wa*, lamenting the politicization of political Islam. Some would become "post-Islamists," as in Turkey—effectively giving up the dream of an Islamic state—while others tried to redefine what that Islamic state might look like, bringing it into sync with modern notions of pluralism and human rights.

In their early, formative decades, Islamist groups put little focus on democracy and political reform. They were, first and foremost, religious movements. Politics only mattered insofar as it served explicitly religious ends. Groups like the Brotherhood had little to gain from democracy during the 1950s and 1960s, when they remained niche parties with small, albeit dedicated followings. In Jordan's last free and fair elections in 1956 before the imposition of martial law, the Jordanian Brotherhood won only four seats out of 40. At a time when secular nationalism was gathering strength across the region, a coalition of leftist groups rode to victory, with a socialist, Sulayman al-Nabulsi, taking the position of prime minister. But, after just a year in government, King Hussein forced Nabulsi's resignation, arresting his supporters and banning all political party activity. The Brotherhood responded by organizing mass rallies in support of the monarchy.[9] Parliament was of little concern to Jordan's Islamists, especially since they had so few seats. The Brotherhood was well aware that it stood to benefit from a party ban and that, as a charitable organization, it would be exempt. In return for its allegiance to the Crown, the Brotherhood was permitted to continue its social and educational activities. The leftists, meanwhile, were shut out of the political arena.

With the Islamic revival of the 1970s and small but significant democratic openings in the 1980s, the political context across the region changed dramatically. Arabs were becoming more religious and more interested in the implementation of sharia, or Islamic law. Political parties, in turn, needed to adapt and respond to the preferences of an increasingly conservative electorate. This put Islamist groups in a strong position. Sensing an opportunity to attract new recruits and gain greater prominence, Islamists either entered the parliamentary fray for the first time, as in Egypt, Tunisia, and Morocco, or made parliamentary participation their top priority, as in Jordan.

For groups with a longstanding suspicion of multipartyism (or the more pejorative *hizbiyya* in Arabic), the leap into electoral politics was fraught with controversy. When the Brotherhood in Egypt formed an electoral alliance with the liberal Wafd party in 1984, the group's leadership struggled to offer a coherent justification. They made the case that working through political parties had nothing to do with any purported belief in the *idea* of political parties. "The Brotherhood have made clear more than once," Brotherhood leader Umar al-Tilmisani explained at the time, "that it is not a party . . . It is an organization that calls for accepting God's law in all facets of life."[10] For decades, democracy was seen as a foreign import. Central to democracy was the notion that legitimacy came from the people, rather than God. The "people" were especially dangerous, particularly since they were more likely to vote for socialists than Islamists. The will of the majority would easily come into conflict with that of God's.

Yet, as society "Islamized," Islamist groups grew more confident that democracy would help them realize their ultimate goals. What was first a tactical concession became, in time, something deeper. In the subsequent years, Islamist groups committed themselves to many of the foundational aspects of democratic life. They contested elections with unprecedented fervor. Where they had once shunned the word "democracy," they now peppered their statements with it. Islamists came to believe not just in the power of democracy but in the power of politics. In the process, they went from being niche parties—with a narrow focus on public morality and applying sharia—to truly national parties with wide-ranging, ambitious agendas.

Partly due to these changes, Islamist parties were often characterized as obsessed with power. Rarely did observers dwell on an intriguing possibility—that Islamist parties weren't particularly interested in winning elections in the first place. A careful consideration of their pre-Arab Spring electoral strategy suggests an ambivalence and even aversion to power. It is not a stretch to say that Islamists lost elections on purpose. With surprising frequency, they did (and, in some countries, still do).

Across the region, Islamist movements became known for their caution and slow deliberation. Notwithstanding their increasing calls for democratic change, they feared outright confrontation with powerful regimes, avoiding it at all costs. This was, in part, a legacy of Algeria and what Islamists call the "American veto"—the conviction that the United States and other Western powers simply would not allow them to win. In January 1992, Algeria's largest Islamist party—the Islamic Salvation Front (FIS)—found itself on the brink of an historic victory. In the first round of elections, FIS won 47.5 percent of the vote and 188 of 231 seats, while the ruling party won a dismal 15. However, there were mounting fears that the military was preparing to move against them. In the tense days that followed, FIS leader Abdelkader Hachani addressed a crowd of supporters. "Victory is more dangerous than defeat," he warned, urging them to exercise restraint to avoid giving the army a pretext for intervention.[11] But it was too late: the military aborted the elections and launched a massive crackdown that plunged Algeria into a bloody civil war which would claim more than one hundred thousand lives.[12]

Islamist movements came to realize that winning before the time was right could threaten to undo decades of painstaking grassroots work and organization building. Hachani's warning would soon evolve into a sort of unofficial Islamist motto: "Participation not domination" (*al-musharika wa laisa al-mughaliba*). If there was any doubt about such an emphatic embrace of gradualism—to the point of even timidity— the Algerian narrative was reinforced, this time in vastly different circumstances, by the intense international opposition that Hamas encountered after its surprise electoral victory in 2006.

To understand the Islamist ambivalence to power, a closer look at the nature of these groups is needed. These are not traditional Western-style political parties. Most political parties, after all, do not double as states-within-states, with parallel networks of mosques, clinics, banks, businesses, day care centers, and even Boy Scout troops. Islamist parties do. They must therefore tread carefully to avoid provoking regimes, as the costs of a crackdown on their social, educational, and preaching activities—effectively the Islamist lifeline—can be severe. The effects of state repression on Islamist groups, then, are critical to understanding why Islamist groups do what they do. Analysts may have assumed Islamists would always display such calm and caution. What they likely missed is that such caution was a result of, and a reaction to, repression. Once the repression ceased, Islamists could just as easily show a knack for political power, sometimes bordering on the cutthroat. Was the party the end or the means? The line could become blurry, particularly when the party felt its very existence threatened.

This was precisely what some Islamist figures like Abdel Moneim Abul Futouh feared most. "Putting religion and political authority within one hand is very dangerous. That's what happened in Iran," he told me just months before Mubarak was ousted. "Historically, famous preachers were not part of the power structure."[13] The precise relationship between religion and politics—even for groups that claimed that they were one and the same—would prove one of most enduring and thorny challenges facing Islamist movements.

As early as the 1980s, religious movements began exploring the possibility of establishing political parties. The Islamic Action Front (IAF) was one of the first to be legalized thanks to Jordan's political opening of 1989. The IAF, although initially meant to be a broad front for Islamists of various stripes, failed to assert its independence from the Jordanian Muslim Brotherhood. While technically separate, party and movement in Jordan became difficult to distinguish. They were, in effect, two arms of the same body.

After the 2011 revolutions, Egyptian and Tunisian Islamists followed suit. In Tunisia, the Ennahda movement and the Ennahda party were effectively the same organization. At Ennahda headquarters, the sign at the entrance seemed almost designed to cause confusion over the matter. "The Party of the Ennahda Movement," it read. As one Ennahda member put it to me, "the party is the movement and movement is the party."[14] In the party's ninth national congress, which took place in July 2012, members and officials, recognizing the contentious nature of the matter, decided to postpone the discussion until after the transition period. In Egypt, there was less debate: the Brotherhood's leadership forbade its members from joining any other party but its own, the Freedom and Justice Party.

For Islamist movements that had, for decades, sought to maintain some degree of political "purity," these were fateful decisions. It was one thing to have a say in national politics; it was quite another to tie a broad-based religious movement to a particular partisan vehicle. Some were more attuned to the dangers than others. Umar al-Tilmisani, fearing party politics would corrupt the Brotherhood's original purpose, prevented the organization from contesting elections for the entirety of the 1970s. Ironically, it was under his tenure as general guide that the group ran in parliamentary elections for the first time in 1984.

The story repeats itself. The "other" Islamists—ultraconservative Salafis—are struggling with the same questions that long plagued their more moderate counterparts. Salafis, being textual literalists, have less room for maneuver. For them, the very decision to participate in elections is steeped in controversy. After all, God—not parliament and not the people—is the sole lawgiver. But this "purity," to the extent that it lasts, is why Salafi groups were able to gain ground in Egypt and, to varying degrees, in Tunisia, Libya, and Syria. Where mainstream movements like the Brotherhood made compromise after compromise, diluting the Islamic components of their message in the process, Salafis claimed to be the true purveyors of God's word and, just as importantly, God's law. Sharia wasn't just a vague catchphrase; they really believed that the strict application of Islamic law was the only legitimate way to order society. But it was just a matter of time before the demands of politics—and the temptations of power that come along with it—plunged Egypt's Salafis into disarray.

Compromising on core ideals—and deciding what those are in the first place—is a fraught process for any party, but more so for self-proclaimed puritans. The gap between the ideal they aspire to and the messy nature of real, everyday politics grows larger the closer they are to power. The tensions between the country's largest Salafi movement, the Salafi Call, and its political party, al-Nour ("the light"), came to a head in late 2012, when the latter experienced its first major split. A number of prominent officials, including the party's president, resigned in protest over the party's lack of independence. In their view, the preachers

and clerics of the Salafi Call—men of religion rather than politics—
were inappropriately meddling and micromanaging the party's affairs.

For all Islamist groups, no matter how liberal or conservative, the
fundamental problem is that they are neither movements nor parties
but a confusing mixture of both. Even with what seemed like a single-
minded devotion to electoral politics over the course of the 2000s and
early 2010s, it would be a mistake to view organizations like the Muslim
Brotherhood as parties in the traditional mold. Elections are just one
facet—albeit the one most visible to outside observers—of what they
do. Millions depend on their vast social infrastructure for anything
from access to jobs and affordable health care to small grants for opening up businesses and even financial support to get married.

There is also the preaching, or *da'wa*, wing of the organization, which
in many ways is the foundation upon which everything else is built. The
Brotherhood and its affiliates across the region seek to strengthen the
religious character of their members through an extensive educational
process with a structured curriculum. As one Brotherhood official put
it to me, many join the group so they can "get into heaven." That same
official, discussing his own reasons for joining the group, explained:
"I was far from religion and this was unsettling. Islamists resolved it for
me."[15] Unlike in traditional parties, becoming a brother is a choice that
brings with it a series of obligations, expectations, and strict standards
of moral conduct. Each member is part of an *usra*, or "family," that
meets on a weekly basis to read Islamic texts and discuss religious and
political topics.

Whether stated or unstated, the goal of Islamist groups is the "Islamization" of society, and that's a task that goes well beyond the political
realm. As Adnan Hassouneh, who was responsible for education policy
in Jordan's IAF, explains it, "the final goal is the return of the Islamic
way of living in society. This is accomplished through the gradual Islamization of laws, in politics, economics, and society."[16] Power, then, is
not just an end in and of itself but also a means to something greater—
and, incidentally, harder to measure.

In any Islamist movement, the relationship between religion and politics is far from clear-cut and flows in both directions. Even those members who have little explicit interest in politics end up playing a political
role, because that is what the organization requires. If the Brotherhood's

leadership tells members to gather signatures for a reform petition or to vote for a specific candidate, then they will. As a result, political and religious decisions are blurred beyond distinction. As one former Brotherhood member remarks, "members take part in protests because they are asked to; they go there as a religious obligation. They don't understand why they are there politically."[17]

In practice, an Islamist group's political concerns must compete with its educational and religious activities. A traditional political party acts in the party's interest. However, a social movement acts in the *movement's* interests. However, the temptations of power—a recurring theme of this book—threaten to distort Islamist priorities and undermine the delicate balance between preaching and partisan politics that has persisted for decades.

Islamists could not claim ignorance. They had grown accustomed to the limits and seemingly internalized them. "The regimes won't let us take power," Hamdi Hassan, head of the Brotherhood's parliamentary bloc, told me during that doomed 2010 election campaign. What was the solution then, I asked him. "The solution is in the 'Brotherhood approach.' We focus on the individual, then the family, then society." "In the lifespan of mankind," he reasoned, "80 years isn't long; it's like eight seconds."[18] Politics was important but it wasn't necessarily vital. After all, the movement had survived and even prospered for long stretches without any presence in parliament.

As a social movement, the Brotherhood's goal was nothing less than the revival of Islam and Islamic civilization in an age of secularization. This notion, at least in its initially vague formulations, had widespread appeal. But the more the Brotherhood got involved in politics, as it did in the 1980s and 1990s, the more it came under pressure to clarify its positions, some of which were unlikely to satisfy all of its members. The process of politics threatened to take a mass movement and make it into something more narrow and limiting. There was a time when an ordinary Egyptian could join the Brotherhood and leave it at that. The political side was there, but it was secondary. Politics, after all, was just a means to a greater end. But, in power, the opposite could just as easily be true: a broad-based religious movement was being used to support and serve divisive government policies, most of which had nothing to do with religion.

Islamists were ambivalent about power for many reasons, and this was one of them. It was Rachid Ghannouchi who issued perhaps the most prescient warning: "The most dangerous thing for the Islamists is to be loved by the people before they get to power and then hated afterward."[19] The stakes were considerable. If Ennahda was voted out of office in disgrace, it wouldn't just mean a failure for Ennahda but a failure for the broader Islamic project, or perhaps even Islam itself. Other times, as in Egypt in 2013, there wouldn't even be a vote. Islamists would be removed by force, bringing back eerie echoes of the Algerian tragedy and a long list of past confrontations with regimes, militaries, and a hostile regional order.

Why Islamists Matter

Whenever Islamists rise to prominence, there are those who argue that their popular support is an illusion and that their demise is just around the corner. Once, the thinking goes, Islamist parties saddle themselves with the difficult and thankless task of governing, they will run into one failure after another. As the leader of Tunisia's first Salafi political party, Mohamed Khouja, told me, "it's well known that the first government after a revolution is bound to fail."[20] Why, he wondered, was Ennahda so intent on assuming power so quickly? The same could be said for Mohamed Morsi and the Brotherhood, who did, in fact, fail, much as Khouja would have predicted.

But premature obituaries of political Islam, a running feature of commentary for decades, usually turn out to be just that—premature. In 1963, Manfred Halpern concluded that "there will still be battles, but this particular war [between secular nationalism and political Islam] is over in the greater majority of Middle Eastern states."[21] Even Richard Mitchell, author of the classic work on the Muslim Brotherhood, wrote as if he were trying to make sense of a past relic. That was 1969. In the heyday of modernization theory and with a seemingly unlimited faith in secularization, it seemed as if the Brotherhood would never again achieve dominance. As Mitchell wrote, "the essentially secular reform nationalism now in vogue in the Arab world will continue to operate to end the earlier appeal of [the Muslim Brotherhood]."[22] After Mohamed Morsi was deposed more than four decades later, many opponents of political Islam held out hope that his defeat wasn't that of a man or an organization but of a worldview and a way of thinking.[23] But, just as before, they were likely to be disappointed.

Of course, Islamist parties will not always win elections. Even when they do, it remains an open question to what extent militaries (as in Egypt) and monarchies (as in Morocco) will allow them to govern. Other times, Islamists will find themselves in the ranks of opposition. They will shed their "purity" and perhaps their coherence. But they will remain a strong current in their societies and one of the most important.[24] In some contexts, the most spirited competition will not be between Islamists and liberals, but between some Islamists and other Islamists, with each group hoping to "outbid" the other on faithfulness to the cause.

One thing to look at is the distribution of voters. For example, if Egyptians are religiously conservative—and nearly every poll suggests that they are—then Islamist parties, whatever their moderate inclinations, may feel compelled to adopt a more conservative discourse. In one survey after another, large majorities say they want Islamic law to be the principal or even the *only* source of legislation[25] and favor the application of the *hadd* punishments, which include cutting off the hands of thieves, stoning for adultery, and the death penalty for leaving Islam.[26] According to a 2011 survey, an overwhelming majority of Egyptian Muslims either mostly or completely agree that a "wife must always obey her husband," while 94 percent say religious judges "should have the power to decide family law and property disputes."[27]

The pervasiveness of religion and rhetorical support for sharia produces a skewed playing field, with Islamists enjoying a built-in advantage in electoral contests. In the series of elections that took place in 2011 and 2012, non-Islamist parties in Egypt found themselves under pressure to use the language of religion, to the extent that some liberal parties refused to identify as such. As Mustafa al-Naggar, founder of the Justice party, explained it to me, "we help people understand liberalism through behavior and example, through an understanding of citizenship."[28] At the same time, he said, "none of us are using the word 'liberalism' because for the Egyptian street 'liberalism' equals disbelief."

It is somewhat ironic that, in countries plagued by economic crisis, the one thing that dominates public discourse is the role of religion in politics, something that has relatively little day-to-day impact on the lives of ordinary people. In Egypt and Tunisia, the first post-revolution elections were defined by identity-based rather than issue-oriented campaigns. These narratives were driven by elites on both sides, with each turning to an echo-chamber of parallel media outlets, preachers, and politicians. Of course, candidates routinely promised more jobs, better wages, and poverty-reduction initiatives. Yet, it was hard to pinpoint significant differences among the circulating economic programs, which, with few exceptions, offered variations on the same theme: market-driven growth coupled with protections for the poor and social justice for all.

Arguing for boosting employment and combating poverty was no way to run an effective campaign. Parties needed to distinguish themselves from each other. Religion and identity offered clear narratives. If deployed effectively, they could mobilize otherwise skeptical voters. These were issues that were raw, personal, and deeply felt: the desire to promote an "Islamic" way of life, on one hand, and the fear that it might fundamentally alter, or even tear, the country's social fabric, on the other.

As one liberal candidate in Egypt's 2011 parliamentary elections put it: "I didn't run a political campaign; I was running a campaign that depended on me telling voters I wasn't an atheist."[29] Shadi Taha, a member of the liberal Ghad party who ran under the Brotherhood's electoral list, described the scene at a Muslim Brotherhood rally. "When the ones before me spoke, their entire message was about religion or how they're religious men. So I thought maybe they would need another voice, something else. This is a political rally, you know," he said. "So I picked up the mike and started talking about politics. I didn't get a single cheer. Nothing . . . It's like doing stand-up comedy and nobody's laughing."[30] If religious rhetoric wins votes, then how do you avoid it?

Mainstream Islamist groups had long had a monopoly on the support of the Islamist faithful. With the emergence of Salafi parties, however, this was no longer the case. If groups like the Brotherhood or Ennahda failed to reassure conservative voters of their Islamic credentials, then those voters would have a number of other options (including, of course, the option of just staying home). This "tea-party effect" influences not just the daily grind of politics but the general tenor of political discourse.

For example, during the charged negotiations in 2012 over a new Egyptian constitution, the most consequential debates on Article 2—which states that the principles of sharia are the primary source of legislation—were between the Brotherhood and Salafis. None of the major liberal parties proposed any significant changes to Article 2 and, in fact, went out of their way to affirm that they supported its inclusion.

It was the Salafis who threatened to withdraw from the constituent assembly if the word "principles"—which they felt was vague and effectively meaningless—wasn't changed to "rulings." Since this was a nonstarter for liberals, the Brotherhood sought a compromise by incorporating Article 219, which further defined the principles of sharia as "including holistic evidence, foundational rules, rules of jurisprudence, and credible sources accepted in Sunni doctrines and by the larger community."[31] What was meant to be an internal Islamist compromise became a lightning rod for liberals who feared the article provided a dangerous opening to Salafis to impose their interpretation of Islamic law. Ultimately, in a democratizing Egypt, no one could really afford to oppose enshrining sharia in the constitution; the question was how much of it to enshrine.

The Problem of Islamization

After the 2011 uprisings, a debate raged among Egyptians and Tunisians over the very nature of their societies. How much of the ongoing "Islamization" was imposed and manufactured, and how much of it was an "authentic" representation of society? Without the stifling yoke of dictatorship, some reasoned, Arabs would finally be able to express their true sentiments without fear of persecution. In "secular" Tunisia, the changes were striking. More and more women donned the headscarf (and even the *niqab*, or face veil) and, for the first time, Salafis—with their full, distinctive beards—became a regular sight in the streets of Tunis. In my conversations with Ennahda leaders, they would recall the early days of their struggle in the 1970s, when the most basic acts of religiosity were turned into statements of radical intent. Relatively few Tunisians prayed. The mosques were empty, seemingly relics of a bygone era. The outward observance of Islam became, in effect, a political act and moreover, an act of defiance.

Islamists felt like strangers in their own country, alienated by what they saw as a foreign culture with its various imported habits. But the French colonial influence, regardless of its foreign origins, made a lasting imprint on Tunisian culture. Even in Egypt, where few doubt the pervasiveness of religion, one would often hear claims that while Egyptians may be religious, they are, by their very nature, flexible, open-minded, and nondogmatic, and that Islamism, in its efforts to define and limit acceptable religious practice, is anathema to them.

It came as a surprise to many Egyptians when a coalition of Salafi parties, seemingly out of nowhere, managed to win 28 percent of the vote in the country's first post-Mubarak parliamentary elections. This was not the Egypt they thought they knew and loved. Perhaps, they reasoned, it was due to cash infusions from sympathetic Gulf governments or, more implausibly, that members of the old regime had, in their nimble pragmatism, adopted new political stripes in rather short order. To be sure, external funding may have helped, but funds can only take you so far. The more accurate explanation is that Salafis were already there and had been for some time. In fact, Egypt's first "Salafi" organization—Ansar al-Sunna al-Muhammadiya—was founded in 1926, two years before the Muslim Brotherhood.[32]

The Salafis' political quietism allowed them to pass under the radar during the Mubarak years. While an increasingly politicized Brotherhood challenged the regime's grip on power, Salafis, drawing on classical injunctions of obedience to the ruler, took care to avoid confrontation with the Mubarak regime (which returned the favor). They kept their focus on education, preaching, and charity work. Salafi television channels, with their fiery, charismatic preachers, became some of the most watched in the country. But the popularity of such stations should be seen "as a reflection and not a cause of the shift towards more conservative religious views," as the authors of one of the earliest studies on Salafi media argued in 2009.[33] Salafi religious views had become mainstream, embedded deep within society. For many Egyptians, it wasn't necessarily about being "Salafi" but about choosing to observe a stricter practice of Islam in their daily lives.

Far from an historical aberration, the rise of Salafism and Islamism more generally gave voice to something that was really always there—the simple, popular desire to emulate the religious purity of the Prophet Mohamed and his companions, however one wishes to define that. In most Arab countries, the only period in which Islam and Islamic law faded from public life was during the pinnacle of Arab nationalism in the 1950s and 1960s. Even in Turkey, where there was an unprecedented and sometimes brutal effort to erase religion from the public domain under Ataturk's rule, religion-friendly conservative democrats (starting with the Democratic Party of Adnan Menderes, who was executed in 1961 after a military coup) as well as more orthodox Islamist movements quickly reemerged.

Viewed through such a prism, the ascendance of Islamism seems less like an accident of particular economic and political circumstances and more a reflection of a widespread tendency toward religious practice and observance. As Richard Mitchell reflected in the 1980s, the Islamic movement "would not be a serious movement worthy of our attention were it not, above all, an idea and a personal commitment honestly felt."[34] Anything that is "honestly felt" by enough people will be difficult to dislodge from the popular consciousness. Taking an historical long view, it seems unlikely that Islamism or its milder cousin, Turkish-style "conservative democracy," will suffer decisive ideological defeat anytime soon.

It seemed to help that Islamists found themselves in a dominant position at the start of transitions across the region. What happens during the early phase of democratization is not incidental, nor can it easily be reversed. This is what makes transitional periods particularly tense and polarizing. Writing on Brazil's transition, Frances Hagopian points out that "individuals rise who are adept at the political game as it is played, and they use their positions to perpetuate modes of political interaction that favor them."[35] There is something to say, then, for path dependence, the notion that the longer one spends on a given road, the more difficult it is to turn around.[36] That Islamist parties in Egypt and Tunisia successfully pushed for a transitional process that played to their strengths—for example, by holding earlier rather than later elections—made their future entrenchment more likely. But, as we will see in the case of Egypt, the fear of Islamist entrenchment hastened an anti-Brotherhood backlash that aborted their seemingly unstoppable rise.

The fluidity and fickleness of Arab politics during transitions, with their many thrusts and reversals, makes definitive predictions unwise. Instead of assuming that Islamist movements are trapped in steady decline, it may be more useful to understand how they will evolve in a number of different directions, reshaping the very meaning of the "Islamic project" in the process. This is what the Arab world's post-revolution era has in store. Islamists matter not just because of their permanency but because, as they change, societies will change along with them, for both better and worse.

Bringing the International Community Back In

Much of the analysis of how and why Islamists change tends to overlook international factors, despite the controversial role of the United States and Europe in constraining and, at times, blocking the rise of Islamists. Of course, Islamist parties are a product of the complex interaction of economic, political, and social forces in their own societies. Yet, in the particular case of Islamists in the Arab world, there is a need to bring the international community back in.

An extensive literature has tried to make sense of the Middle East's "democratic exceptionalism" (even after the Arab Spring, autocracy remains the predominant form of government). Where the rest of the world, including the least developed regions of Africa, had seen significant democratization, the Arab world had not. Scholars have considered a variety of factors, whether economic underdevelopment, illiteracy, oil rents, or lack of a middle class, not to mention political culture and the influence of Islam. In one of the few articles that examines international factors, the political scientist Eva Bellin comes closer to the mark. She focuses on the Arab state's coercive capacities and asks why they remained so robust for so long. "In contrast to other regions," she writes, "the authoritarian states in the Middle East and North Africa did not see their sources of international patronage evaporate with the end of the Cold War or with America's subsequent reanimation with democracy."[37] The Middle East remained vital to U.S. strategic interests. As a result, autocratic regimes could continue counting on American largesse to the tune of billions of dollars in economic and military support. In his suggestively titled book *Democracy Prevention*, Jason Brownlee characterizes the American role this way: "The United States is less like an external force and more like a local participant in the ruling coalition. The U.S. government plays a role analogous to those of domestic coalition members (the director of intelligence, the minister of the interior, the minister of defense), shaping the calculations, priorities, and resources of the regime."[38]

In a number of Arab countries, the Islamist struggle against authoritarian regimes was effectively internationalized. Islamist groups eventually came to see the international community, and particularly the United States, as an important audience in its own right and one worth courting. They came to believe that acquiring real power—or even securing basic freedoms—would remain unlikely, if not impossible, without American encouragement or, at the very least, neutrality.

With the uprisings of early 2011, Islamists in Egypt and Tunisia discovered that they did not need the United States or Europe to overthrow their regimes. As American officials were fond of saying, "it's not about us; it's about them." Yet such truisms obscured an unsettling reality: international support remained critical to the success of democratic transitions *after* a revolution.[39]

For successive U.S. administrations, deciding what to do about Islamist parties has been a particularly thorny challenge. Because of the region's importance, and the fact that Islamists were seen as vehemently anti-American, policymakers found themselves in a bind. Free and fair elections were likely to bring Islamist groups to power, perhaps at great consequence to U.S. security interests. It was difficult, if not impossible, to resolve America's "Islamist dilemma," because the tradeoff, at the least in the short term, was indeed real: democratically elected Islamist governments would be less deferential to American interests than secular dictators. The Arab revolts, however, ushered in the demise of longtime allies like Hosni Mubarak. In the ensuing power vacuum, Islamists rose to power and prominence, and there was nothing the United States could do about it. The Obama administration had little choice but to reconcile itself to the region's new realities, although, here too, it would struggle to find the right balance between supporting democracy and preserving its security interests in the region.

Illiberal Democracy and Arab "Exceptionalism"

The prominent role of Islamists in the battle for regional supremacy puts Western analysts and policymakers in the uncomfortable position of having to prioritize some values they hold dear over others. In the Western experience, democracy and liberalism usually went hand in hand, to the extent that "democracy" in popular usage became short-hand for liberal democracy. Liberalism preceded democracy, allowing the latter to flourish. As the scholars Richard Rose and Doh Chull Shin point out, "countries in the first wave [of democracy], such as Britain and Sweden, initially became modern states, establishing the rule of law, institutions of civil society, and horizontal accountability to aristocratic parliaments. Democratization followed in Britain as the government became accountable to MPs elected by a franchise that gradually broadened until universal suffrage was achieved." In contrast, they write, "third-wave democracies have begun democratization backwards."[40]

Getting democracy backwards has led to the rise of "illiberal democracies," a distinctly modern creation that Fareed Zakaria documents in his book *The Future of Freedom*. Zakaria seeks to disentangle liberalism and democracy, arguing that democratization is, in fact, "directly related" to *illiberalism*.[41] On the other hand, "constitutional liberalism," as he terms it, is a political system "marked not only by free and fair elections but also by the rule of law, a separation of powers, and the protection of basic liberties of speech, assembly, religion, and property." "This bundle of freedoms," he goes on, "has nothing intrinsically to do with democracy."[42]

Michael Signer makes a similar argument in his book charting the rise of "demagogues," who accumulate popularity and power through the ballot box. Like Zakaria, Signer acknowledges the inherent tensions between liberalism and democracy, noting that early generations of Americans were particularly attuned to these threats. He writes, for instance, about Elbridge Gerry, a representative from Massachusetts who declared that "allowing ordinary Americans to vote for the president was madness."[43] Drawing on such examples, Signer argues that "at its simplest level, democracy is a political system that grants power based on what large groups of people want."[44] And what these large groups want may not be good for constitutional liberalism, which is more about the ends of democracy rather than the means.

The emergence of illiberal democracy in the developing world saw democratically elected leaders using popular mandates to infringe upon basic liberties. Elections were still largely free and fair and opposition parties were fractious but viable. But ruling parties, seeing their opponents more as enemies than competitors, sought to restrict media freedoms and pack state bureaucracies with loyalists. They used their control of the democratic process to rig the system to their advantage. In some cases, as in Venezuela under Hugo Chávez, a cult of personality became central to the consolidation of illiberal democracy. Sometimes it bordered on self-parody, taking the form of highway billboards announcing that "Chávez is the people."[45]

Illiberal democracy has risen to prominence in part because Western Europe's careful sequencing of liberalism first and democracy later is no longer tenable—and hasn't been for some time. Knowing that democracy, or something resembling it, is within reach, citizens have no interest in waiting indefinitely for something their leaders say they are not ready for. Democracy has become such an uncontested, normative good that the arguments of Zakaria seem decidedly out of step with the times. Zakaria argues, for instance, that "the absence of free and fair elections should be viewed as one flaw, not the definition of tyranny . . . It is important that governments be judged by yardsticks related to constitutional liberalism."[46] Interestingly, he points to countries like Singapore, Malaysia, Jordan, and Morocco as models. "Despite the limited political choice they offer," he writes, "[they] provide a better environment for life, liberty, and happiness of citizens than do . . . the illiberal democracies of Venezuela, Russia, or Ghana."[47]

The phenomenon of Islamists seeking, or being in, power forces us to rethink the relationship between liberalism and democracy. As I will argue in later chapters, illiberal democracy under Islamist rule is different from the Venezuelan or Russian varieties for a number of important reasons. In the latter cases, illiberal democracy is not intrinsically linked to the respective ideologies of Hugo Chávez or Vladimir Putin. Their illiberalism is largely a byproduct of a more basic, naked desire to consolidate power. In the case of Islamists, however, their illiberalism is a product of their Islamism, particularly in the social arena. For Islamists, illiberal democracy is not an unfortunate fact of life but something to believe in and aspire to. Although they may struggle to define what it entails, Islamist parties have a distinctive intellectual and ideological "project." This is why they are *Islamist*.

The Immoderation of Islamists

Under autocracy, leaders can more easily insulate themselves from the popular will. Islamists, to the extent they are tolerated, are so busy with mere survival that ideological demands are pushed to the side and postponed. They counsel patience, telling over-exuberant followers to wait, that the application of sharia is simply not possible now. Democracy, for both the secular and Islamist opposition, becomes the overarching imperative, because, without it, nothing else can really happen. Repression brings them together, giving them a shared enemy and a shared goal—toppling the dictator.

After their revolutions succeed, Islamists, liberals, and leftists find that they have less reason to work together. At best, they become bitter adversaries but agree to resolve their differences within the democratic process. Other times, they become implacable enemies in a zero-sum battle, one that can descend into political violence and military intervention. Either way, both sides become consumed by a struggle for the spoils of revolution, including, most importantly, control of the state and its resources. Sometimes, then, it is about power. But underlying the battle for power is a more fundamental ideological divide over the very meaning of the modern nation-state. Before the uprisings, most Arabs hadn't really had this conversation. The intellectual and political elites who did, did so in the abstract. None of them were going to be in power any time soon; it was a debate for their children or their grandchildren after them. But with the Arab revolutions, the essential questions of identity and ideology, of God and religion, of the conception of the good, assumed a newfound urgency.

In short, democratization does not necessarily have a moderating effect on Islamist parties, nor does it blunt the importance of ideology. There are no easy answers and, at some point, it may very well come down to a matter of faith. What if Tunisians, Egyptians, Libyans,

Yemenis, or Syrians decide, through democratic means, that they *want* to be illiberal? Is *that* a protected right? For its part, the Universal Declaration of Human Rights (UDHR) is clear on the matter. A United Nations background note discusses the "red line": "The right to culture is limited at the point at which it infringes on another human right. No right can be used at the expense or destruction of another, in accordance with international law."[48] For Western policymakers and Arab liberals alike, the notion that there should be supra-constitutional principles binding on all citizens seems self-evident. Liberal democracy depends upon the recognition of inalienable rights. But if Islamists do not consider themselves party to this consensus—and many do not—then the matter becomes a more basic one of colliding worldviews. This divide was evident in the contentious debates over first constitutions in Egypt and Tunisia. Egypt's first post-revolution constitution, passed by referendum in December 2012, seemed to violate the UDHR or at least failed to offer sufficient rights protections in numerous instances, including on gender equality, freedom of expression, and freedom of conscience and religion.

Even what may have seemed, in retrospect, like minor quibbles— over the particular wording of sharia clauses, for example—reflected fundamental divides over the boundaries, limits, and purpose of the nation-state. For liberals, certain rights and freedoms are, by definition, nonnegotiable. They envision the state as a neutral arbiter. Meanwhile, even those Islamists who have little interest in legislating morality see the state as a promoter of a certain set of religious and moral values, through the soft power of the state machinery, the educational system, and the media. For them, these conservative values are not ideologically driven but represent a self-evident popular consensus around the role of religion in public life. The will of the people, particularly when it coincides with the will of God, takes precedence over any presumed international human rights norms.

As much as Islamist groups moderated their rhetoric and practice from the 1970s through the 2011 uprisings, they did not become liberals (here, as ever, the distinction between being a "liberal" and a "democrat" is worth emphasizing). There was a time when the notion of "post-Islamism" gained popularity in academic circles. Turkish Islamism—which had ceased to be

Islamist in any real sense—showed the way to a brave new future where Islamists would agree to work within the framework of secular democracy. However, such hopes, when applied to the Muslim Brotherhood and like-minded groups, were misplaced.

At the same time, it would be a mistake to view Islamists as radicals bent on introducing a fundamentally new social order. Even the Brotherhood's most controversial positions—such as its opposition to women and Christians becoming head of state—fell well within the region's conservative mainstream. The irony of Islamist victories at the polls is that they did not announce a break with the past; they confirmed something that was already there and had been for some time. The goal of Islamists is the Islamization of society, in thought and practice, and in the standards that people hold themselves to. In some countries, like Egypt, the extent of Islamization on the societal level was striking well before Islamists even came to power; in other countries, Islamists were creating something from nearly nothing. In post-revolution Tunisia, the level of Islamization was remarkable, considering how much ground Islamists had to cover in such a short period of time. In Tunisia, Ennahda had been effectively eradicated in the early 1990s. After that, the group had no organized presence in the country, with its leaders in prison or in exile.

After the demise of strongman Zine al-Abidine Ben Ali in January 2011, the changing character of society was immediately apparent, with a growing number of Tunisians dressing, speaking, and living differently. Mosque preachers, not accustomed to large crowds, reported rows of the devout lining up for prayer. It was almost as if the removal of a dictator allowed society to return to a more natural equilibrium. Certainly, the return of Ennahda members and leaders to Tunisia helped spur these changes, but the party's quick return to prominence reflected a seemingly widespread desire to reconnect with the country's Islamic roots. Just months after Rachid Ghannouchi and other leaders returned, triumphant, to Tunis in early 2011, they won by a landslide in the country's first elections, with 37 percent of the popular vote and 41 percent of the seats. (The second largest party, the secular Congress for the Republic, won only 8.7 percent of the vote and 13 percent of the seats.)

Tunisia, with its sizable middle class, high level of literacy, and one of the region's best educational systems, was thought to be less hospitable to the specter of religious politics. Ennahda's success couldn't simply be explained by superior organization, as the party could claim virtually no preexisting organizational structures. To be sure, Ennahda members proved far more effective at campaigning than their secular counterparts. They drew on the legitimacy of their decades in prison under the previous regime. But they also drew on a latent Islamization of attitudes and a popular predisposition toward the mixing of religion and politics.

Immediately after the revolutions, Islamists in Egypt and Tunisia were careful to portray themselves as responsible actors. This relative sobriety was in constant tension with their stated, and unstated, ambitions for their respective societies. Egypt's Muslim Brotherhood, in particular, spoke of a comprehensive "civilizational" project. While this vague aspiration, embodied in the Brotherhood's so-called Renaissance Project,[49] had technocratic reform components, it also sought something more transformational. This part was less defined, in part because the Brotherhood had not given it the careful thought it deserved. Or perhaps, for them, it was so self-evident that it needn't be detailed in a program. Within the framework of democracy, they hoped to offer a spiritual and philosophical alternative to Western liberalism. For Islamists as well as their liberal opponents, it was a question—one that was intensely personal—of how societies would be ordered. Any moral project could be counted on to intrude on private conduct and personal freedoms, on the very choices that citizens made, or didn't make, on a daily basis.

In their original guise, the Muslim Brotherhood and other Islamist movements believed in a bottom-up approach, beginning with the individual. The virtuous individual would marry a virtuous wife and, together, they would raise a virtuous family. Those families, in turn, would transform culture and society. Once society was transformed, the leaders and politicians would follow. No one was quite sure exactly what this looked like in practice—it had never actually been done before.

Taking the long view, the struggle for and within political Islam is not just important for understanding the evolution of Arab societies; it is important for what it can tell us about how beliefs and ideology are mediated and altered by the political process. At the end of history, Fukuyama wrote, "the state that emerges . . . is liberal insofar as it recognizes and protects through a system of law man's universal right to freedom, and democratic insofar as it exists only with the consent of the governed."[50] But what Fukuyama failed to grapple with is whether a state could claim the latter without enjoying the former. The question here is whether the democratic process, in the long run, will blunt the ideological pretensions of Islamist groups, forcing them to move to the center, back into the confines of the liberal democratic consensus.

In the modern period, religiously based states are rare. The few that do exist, or have existed, do not have a good track record. Afghanistan, Iran, and Saudi Arabia are the obvious examples, but they are of limited value in making sense of Islamism after the Arab Spring. None of them were democratic. Although they enjoyed various degrees of popular support, there was no, in Fukuyama's words, real consent of the governed. In contrast, Islamist parties today are interested in fashioning religiously oriented states through democratic means and maintaining them through democratic means. They took this to levels of near self-parody in Egypt, where elections became a sort of crutch. Whenever the Brotherhood faced a crisis, its immediate instinct was to call for elections, thinking that electoral legitimacy would stabilize Egypt and solidify its rule (it didn't).

Throughout the 20th century, alternative ideologies, such as socialism, communism, and Christian Democracy, all attempted to secure power through the ballot box. But these were movements with built-in limitations. Islamist parties may be divisive for other reasons, but they do not struggle with the same limitations. The vast majority of Arabs have no *a priori* ideological opposition to Islamism as such. Most, after all, support a prominent role for Islam and Islamic law in political life. On the other hand, the natural constituencies of socialists and Christian Democrats—workers and social conservatives, respectively—were inherently limited. To win elections, these movements needed to deemphasize ideology and move to the center, where presumably the median voter would be found. This is how democratization produced ideological moderation, leading many analysts to assume that the same process might tame Islamist parties.

Islamism and the New Center

Where it is allowed to proceed, democratization will reorient political life in Arab societies. But how? In a country like Tunisia, the center of Arab politics shifted to the right. In Egypt, it shifted to the right before retreating in the face of mounting opposition to the Muslim Brotherhood and Islamists more generally.

Some "liberal" Islamists have made the case that religion should no longer be such a divisive issue. During his insurgent campaign for president, former Brotherhood leader Abdel Moneim Abul Futouh explained it this way to a Salafi television channel: "Today those who call themselves liberals or leftists, this is just a political name, but most of them understand and respect Islamic values. They support the sharia and are no longer against it."[51] In a creative attempt at redefinition, Abul Futouh noted that all Muslims are, by definition, Salafi, in the sense that they are loyal to the *Salaf*, the earliest, most pious generations of Muslims. He seemed to be saying: we are all, in effect, Islamists, so why fight over it?

Abul Futouh, for all his purported liberalism, believed that the Egyptian people (and perhaps all Muslim-majority populations) had a natural inclination toward Islam. Here, the tensions between liberalism and majoritarianism became more evident. When I asked Abul Futouh in 2006 what Islamists would do if parliament passed an "un-Islamic" law, he dismissed the concern: "Parliament won't grant rights to gays because that goes against the prevailing culture of society, and if [members of parliament] did that, they'd lose the next election," he said. "Whether you are a communist, socialist, or whatever, you can't go against the prevailing culture. There is already a built-in respect for sharia."[52]

Over the course of my interviews in Egypt, Jordan, and Tunisia—both before and after the Arab Spring—this particular sentiment was repeated so often that it began to sound like a cliché: freedom and Islamization were not opposed but rather went hand in hand. As Salem Falahat, the former General Overseer[53] of Jordan's Muslim Brotherhood, put it, "if they have the opportunity to think and choose, [the Arab and Muslim people] will choose Islam. Every time freedom expands among them, they choose Islam."[54] In other words, Islam didn't need to be enforced. The people, to the extent they needed to, would enforce it themselves—through the binding nature of the democratic process.

This notion has a long pedigree in Islamic thought: the Prophet Mohamed is reported to have said, "my *umma* [community] will not agree on an error." Depending on where exactly you stand on the political spectrum, this sort of belief in the wisdom of crowds is either reassuring and somewhat banal or mildly frightening. It either hints at a new conservative consensus or at an exclusionary politics that has little space for liberal dissent.

A Tunisian Exception?

Tunisian Islamists, like all Islamists, have an "Islamic project," but their project looks different, in part because the society of which they are a part has diverged so significantly from regional norms.

Early on in the country's democratic transition, the limits of Islamization became evident. There were three controversial clauses in earlier drafts of the constitution, one on blasphemy (prohibiting "attacks on the sacred"), one on the place of women in society ("their [men's and women's] roles complement one another within the family"[55]), as well as a proposed clause that would enshrine sharia as "a source among sources" of legislation. In each case, particularly the latter two, the response from the secular opposition as well as civil society was unmistakable; the pushback forced Islamists to withdraw the clauses. The costs of going forward, in the face of a mobilized opposition, were simply not worth it.

What Tunisia has that most others in the region do not are strong, vibrant—and unabashedly secular—civil society organizations, media outlets, and opposition parties. Even the most mild, symbolic sort of "Islamization" will face considerable resistance at every turn. In Tunisia, the country's "founding father" Habib Bourguiba and then President Ben Ali were not only autocrats, but autocrats strongly influenced by the French tradition of *laïcité*, the notion that religion should be entirely separate from politics (in contrast to the Anglo-Saxon model, which allows ample space for expression of religion as long as the separation of church and state is respected).[56] Religion was to be a private matter, one that concerned the individual and God (and, even then, excessive displays of "private" religiosity could prove risky). Mosques were monitored for those who appeared especially devout. Women were prohibited from wearing the headscarf in public schools and universities. It was Bourguiba who infamously appeared on television during the Ramadan fast and drank a glass of orange juice, saying that work and productivity took precedence over any presumed religious obligation.

The cultural re-rendering of Tunisian society, taking place over decades, cannot be ignored or reversed, as many in Ennahda seem to recognize. Tunisia's Code of Personal Status, for example, is one of the most progressive in the region and enjoys broad public support. Rachid Ghannouchi grew up in a polygamous household, showing deep affection for both his biological mother and his stepmother (whom he also called "mother").[57] The code, however, would ban marrying more than one wife. Despite other controversial provisions, Ennahda members eventually made their peace with the personal status code not because they wanted to necessarily, but because they had to. In his biography of Ghannouchi, Azzam Tamimi notes that Ghannouchi "strongly opposed" the code until 1984 but withdrew his opposition in the hope that it would facilitate the party's legalization.[58] By then, the personal status code had become part of Tunisian culture, even though it may have at first been "imported" or "imposed." Women had made considerable gains and, as a result, enjoyed greater rights and protections than the vast majority of their counterparts in the region. As Meherzia Laabidi, leading Ennahda figure and vice president of the constituent assembly, explained, "the personal status code is my heritage as a woman. It is my daughter's heritage and my sister's heritage."[59]

With the advent of democracy, the tradition of *laïcité* will weaken, but it will remain an inexorable part of the Tunisian social fabric. That is not necessarily something that Ennahda wants to challenge, at least not yet. To do so would require a transformation of society, and that is the stuff of long-term social projects rather than short-term electoral platforms.

Egyptian Islamists, meanwhile, had a head start. Before Egypt's Muslim Brotherhood came to power in 2012, it had spent nearly four decades organizing among the people and spreading its message. In the 1940s, as many as 600,000 Egyptians[60] (in a population of only around 20 million) were Brotherhood members, before the organization was effectively dismantled during the mihna. In short, Egypt already had a history of Islamization before Islamists became leading political actors. Tunisia's very different circumstances compelled Islamists to adopt a different, subtler approach and a more modest set of ambitions in tune with the realities of Tunisian culture and society. Tunisia's transition ended up the better for it.

The important point here is that context and constraints matter. While Ennahda may have started out with the same ideology as its counterparts in Egypt, Jordan, and elsewhere, the party ended up following its own distinct path. It has often been argued that radicalism produces radicalism, but this clearly wasn't the case in Tunisia. Tunisia was one of the environments most inhospitable to Islamists. Not only was there repression but there was a systematic attempt to erase Islam from the public sphere. Radical secularism did not produce its mirror image, as one might have expected.[61] If anything, Ennahda has long been regarded as one of the most "moderate" Islamist movements in the Arab world.

Ennahda's starting point, then, is different, but the overall direction is much the same. As Tunisians become more religiously observant—and as popular support for sharia grows—Ennahda will have more room to push a more explicitly Islamist agenda; its conservative base will demand it. It is here, though, that we can see the rough outlines of a party–movement compromise, one that any number of Islamist groups might wish to consider. The movement removes itself from politics and gets back to the basics religious education and charity work. It serves as a sort of "sharia lobby," putting pressure on the party—mostly made up of professional politicians—to reflect the movement's conservatism. If the party "fails," however, the movement will be somewhat insulated. It will continue to promote its broader cultural and societal project regardless.

The Book

What follows is informed by hundreds of hours of interviews, discussions, and informal conversations with mainstream Islamists as well as Salafis across the region, primarily in Egypt and Jordan, as well as in Tunisia. I spent a period of over 20 months in Egypt and Jordan, in

2004–6, 2008, and 2010–3. I make extensive reference to these interviews, which were often candid and revealing, offering an account of events that, I hope, will provide new perspectives to Western and Arab observers alike. I have chosen to emphasize these interviews and conversations for reasons that will become apparent in the coming chapters. I am interested not only in whether Islamist groups change but also in how and why. One way to understand why Islamists adopted certain positions is to ask them to explain the strategic logic behind their decisions, particularly those that were controversial at the time. For this reason, I tended to focus my attention on leaders as well as activists who were privy to the decision-making process. Much of my early field research was conducted at a time when Islamists were under far less scrutiny than they are today. In Egypt, I met with many Brotherhood figures who could, at any moment, be whisked away to prison, including Khairat al-Shater, Mohamed Morsi, Mahmoud Ghozlan, Essam al-Erian, and Abdel Moneim Abul Futouh—all of whom spent stints in jail during my research. They figured that it couldn't get any worse, and for this reason, I suspect, they were often quite forthcoming.

In Jordan, the situation wasn't quite as dire. Still, Brotherhood leaders there felt underappreciated and, this too, led to its own kind of openness. They often pointed to what they felt were the unique accomplishments of their movement and its political arm, the IAF. They were especially proud of the IAF's admittedly impressive internal democracy. This was partly a function of housing two competing factions within the same movement, dubbed the "hawks" (suqour) and "doves" (hama'im).[62] Somewhat to my surprise, members of both factions spoke about each other with open disdain (sometimes on the record). Unlike the Brotherhood in Egypt, which put a priority on closing ranks, Jordan's Islamists were a more raucous bunch. They didn't seem particularly interested in pretending otherwise. Generally, they appreciated that I seemed to care. I often got the sense that they found it odd that I had decided to live in Jordan for the express purpose of studying them. While other academics would visit often, I was, to my knowledge, the only American researcher of Islamist movements living in Amman in 2004–5, which also happened to be a tense time, with the relationship between the regime and Islamists continuing to deteriorate.

I have also made use, particularly in the Jordanian case, of first-hand accounts of the Islamic movement. Due to the less secretive nature of the Jordanian Brotherhood, current and former members have been more willing to write down its history.[63] Published in 2008, Bassam al-Emoush's *Stations in the History of the Muslim Brotherhood* adds a wealth of knowledge and understanding to key moments in the group's relationship with the Jordanian monarchy.[64] Regarding Egypt, I have chosen to devote significant attention to episodes in the Brotherhood's history that have received little attention in Western scholarship. These include the Egyptian government's ambitious (but now forgotten) endeavor to reconcile Egyptian law with sharia, headed by the powerful speaker of parliament Sufi Abu Talib, as well as the Brotherhood's decision in 1984 to form an electoral alliance with the Wafd party, the once venerable bastion of liberal politics. All translations of Arabic sources are my own unless otherwise noted.

This book takes both a chronological and thematic approach to the topic at hand. In the first part of the book, I discuss the behavior of Islamist groups in opposition as they faced intensifying repression. I survey how Islamists' experiences under autocracy shaped their behavior, and what that tells us about how they perceive and respond to various political pressures and threats. Here, I have chosen to focus on Egypt and Jordan, two countries that in the pre-2011 period experienced both significant political openings as well as sharp increases in repression. This variation, over time, in the level of repression and political exclusion allows us to explore how Islamists shifted their positions and priorities as a result.[65]

The pre-Arab Spring Middle East is sometimes treated as a mono-lithic mass of autocracy. Yet, in Egypt and Jordan, regimes briefly opened up in the 1980s and early 1990s before turning decisively toward repression. Both cases feature unexpected shocks to the political system. These shocks, in turn, led to significant shifts in Islamist behavior. But what exactly caused these shifts? This book challenges existing theories of Islamist moderation and argues that increasing levels of repression, rather than resulting in radicalization, can have a moderating effect on Islamist groups, pushing them to reconsider and redefine their policy priorities.

The book then moves on to another unexpected shock—the 2011 uprisings. In Egypt, we see a striking shift from one of the worst periods of anti-Islamist repression to an unprecedented democratic opening, where the Muslim Brotherhood found itself free to operate as never before. It is worth remembering that just months before the revolution, the Mubarak regime presided over the most fraudulent elections in the country's history.

The pre- and post-revolution contrasts were even starker for Tunisia's Islamists. In Egypt as well as most other Arab countries, the repression was bad, to be sure, but it was never total. In Tunisia, the Ben Ali regime had eliminated its Islamist opposition in the early 1990s, to the extent that Ennahda ceased to exist in any real sense. After Ben Ali's fall, Tunisia's Islamists, quite literally, had to start from scratch.

2

Can Repression Force Islamist Moderation?

I BEGIN THIS CHAPTER with a puzzle. In the early 1990s, Arab regimes descended into full-blown authoritarianism, launching aggressive crackdowns against the Islamist opposition, including in Egypt, Jordan, and Tunisia. According to what scholars call the "inclusion-moderation hypothesis," mounting repression could have been expected to lead to Islamist radicalization. While this period did indeed see militant groups engaged in violent struggles with Arab regimes, the story of mainstream Islamist movements was rather different. Just as regimes grew increasingly repressive, these groups—most of which are affiliated with or inspired by the Muslim Brotherhood—accepted many of the foundational tenets of democracy, including popular sovereignty and alternation of power. Across the region, they adopted increasingly moderate positions on political pluralism and women's and minority rights. Moreover, they moved to democratize their organizational structures. Jordan's Islamic Action Front, for example, achieved a level of internal democracy that remains unparalleled in the region.

This isn't what we would have expected: Islamists moderated not only in the absence of democracy but as repression was getting worse. Much of the academic literature posits or simply assumes that the moderation of Islamist groups occurs as a result of political participation and inclusion. Meanwhile, repression has a radicalizing effect. The thinking here centers on the idea that ideological parties prosper in open, participatory politics by moving to the center and reaching out to the broadest cross-section of the electorate. But, here,

Islamist parties appear to have moderated not because of democracy, but before it. They represent an intriguing and often misunderstood phenomenon—the emergence, in the Middle East, of democrats without democracy.

With Islamists likely to be in positions of political influence if not power for decades to come, understanding how and why moderation takes place is as critical as ever. It is striking just to what extent assumptions about Islamist moderation have come to dominate both the academic and policy discourse. After the Arab uprisings, Quinn Mecham, an academic who led the interagency working group on political Islam in the U.S. State Department in the first years of the Obama administration, captured what had become a wide-ranging consensus: "Considerable research has shown that often Islamists will 'moderate' their ideology and behavior the more they directly participate in their political systems."[1] Indeed, the "inclusion-moderation hypothesis" has gone mainstream and mutated into various related forms. One of these is the so-called pothole theory of democracy—the notion that the responsibilities of governing force Islamists to move away from ideological appeals and deliver on the bread-and-butter issues that voters presumably care about most (including fixing potholes).[2]

The "pothole theory" has found its way into the statements of numerous policymakers and politicians, including, oddly enough, President George W. Bush. Responding to a question about Hezbollah in 2005, Bush had this to say: "I like the idea of people running for office. There's a positive effect . . . Maybe some will run for office and say, vote for me, I look forward to blowing up America . . . I don't think so. I think people who generally run for office say, vote for me, I'm looking forward to fixing your potholes."[3]

In Egypt's first ever presidential debate on May 10, 2012, Islamist candidate Abdel Moneim Abul Futouh called Israel an "enemy," causing some concern in Washington. But State Department spokeswoman Victoria Nuland brushed it aside. "People say things in a campaign and then when they get elected they actually have to govern," she said.[4] This is, understandably, what we would all like to believe. Many Western analysts, including this author, have written at length on the need for the United States to more proactively support democracy in the Arab world. Their argument, however, is undermined if those most likely to win elections govern in ways that seem, in Western eyes, aggressive, intemperate, and intolerant. Policymakers, meanwhile, have little choice but to work with Islamists when they do reach the halls of power. Still, it is always easier to engage—and justify it to domestic constituencies— if there is a sense that Islamists will become more "moderate" as a result of being engaged.

Even Islamists themselves have dutifully promoted the idea that more political participation leads to moderation.[5] The reverse, they insisted, was also true. In dozens of interviews I conducted in Egypt and Jordan during the crackdowns of 2008, Brotherhood officials warned that their supporters would radicalize if regime repression continued. Islamists—as well as ordinary Egyptians—would lose faith in the little that was left of the democratic process. They might give up on the gradualism of the Muslim Brotherhood and embrace extremism and perhaps even violence, the argument went. Similarly, after the Tunisian revolution, Ennahda justified its decision to legalize two Salafi parties by arguing that inclusion in the political process would have a moderating effect.

Such notions are as intuitive as they are convenient. They also happen to draw from decades of research and experience with ideological currents in Western Europe and Latin America, including socialists, communists, and Christian Democrats. Samuel Huntington further popularized the idea with what he called the "participation-moderation tradeoff." He saw ample evidence of the tradeoff in the third-wave democracies of Latin America, Asia, and Eastern Europe. "Implicitly or explicitly in the negotiating processes leading to democratization," Huntington wrote, "the scope of participation was broadened and more political figures and groups gained the opportunity to compete for power and to win power on the implicit or explicit understanding that they would be moderate in their tactics and policies."[6]

While applying these ideas to the Middle East is a welcome antidote to the anti-Islamist scaremongering of old, they oversimplify complex causal processes. There is, of course, a natural tendency to try to find analogues for Islamism in other regions. And while there are no doubt similarities, there are also important differences.

Does Inclusion Lead to Moderation?

Proponents of "inclusion-moderation" argue that the more democracy there is in a given country, the more Islamists will moderate and internalize democratic values and commitments. The corollary of this is the "exclusion-radicalization" hypothesis, which argues that, as political opportunities for opposition actors close, the risk of radicalization increases.

There are two sets of related causal mechanisms, one having to do with electoral pressures and the other with regime pressures. They are worth outlining in brief. Median voter theory helps us understand how revolutionary socialist parties in Western Europe became, in due time, social democrats wholly committed to the parliamentary process.[7] (Many of the same doubts expressed about Islamists' commitment to democracy were expressed about socialists decades ago.) As Adam Przeworski and John Sprague note, "the quest for electoral allies forced socialist parties to deemphasize that unique appeal, that particular vision of society."[8] Because socialists did not command a numerical majority, they needed to reach out beyond their natural constituency of wage earners and workers and move to the "center," where the median voter could be found. Stathis Kalyvas recounts a similar movement toward moderation among religiously oriented Christian parties. "The realization that power is within reach," he writes, "creates the incentive to moderate so as to appeal to broader sections of the electorate."[9] Building on these arguments, Vali Nasr argues that "as was the case with Christian Democracy in Europe, it is the imperative of competition inherent in democracy that will transform the unsecular tendencies of Muslim Democracy into long-term commitment to democratic values."[10]

Not only do parties want to win elections; after they have won and assumed power, they want to keep on winning. Voters, the thinking goes, cannot live on empty ideological appeals. As James Carville put it, "it's the economy, stupid." They need to see tangible changes in their standard of living, whether that means better access to jobs and health care, lower food prices, increased educational opportunities, or improved public transportation. And they want to see their potholes fixed.

Underlying these specific claims is the deeper, often unstated recognition that politics, at its very essence, is about getting things done,
which, in turn, requires making difficult compromises, often with
people you don't like very much. Where religion operates in the realm
of purity and absolute concerns, politics is about the daily grind of dis-
pensing favors, serving constituents, and doing what it takes to push a
tough piece of legislation through parliament. Through the messiness of
everyday politics, a process of political learning takes place.

The second set of causal mechanisms has to do with regime pressures in an autocratic environment. Repression, the thinking goes, has
a distorting effect on political participation, pushing groups to adopt
policies and positions less moderate than those they would adopt under
democracy. As Muriel Asseburg notes, "measures aimed at exclusion
threaten to re-radicalize these groups and ultimately pose the dangers
of a surge in violence and a reorientation of Islamist movements from
governance and human rights issues towards a predominantly religious
and moral agenda."[11] As mentioned earlier, this is the argument that
Islamists tend to make when speaking to Western audiences. The idea
here is that when opposition groups and their supporters lose faith in
the political process, they are more likely to fall back on divisive cultural issues and perhaps even resort to violence. If regime repression
has a radicalizing effect on Islamist groups, then it follows that a de-
crease in repression—or no repression at all—would have a moderating
effect.[12]

In either scenario, whether the focus is on the relationship between
Islamists and the regime or Islamists and the electorate, a causal link
is posited. As democratic space expands, Islamist groups will continue
moving boldly along a linear projection, embracing an increasingly moderate politics, one much more focused on political reform than on a religious agenda. Space limitations do not allow for a thorough consideration
of the many arguments of this nature, but a few are worth citing here.
Daniel Brumberg writes, for instance, that "because it is only through
the carrots and sticks of real political competition that Islamists will see
the logic behind shelving their ideological priorities in favor of a system
of compromised and multiparty coalition government."[13] Graham Fuller
argues that "the existence of a reasonably open political system places a
greater onus on Islamist organizations to accept some kind of ideological

flexibility, moderation, and pluralism—characteristics easier to reject when the system is closed."[14] In a post-Arab Spring context, a paper from the Center for a New American Security notes that "pressures to produce socioeconomic gains and maintain a broad coalition, including their own younger generation, can provide moderating forces that U.S. policy can reinforce."[15] Meanwhile, referring to Salafi groups, Jonathan Brown writes that "the democratic process, political involvement, and electoral accountability will continue to moderate Salafi views and policies over the long term."[16]

Not all of these assertions are off the mark. It goes without saying that the practice of politics does instill a kind of pragmatism, and extreme levels of repression do, in fact, lead to radicalization, as I will discuss later. But as intuitive as they may appear, such arguments demand further scrutiny. More often than not, the relationships and causal mechanisms in question are not explored in any great depth.

One of the most notable attempts to address these limitations is Jillian Schwedler's 2006 book *Faith in Moderation,* but even here major questions remain unanswered. Her goal, as she explains it, is to determine to what extent Islamists have moderated as a result of political inclusion, using parties in Jordan and Yemen as case studies. Toward the end of the book, Schwedler argues that the "most pivotal factor that explains moderation is that the IAF leadership as a whole has sought to justify new practices in terms of the party's central ideological commitments while Islah [Yemen's major Islamist party] has not."[17] But *why* did the IAF leadership seek to justify new practices according to the party's ideological commitments? Furthermore, Schwedler and others tend to treat "moderation" as an aggregate outcome, so we only really end up with one observation per case and one final outcome that is the product of a slow, gradual process. What we don't have is a more fine-tuned understanding of when and where exactly, along this long process, Islamists moderated.

Surprisingly, there are few articles where the link between repression and moderation is explicitly discussed. The possibility of such a link is sometimes alluded to in passing. Carrie Wickham, for example, finds that the experience of Wasat, the party that split from the Brotherhood, defies some of the core assumptions of how moderation occurs. "On the face of it," she writes, "the formation of the Wasat party under conditions of increased repression is surprising, not only because the incentives for moderation created by democratization elsewhere were absent but because repression might more logically trigger Islamist radicalization."[18]

Far from an outlier, the experience of Wasat gets us closer to the reality of Islamist political behavior and the role that repression plays. The case of Wasat mimics, to a large degree, the process of "forced moderation" that made Turkish Islamists into what they are today. As M. Hakan Yavuz writes, "the coup [against the elected Islamist-led government in 1997] taught [AKP leader Recep Tayyip] Erdogan to realize the parameters of democracy and the power of the secularist establishment, and forced him to become a moderate and a democrat."[19]

Repression and "Eradication"

Turkey's successive coups—damaging as they were to Turkish democracy—did indeed push Islamists toward greater moderation, including the acceptance of the secular foundations of the Turkish state. But extreme levels of repression—deployed in an attempt to eradicate a particular social or political group—are a different matter.

In 1954, few could have guessed that the brutal crackdown against the Egyptian Brotherhood would set into motion a chain of events that would have such devastating consequences for the region. Prison had a radicalizing effect on Sayyid Qutb, a leading Brotherhood ideologue, who experienced torture at the hands of his captors before being executed in 1966. Many of Qutb's followers later left the Brotherhood's embrace and went their own way, setting up militant organizations and perpetrating acts of terrorism.

In Algeria, the army's decision to eradicate the Islamic Salvation Front after it won the first round of landmark elections in 1991 caused many Islamists to give up on the political process and take up arms against the Algerian regime. Beyond these obvious examples, there is a growing academic literature that suggests strong "tyranny–terror" linkages. In a widely cited 2003 study, for example, Alan Krueger and Jitka Maleckova conclude that "the only variable that was consistently associated with the number of terrorists was the Freedom House index of political rights and civil liberties."[20] Steven Brooke and I survey this literature in greater detail in an article we wrote in 2010.[21]

What I am focused on here, however, is low to moderate levels of repression short of outright eradication, which has actually been relatively rare in the Middle East.[22] In much of the region, Islamist parties have been allowed at least some room to operate, to contest elections, and to win seats in parliament—as long as certain lines weren't crossed. Mubarak, Yemen's Ali Abdullah Saleh, the kings of Morocco and Jordan, and the rulers of Kuwait may have been autocrats but they were not radicals. Eradicating groups that enjoy significant popular support is extremely challenging from a logistical standpoint and is almost certain to have devastating consequences, leading to the unraveling of the social fabric and prolonged civil conflict, as occurred in Algeria in the 1990s and in Egypt after the 2013 coup. For most autocrats, it is simply not worth the heavy economic and political cost. It is usually preferable to employ low to moderate levels of repression and to use political incentives and the threat of sanction to co-opt and divide opponents.

What Is Moderation?

The word "moderation" has become something of a cliché and a tiresome one at that. In popular discourse, it tends to translate roughly into doing the things we want Islamist groups to do. Its usage in the academic literature lends itself to similar confusion.

Moderation is often conflated with "pragmatism" and "non-confrontation," two other related but distinct ideas. Pragmatism entails flexibility and willingness to compromise, which would appear to imply moderation. Muriel Asseburg says as much: "The more competitive the political system and the more incentives for democratic agendas, the greater the chances that Islamists will adopt pragmatic positions and prove themselves to be reform actors."[23] But pragmatism is more about means than ends. It entails a willingness to take on political positions irrespective of beliefs. Understood this way, pragmatism can lead moderates—out of political expedience—to take on conservative or radical positions, or, alternatively, for radicals to adopt moderate positions. For example, if an Islamist party in a conservative country decided to pass a law restricting alcohol consumption, it could very well be a pragmatic political winner with a large segment of the population. But Western media coverage would probably not use the word "moderate" to describe it. Similarly, by working within democratic structures,

Salafi parties can learn how to play the game better, while not necessarily giving up on their longer-term goals. It's possible in other words for Salafis to be "pragmatic" in the pursuit of a gradual move toward a strict, exclusionary Islamic state.

Moderation is also often conflated with non-confrontation. Janine Clark, in one article, defines "moderates" as those willing "to accept whatever restricted space is granted to them by the regime," while "radicals" are "those who are unwilling to enter agreements with authoritarian regimes until restrictions they consider inherently undemocratic have been lifted."[24] But this would be an odd way of looking at things, with radicals demanding that undemocratic restrictions be lifted and moderates accepting restrictions on their rights in deference to an authoritarian regime.

Similarly, playing by the "rules of the game" is often considered an indicator of Islamist moderation. It is not, however, clear why accepting existing rules—rules often imposed by authoritarian regimes by force—would suggest moderation. For example, if an Islamist party boycotts an election because it refuses to play by the rules of the game—a game it views as fundamentally unfair and rigged—does this make it radical or moderate, or neither? Indeed, "confrontational" political approaches have been viewed by both regimes and the international community as a sign of radicalism, which is one reason why Islamist groups generally avoided civil disobedience and mass mobilization before the Arab Spring.

Scholars may mean different things by moderation, but, ultimately, it is used almost exclusively as a positive term. Moderation is something to be understood in part because it is something to be pursued. The intent is to capture a progression in the way Islamists relate to their surrounding environment, a progression that makes a preferred outcome—usually political reform and democratization—more likely to occur. With this in mind, moderation takes place when Islamists deemphasize the application of Islamic law and the establishment of an "Islamic state" and commit to the foundational components of democracy, including alternation of power, popular sovereignty, and freedom of speech and religion.

Rather than treating moderation as a binary variable—in other words, did they or didn't they?—I am more interested in *relative moderation*, which asks whether a party in one time period becomes more or less moderate on particular issues in relation to a previous time period. In tracking Islamist moderation, I will consider several indicators, including their approach to democracy and the democratic process and, relatedly, the primacy of Islamic law in the political order; cooperation with non-Islamist groups; their positions and policies toward women's and minority rights; and degree of internal organizational reform. These four indicators help capture critical shifts in an Islamist party's broader agenda and strategic orientation. It is worth recalling that most Islamist groups were founded as *niche parties*, a term used to describe "single-issue" parties whose raison d'être is to inject a particular issue—one neglected by mainstream parties—into the public discourse.[25]

Although the term "niche party" was originally intended for Green parties and the radical right in Europe, it is also useful for understanding the distinctiveness of Islamists. Mainstream Islamist groups such as the Muslim Brotherhood were founded for a specific reason: to promote religious values in society and the application of Islamic law, which, in turn, would lead to a fundamental transformation of the social order. In their formative decades, they exhibited a relative disinterest in most domestic political issues unless they were specifically tied to Islamic law. Even when Islamist groups began entering parliaments for the first time in the 1980s, they continued to operate as a "sharia lobby." However, over decades, Islamist groups not only became more "moderate," but their basic orientation shifted and their hierarchy of priorities changed. Some scholars have called it a "metamorphosis."[26] This may be overstating things, but there is little doubt: Islamist groups in the 1990s looked quite different from what they were in the 1940s or 1970s. And, on the eve of the Arab uprisings, Islamist parties looked quite different from their predecessors of the 1990s.

Islamists and the State: An Unfair Bargain

What is surprising about Egypt and Jordan—two of the region's most strategically vital countries—is the extent to which they seem to contradict the conventional wisdom of how Islamists change. In a span of more than three decades, Islamist groups in both countries publicly embraced what, decades ago, would have been seen as controversial—and even un-Islamic—positions. But they did so not in the context of democratization but rather in its absence.

Political repression is defined as "the use or threat of coercion in varying degrees applied by government against opponents or potential opponents to weaken their resistance to the will of authorities."[27] The means of repression took on various forms in Jordan and Egypt. In the latter, the turn to repression began in the early 1990s, while in Jordan it began in 1993. Despite very different local circumstances, the two countries featured leaders—Hosni Mubarak, King Hussein, and King Abdullah—who made a conscious, strategic decision to constrain Islamist influence, to exclude them not only from power but from having even a small say in the decision-making process. Mainstream Islamists in Egypt were subject to mass arrest, indefinite detention, and blatantly rigged elections. In Jordan, repression included intermittent arrests, regime intimidation, purging of government ministries, and the denial of public sector jobs to Muslim Brotherhood members. Islamists' ability to win large pluralities in elections was circumscribed. Parliament's jurisdiction was restricted, with power becoming increasingly concentrated within the royal court.

In both countries, for much of the time period in question, the level of repression gradually intensified. For example, as bad as the early to mid-1990s were for Egypt's Islamist opposition, things managed to get even worse. According to various observers, 2006 to 2008 was the worst period of anti-Islamist repression since the 1960s (only to be superseded just a few years later by the devastating post-coup crackdown of 2013).[28]

Jordan's political deterioration never quite reached the level of Egypt, but on its own terms—comparing Jordan to what it had been rather than to what Egypt was—the country's descent into autocracy was just as striking. Jordan, after all, could once claim one of the region's most promising democratic experiments in the late 1980s and early 1990s. It was, among other things, one of the first countries in which a Muslim Brotherhood branch held executive power, with the group claiming five ministries during a brief six-month period in 1991. Those early days of optimism, however, would become a distant memory. The 2007 parliamentary elections were the culmination of a reversal that had begun long before in 1993. Like Egypt's 2010 elections, Jordan's 2007 contest was arguably the most fraudulent in the country's history.

Yet just as regimes turned to greater repression, Islamists affirmed and reaffirmed their commitment to a moderate course. They made democracy their call to arms, going out of their way to present themselves as responsible, mature actors on the regional and international stage. The decision of Islamists to continue working within such a restricting political system with little meaningful progress on political reform is vexing. In a "participation-moderation tradeoff," there is, as the phrase suggests, a tradeoff. Islamists agree to abide by the rules of the game and give up revolutionary designs against the regime. In return, they are promised a stake in the system, including the ability to form legal parties and otherwise gain recognition as legitimate political actors. Implicit in the tradeoff are increased political gains and the prospect of holding power at the local or national level.

On the part of the state, this is a prudent course of action, part of a broader process whereby democratization is "defensive" and "managed." Democratization, in these cases, does not necessarily lead to democracy. Bringing Islamist parties into the political process is one way to wed them to an elaborate structure of institutional constraints. Under the watchful eye of the state, they can be manipulated and controlled.[29] Of course, the "tradeoff" only works if Islamists believe participation will lead to an improvement in their political situation. However, in both Egypt and Jordan, their situation not only failed to improve; it deteriorated significantly. In exchange for committing to the rules of the game, Islamist groups were met with more, not less, repression. This wasn't a fair bargain, but the bargain nonetheless held. The radicalization and the exodus from politics that so many warned about—including Islamists themselves—simply did not come to pass.

Islamist Exceptionalism

The starting point for addressing the puzzle of moderation is to view Islamist groups as fundamentally different from traditional political parties. A movement that essentially operates as a mini-state, with a network of parallel institutions, is particularly sensitive to repression. Repression is not just a matter of rigging elections, punishing speech, or arresting dissidents—although that is all bad enough—but of under-mining the vast organizational structure that serves as the engine of the Islamic movement.

In this respect, Islamist groups bear some resemblance to what Robert Michels calls "subversive parties," which are interested not only in replacing the current order but in transforming it. The subversive party, Michels writes, "organizes the *framework* of the social revolu-tion. For this reason it continually endeavors to strengthen its positions, to extend its bureaucratic mechanism, to store up its energies and its funds."[30] Ironically, the revolutionary component of the party's activi-ties leads it to seek accommodation with the state, as has been the case in Egypt, Jordan, Morocco, and elsewhere. It also leads the party to be more "moderate" than it might otherwise be.

Whether repressive measures are actually exercised is not the point; the point is that they *can* be. This fear creates self-enforcing norms that encourage accommodation with the state and discourage confronta-tion. As Michels notes, "the party, continually threatened by the state upon which its existence depends, carefully avoids . . . everything which might irritate the state to excess."[31] The fear of repression has a power-ful effect on Islamist behavior. It explains, among other things, why Islamist groups have so insistently sought both legalization and legiti-macy from regimes. Legal status, while offering no guarantees, at least offers some protection. It is obviously more difficult to repress a legal organization than to repress one that is breaking the law through its very existence.

In more repressive contexts, such as Egypt in the late 2000s, Is-lamist groups do whatever is in their power to minimize repression, by absorbing blows and avoiding further escalation. In an effort to paint government crackdowns as unjustified and disproportionate, Islamists became even more adamant about not resorting to violence precisely as the level of repression increased. Both at home and abroad, they went out of their way to portray themselves as committed to democ-racy, pluralism, and women's rights. Such an approach was meant to solidify their moderate credentials in the eyes of important observers, including liberal parties whose support they needed to stave off politi-cal isolation, and perhaps even reformers or sympathizers within the regime itself. They also hoped to send a message to the international community that mainstream Islamist parties had made a strategic, rather than tactical, decision to support democracy even in the most trying circumstances.

Let us now more carefully consider some of the key factors and causal mechanisms that explain the puzzle of moderation in the absence of democracy.

Moderation as Protection

Under authoritarian rule, and facing mounting repression, Islamist groups cannot afford to be isolated from other political forces. Forming coalitions offers protection against government crackdowns, making it harder for regimes to portray Islamists as extremists or terrorists. In one sense, working with other, more "liberal" and "respected" political forces gives Islamists the political cover they need. This logic was clearly explained in an internally circulated working paper by Bassam al-Emoush, then one of the most prominent IAF leaders before leaving the party in 1997. As relations between the regime and the Brotherhood soured, Emoush argued that it was "important to establish coalitions with pan-Arabist and nationalist forces that reject the western plan to impose Israel as a hegemonic force in the region." "These coalitions are important," he goes on, "since they protect us from the perception that we are the sole power, which leaves us open to repression."[32]

As King Hussein reversed his earlier political reforms, Emoush and his fellow Islamists worried that the regime would intensify its attack. In another internal working paper, he warns his colleagues to prepare for the worst, including "the dissolution of the Islamic Center Society on the grounds of violating the Associations Law."[33] The Islamic Center Society (ICS), Jordan's single largest nongovernmental organization, is the umbrella for the Brotherhood's institutional empire, the financial heart of the organization, and an important funding source for IAF election campaigns. It has run schools, colleges, medical clinics, as well as two hospitals, including the Islamic Hospital, regarded as one of the best in the country.[34] If anything happened to the ICS, it would be a devastating blow. The Brotherhood, of course, knew this. Emoush suggested that "one way to combat this possibility [of a crackdown] is to make a greater effort to reach out to influential individuals in the government and among the tribes so that they form a layer of protection for the ICS."[35] (Emoush's concerns were quite prescient: the regime dissolved the ICS board—effectively a hostile takeover—in July 2006.[36])

Better relations and greater cooperation with secular groups were, as Islamists saw it, critical to increasing the costs of repression for the regime. In partnership with others, including even certain establishment figures, the authorities would need to think twice before cracking down. On the other hand, isolated from other parties and civil society groups, Islamists were easy targets. Without reliable allies, they would have few defenders to organize on their behalf and promote public awareness of their plight. This is what Emoush means by "layers of protection." Allies meant protection. And adopting a more recognizable pro-democracy posture—and saying the right things on women, minority rights, and basic freedoms, for instance—presumably meant more allies. In practice, it did not always work this way, but this did not prevent Islamists from expecting, or hoping, that it would.

Democracy as Something Worth Fighting For

A second reason for Islamists' accommodation with democracy—and later their forceful advocacy of it—is deceptively simple and intuitive: in the absence of democracy, it becomes something worth fighting for. Calling for separation of powers, alternation of power, judicial independence, and popular sovereignty makes sense only if those things are perceived as being taken away or destroyed. When Islamists see themselves as under political siege, the necessity and urgency of democratic reform becomes an almost existential concern.

Nancy Bermeo, who has written extensively on the political learning that results from the experience of autocracy, argues that "dictatorship can force us to reevaluate the nature of particular regimes or enemies, and our own goals and behavior . . . Tactics, or the conscious behaviors one uses to obtain a desired goal, may also be altered as a result of political shocks, crises, and frustration."[37] In other words, political attitudes are far from static, and they are very much dependent on political circumstances. And, in Egypt and Jordan, those circumstances changed markedly.

The descent into authoritarianism in the 1990s caught Islamists off guard. The previous decade had seen unprecedented levels of Islamist political participation. There was a real sense that the democratization process, however flawed, would continue. It didn't. In the subsequent years, Islamists struggled to fashion a coherent response for their new predicament. Political shocks forced Islamists to think again about their priorities and about what really mattered to them.

Such cognitive shifts have happened elsewhere. As the Chilean socialist Jorge Arrate wrote in 1982, "the authoritarianism [of the Pinochet regime] has meant the consolidation of antiauthoritarianism in the heart of the left . . . The loss of democracy and its denigration in the official discourse [of the dictatorship] induce a more profound appreciation of the value, meaning, and contents of political democracy."[38] Islamist leaders have given voice to this dynamic in similar terms. In 2005, I asked the IAF's Jameel Abu Bakr why Jordan's Islamists had adopted a more democratic discourse while deemphasizing Islamic law. He had this to say:

> The change is in the experience. There is no doubt that alcohol is forbidden for Muslims. In the beginning, it was necessary to have a discussion regarding alcohol. As we became more experienced, we saw a need to concentrate on the essential issues. And the essential issues are those that have to do with the democratic process—alternation of power, freedoms, application of justice, rule of law, parliamentary elections, a media that represents the people and protects them from authoritarianism and repression, and an independent judiciary.[39]

In another discussion, the Jordanian Brotherhood's Nael Masalha reflected on how his views on "freedom" had changed. Freedom, he told me, is the "opening to everything, but as to whether it's a means or an end, I think it's actually a necessity and one of the essential needs in the building of any nation."[40] In looking back at the evolution of the Brotherhood's position, Masalha says, "I believe the Islamic movement gave priority to superficial issues that were easy to reverse, and now we're paying the price. And if we, from the 1950s on, had raised [the demand for freedom] and went and told the people 'freedom, freedom, freedom,' I don't think things would have gotten to this point."[41]

It is not that Islamists became less interested in their core concerns of preaching and education. But these aspects of their work depended on a certain level of freedom; they were much more difficult to pursue under authoritarian rule. As Brotherhood General Guide Mamoun al-Houdaiby notes, "if the country is controlled with emergency and martial laws, it would naturally restrict the activities of *da'wa* and the *du'a* [people participating in *da'wa*]."[42] As we will see in subsequent chapters, this is the same argument that the Egyptian and Jordanian Brotherhoods make in their political programs of 2004 and 2005, that religious and social reform were dependent on political reform. Without the latter, discussion of the former becomes almost beside the point.

If democracy becomes something worth fighting for the less of it you have, then this is likely to apply not just to Islamists but also to other groups whose political rights are denied. In this respect, regime repression may have the effect of bringing the opposition closer together. The Brazilian politician Francisco Weffort, reflecting on his country's experience, writes that "state terror reduced all its opponents, generally on the left, but also many liberals, to their common denominator as unprotected and frightened human beings. Civil society was born out of this experience of fear."[43] In the Egyptian context, Houdaiby makes a similar point, in discussing the "common denominators" of opposition during the 1990s:

> Since [the time of our alliance with them ended in 1987] we did not have any differences with the [liberal] Wafd party, and this is due to the fact that all of us—the Brotherhood, the Wafd, and all the other political parties with the exception of the ruling party—face the same oppression. The situation is becoming more strained. The elections come out with false results, and any freedom given is restricted and paralyzed. Hence there are main points of agreement between all the parties as they all ask for suitable guarantees for honest elections [and the] cancellation of the emergency law.[44]

This seems somewhat counterintuitive. Democracy, by opening up political space for the opposition and allowing them greater opportunities to interact and learn from each other, is usually thought to encourage cooperation and compromise. However, in contexts of significant ideological polarization, the reverse is likely to hold true. The shared experience of repression, on the other hand, encourages opposition groups to focus on what they have in common. After all, they have a shared enemy—the regime. So they agree to prioritize the fight for basic freedoms and democracy. Ideological divisions are put to the side.

This dynamic reached its high point during the 18-day uprising in Tahrir Square. It is difficult to think of another time in recent Egyptian history where the full spectrum of opposition groups—youth activists, socialists, liberals, the Brotherhood, even Salafis—were able to so completely put aside their differences and work toward a common objective. Organizers in the square ordered their supporters to refrain from using any ideological or partisan slogans. There was no room for ideological displays, which would shatter the unity of the square and provide an opening for the regime to regain the initiative.

Base–Leadership Gaps

In Egypt, the Islamist "base"—the grassroots rank-and-file that forms the core of Islamist movements—was not particularly enthusiastic about the organization's embrace of elections and democracy and the accompanying deprioritization of Islamic law. They seem to have gone along for the ride with a mixture of silence, skepticism, and, occasionally, opposition. In his 2007 "field study" of 50 rank-and-file activists, Khalil al-Anani found that on a number of key issues, there is a "clear division between the discourse and understanding of the Brotherhood's leadership and the discourse and understanding of the base."[45] For example, while there was nearly unanimous support for the right of Christians to participate in political life (98 percent), only 27 percent of respondents support their right to hold the position of prime minister. Similarly, only 40 percent believe a woman can be a member of parliament. Both positions went against the organization's official stance that Christians and women can hold any political office save that of the presidency. These admittedly incomplete findings—the sample is neither random nor large—are corroborated by Islamist leaders themselves. Numerous officials I interviewed over the course of 2006–8 acknowledged growing sentiment among members that the group's focus should shift back toward religion, education, and grassroots social work.

Some, like journalist and former Brotherhood member Abdel Moneim Mahmoud, point out that the political moderation of the 2000s was never accompanied by any intellectual or theological transformation, so "when you discuss issues [such as pluralism, democracy, and women's participation] with ordinary members, you find that they lack a depth of knowledge."[46] When a woman, Jihan al-Halafawy, ran for parliament in the 2000 elections—a first for the Brotherhood—it "caused a lot of consternation among the rank-and-file who weren't aware of the 1994 statement [which affirmed women's right to run for parliament]."[47] There were similar objections to the 2004 reform initiative, a document that read like a pro-democracy manifesto. After its release, 17 young Brotherhood members offered their resignations, criticizing the organization for leaving the path of religious education and straying from the original message of applying sharia.[48] As the Brotherhood's Khaled Hamza remarks, "every time a new document emerges like the reform initiative or the political program of 2007 . . . there are people who say 'where is the *gama'a* [organization] we used to know?'"[49]

Similarly, Schwedler recounts a revealing conversation with Hamzah Mansour, then the secretary-general of Jordan's IAF: "[Mansour] acknowledged to me in June 2003 that the party's support base is largely disinterested in, if not opposed to, the party's commitment to democratic processes. Its constituency is more moved, he argued, by its advocacy for conservative social programs, Islamic education reforms, and criticism of official foreign policy positions."[50]

The existence of such a base–leadership divide should not necessarily be surprising: if repression has a moderating effect, and Islamist leaders are disproportionately affected by repression, then they are likely to be more moderate than their supporters, who, since they tend to be less directly involved in politics, escape the regime's wrath. When ordinary Egyptians and Jordanians opted to join Islamist movements, a slow and apparently fruitless process of regime-led democratization is probably not what they had in mind. Another factor that stands out is the failure of the educational curriculum—which every Brotherhood member is required to go through—to keep pace with the organization's political evolution. As Anani notes, "the political component is the weakest part of the curriculum."[51]

A religious education will naturally be less concerned with the tenets of democracy and more interested in inculcating the values of duty, responsibility, and obedience, all of which are discussed at length in the group's curriculum.[52] As one prominent Brotherhood member notes, "it is a traditional curriculum because those who devised it are traditionalists and have not caught up with the Brotherhood's own statements and documents. This shows that different parts of the organization are going in different directions."[53] There had been some intermittent efforts to close the gap. A committee for political education was established after the 2005 elections, and a new collected volume—*Awraq fi al-Tarbiya al-Siyasiya* (Readings in Political Education) was introduced into the curriculum in 2006.[54]

Normally, an organization's leadership would try to be responsive to the sentiments of its membership, particularly in a mass movement like the Brotherhood that holds internal elections at a number of different levels. Yet repression insulated the leadership from the pressures of the base for several reasons. First of all, the perception of being under siege may make ordinary activists reluctant to express disagreement with their leaders. They understand that these are exceptional circumstances with the survival of the organization at stake. Conflicts over strategy can therefore be deferred until some later juncture.

Interestingly, authoritarian contexts seem to insulate Islamist groups not only from their own base, but from popular sentiment as well. Most available polling for Egypt and Jordan (as well as other Arab countries) makes clear that these are religiously conservative societies, where large majorities favor Islam and Islamic law playing a central role in public life. For example, in a 2012 Pew poll, 72 percent of Jordanians said that "laws should strictly follow the teachings of the Quran."[55] Meanwhile, in the 2010 Arab Barometer, 51 percent of Jordanians said "a parliamentary system that allows for free competition, but only between Islamic parties" is somewhat appropriate, appropriate, or very appropriate.[56] Somewhat remarkably, the comparable number for "a system governed by Islamic law in which there are *no* political parties or elections" was 62 percent. Even if we assume, for whatever reason, that these results significantly overstate support for sharia, the fact of the matter is that there is a large constituency of Jordanians with positions well to the right of the Muslim Brotherhood on the role of religion in politics.

In Egypt, a similar case can be made. According to the 2012 Pew survey, 60 percent of Egyptians say that laws should strictly follow the Quran's teachings, while another 32 percent say that laws should follow the principles of Islam.[57] More strikingly, in a 2011 poll, 80 percent of respondents said they favored stoning adulterers, 70 percent supported cutting off the hands of thieves, and 88 percent supported the death penalty for apostasy.[58] (The comparable numbers for Jordan were 65, 54, and 83 percent, respectively.) Despite such widespread popular sentiment, public calls for getting serious about sharia were—with the exception of some isolated grumbling—relatively rare during the latter part of Mubarak's autocratic rule.

Mainstream Islamist groups were insulated for another reason: they had a monopoly on the Islamist vote. Under dictatorship, the avenues for establishing more purist, Salafi alternatives to the Brotherhood were limited. Any initiative to start a Salafi party was sure to be met with opposition from the authorities. But perhaps more importantly, there would be little opportunity to actually implement Islamic law. All the opposition could do, even if it was allowed in parliament, was complain and criticize. For Salafis, then, their refusal to enter parliamentary politics was both pragmatic and principled. Being part of a system that was, in their view, so blatantly contrary to God's laws would be unforgivable, especially if there was no possibility of changing it from within.

For these reasons, authoritarian regimes provided the ideal conditions for mainstream Islamist groups to ignore pressures from their right flank and to move, instead, toward the middle. This is precisely what they did.

International Factors

For groups that take pride in their staunch opposition to American foreign policy, Islamists are surprisingly sensitive to what Western audiences—and particularly the United States—think of them. It wasn't always like this. In the 1980s, such concerns were an afterthought for both sides. Islamists may have been gathering strength, but they were not yet a serious threat to the American-sponsored regional order. With the close of the Cold War and the growing challenge they posed to U.S. allies, however, the problem of political Islam had risen on the American agenda, to the point where Clinton administration officials made a number of speeches and statements outlining a "policy" toward Islamist groups.

There was of course the Algerian civil war, which broke out in 1992. But the early 1990s also saw Egypt confronting a violent insurgency led by the radical Islamists of Gama'a Islamiya. With the world paying more attention, Muslim Brotherhood leaders came under growing pressure to distinguish themselves from the perpetrators of the increasingly brutal attacks. They needed to make the case to both domestic and international audiences that they were not like the extremists; they were a different breed of Islamist that pursued nonviolence, spoke (at least some of) the language of human rights and democracy, and sought gradual, not revolutionary change.

The fear of being associated with extremism is not just a matter of being tarred publicly, but of the regime using national security as a pretext to extend its crackdown on all Islamists, including even the moderates. This threat of repression hung over the Brotherhood, putting its organizational structure in grave danger. We will see in Chapter 4 how this spurred the group to release a series of declarative statements, laying out in detail the group's positions on issues of controversy, including democracy and pluralism, the use of violence, and the rights of women and minorities.

In the wake of the September 11 attacks, it became even more important for Islamists to present themselves in the most moderate light possible. Arab regimes were using Bush's war on terror to pass draconian antiterrorism legislation with Islamist groups as the primary target. The irony is that the Bush administration's "freedom agenda" also provided an opening for Islamist groups, who stood to benefit most from U.S. pressure on Arab autocrats. Obviously, these two competing impulses of Bush administration policy were often in conflict, but, in tandem, they provided additional incentives for Islamist moderation.

Even Brotherhood leader Mahdi Akef, known for his inflammatory anti-American comments, admitted in August 2006 that the Bush administration's pressure on the Mubarak regime had a positive effect on Egyptian reform.[59] Abdel Moneim Abul Futouh, then a member of the Brotherhood's Guidance Bureau, put it this way: "Everyone knows it . . . We benefited, everyone benefited, and the Egyptian people benefited."[60] The group happened to release its "reform initiative" in March 2004, just as the Bush administration was working to unveil its own "Broader Middle East Initiative." The synergies were as undeniable as they were unlikely. As the Jordanian Islamist writer Jihad Abu Eis said, "It's the right of Islamists to take advantage of American pressure on reform."[61]

The near-obsession with what America said and did would continue, the lasting legacy of decades of U.S. interference in the region. If the "American veto" was enough to block democratic progress, as it had been in Algeria and Palestine, then Islamists had little choice but to hope that, one day, U.S. policy might change. The Bush administration was hated for other reasons—namely the Iraq War and its unflinching support for Israel—but, in the so-called freedom agenda, Islamists across the region found reason to hope. Certainly, it wasn't Bush's intention to empower Islamist parties, but they benefitted nonetheless.

Those hopes, however, were shattered when the Bush administration reversed course in late 2005 and early 2006, dropping its emphasis on democracy promotion. Across the region, in Egypt, Lebanon, Kuwait, Bahrain, and even Saudi Arabia, Islamist groups were claiming one success after another in local and national elections. Perhaps Bush administration officials could have found a way to bear this with their tolerance for "constructive instability."[62] But it went a step too far when Hamas won the Palestinian elections in January 2006. Hamas wasn't just an Islamist group; it was designated as a terrorist organization by the State Department. And then there were other problems. The situation in Iraq, another country where an Islamist party came to power through U.S.-sponsored elections, was descending into civil war. Iran, meanwhile, was throwing its weight around, challenging the United States on its own turf. Soon enough, the Bush administration's idealism gave way to damage control and picking up the pieces left over from its own disastrous policies.

Freed from the withering glare of the international community, Arab regimes judged, correctly, that they had ridden out the storm. The repression returned and it was even worse than before. But instead of turning against the democratic process in desperation, mainstream Islamist groups doubled down on the pro-democracy course they had committed to years before. They continued to position themselves as "moderates" in a region of extremism and instability. That is what they wanted the world to believe.

3

The Promise of Politics

IN 1984 AND 1992, Egypt and Jordan registered their best-ever Freedom House scores.[1] In fact, Jordan's 1992 rating was—and, at the time of writing, still is—the best ever for an Arab country. For Islamists, these were heady times. An Islamic revival was taking hold throughout the region, and the religious fervor of the time would bleed into the political realm. As Islamists entered politics with their idealism and unadulterated commitment to sharia, one may have expected a tempering of spirit. But in societies undergoing cultural and religious transformations, Islamists found themselves not constrained by politics, but empowered by it. Islamists grew more confident and emboldened as they found a public receptive to their brand of assertive religion-infused politics. Islamist groups were reflecting deeper cultural changes already well under way and then amplifying them further. Their societies were transformed in the process.

In this chapter, I will consider some of the key moments in the evolution of the Muslim Brotherhood in Egypt and Jordan. Despite their very different local contexts, the two countries pursued a similar trajectory—an unprecedented democratic "opening" followed by a sudden turn to repression. These periods of opening—and how Islamist groups responded to them—have generally escaped the attention of Western analysts. It is worth revisiting these political openings, however brief and tentative, to see what they can tell us about the new process of democratization—and de-democratization—occurring in the wake of the Arab Spring.

Mubarak Opens Up

Oddly enough, the reign of President Hosni Mubarak began with a newfound sense of possibility. One of his predecessor Anwar el-Sadat's last acts in office was to round up and imprison more than a thousand activists and political figures. After the ensuing trauma—culminating in Sadat's assassination—there was an apparent desire on the part of both regime and opposition to defuse tensions. "Between 1981 and 1983," writes Noha el-Mikawy, "everyone was building bridges of goodwill."[2] Shortly after Sadat's death, Mubarak invited opposition leaders to take part in a national dialogue to discuss the future of political reform.

The opening of political space, and the optimism it helped create, contributed to a perception that Egypt was moving toward democracy. As Anthony McDermott observed, "there was a sense of freedom on a scale which had not been felt for some years."[3] Meanwhile, the parliamentary elections of 1984 and 1987 were the freest Egypt had seen since 1952 (although far from free and fair in absolute terms).

Jordan's "transition" seemed to hold even more promise. Like in Egypt, 1984 proved an important marker. That year, the Jordanian Muslim Brotherhood contested elections on three levels, university, municipal, and national, exceeding expectations in each. The "Islamic trend" swept the elections for the University of Jordan's student union. On the national level, for the first time since 1967, reasonably free by-elections were held for eight vacated parliamentary seats. Three candidates from the Brotherhood ran, with two winning by comfortable margins. But that was just a dry run for the 1989 elections, the freest in Jordan's history. The Brotherhood and independent Islamists won 34 of 80 seats. Along with the leftist and nationalist opposition, they could claim a slight majority. Soon enough, Jordan would see its first Islamist speaker of parliament, as well as five Brotherhood ministers who briefly joined the government in 1991, another historic first.

Religious Revival

In any process of democratization, the role of popular sentiment grows increasingly important. Politicians, assuming they want to get elected again, cannot afford to ignore voters. Where, then, was popular sentiment heading during Jordan's democratic "experiment"? The place to start is with what Islamists call the "Islamic awakening," which permanently reshaped Arab society and continues to make its presence felt to this day.

It is easy to overstate the importance of particular historical junctures. But that doesn't apply to 1967, a year that ushered in a slow but decisive transformation. That year, Egypt, Jordan, and Syria were routed by Israel in the Six-Day War. Millions had placed their hopes in the charismatic Egyptian president, Gamal Abdel Nasser, himself a Brotherhood member turned secular nationalist.[4] Such a stark defeat brought about a collective round of soul-searching. In the mass disillusion that followed, Arabs across the region concluded that the socialist experiment had failed. Many young socialists began flirting with alternative ideologies, including two of most powerful Islamist figures of the Arab Spring, Tunisia's Rachid Ghannouchi and Egypt's Khairat al-Shater. An emerging narrative—which would become the Islamist narrative—was that the Arab world had strayed from the teachings of Islam and that it needed to return. And so the religious revival began in earnest, buoyed by the release of imprisoned Muslim Brotherhood leaders in the early 1970s.

The changes taking hold were compounded by the growing influence of Saudi Arabia and other Gulf countries, which, armed with petrodollars and a Salafi brand of Islam, loaned and granted their poorer Arab neighbors billions of dollars. Meanwhile, hundreds of thousands of Egyptians and Jordanians went to the Gulf for work. They came back not only wealthier but more conservative, helping to create a new Islamically minded bourgeoisie. Remarkably, financial assistance from Gulf donors, along with remittances from Jordanian expatriates, accounted at one point for nearly half of Jordan's gross national product.[5]

Meanwhile, countries that had dabbled in the state control of production gradually liberalized their economies. In Egypt, the Brotherhood would turn against the neoliberalism of Sadat's *infitah*, or opening, railing against the Westernization that seemed to come with it. The irony is that they were among its greatest beneficiaries: the relative economic freedom of the 1970s allowed Brotherhood members to establish new businesses, banks, and other economic ventures. By the late 1980s, the private sector was effectively dominated by a small number of families, eight of which included members or supporters of the Brotherhood, according to one account.[6] With Egyptians increasingly turning to "sharia-compliant" venues for their money, Islamic banks mushroomed.

It is obviously difficult to quantify these sorts of societal changes, but one interesting indicator is the rapid construction of new mosques. In a study of the changing religious architecture of Amman, Eugene Rogan found that "the five years 1980-1984 represent a period of extraordinary mosque construction."[7] In 1973, there was one mosque for every 13,181 residents; by 1984, there was one for every 6,908 residents. Although the government had to approve building requests, most mosque construction was initiated by private citizens and organizations.[8] The Islamic revival, in other words, was an organic, popular one.

No regime, however autocratic, can fully insulate itself from its own people, and it was clear that the groundswell of religiosity was not a passing fad. Even before their respective political openings, Egypt and Jordan had allowed for some civil society participation, particularly with religious groups and charities that eschewed partisan politics. The regimes saw the Islamic revival and cynically tried to manage it, co-opt it, and even ride it to greater popularity. The results were decidedly mixed. Anwar el-Sadat, with a prayer mark—the uniquely Egyptian *zabiba*—on his forehead, styled himself the "believing president." Jordan's King Hussein, a descendant of the Prophet Mohamed who enjoyed a modicum of historical and religious legitimacy, had perhaps a better claim.

In 1979, the Jordanian government exempted citizens from 25 percent of their income tax if they paid *zakat* (a religious obligation requiring Muslims to donate to the poor).[9] Newspapers and state television were instructed to devote more programming to religious issues. Despite having only three self-identified Islamists in a body of 60 representatives, the 1984 parliament was receptive to Islamist initiatives, reflecting the popular reach of Jordan's religious resurgence. A majority of 33 deputies called on the government to implement a mandatory zakat tax, while 22 supported a bid to prohibit the manufacture and sale of alcohol.[10]

Similarly, in Egypt, long before the Brotherhood had any formal presence in parliament, efforts to inject Islamic law into politics were well under way. There were only a handful of Islamists in the 1976 parliament,[11] yet 130 deputies gathered to submit a proposal to the speaker of the house in February 1976 requesting that the constitution be amended to make the principles of sharia "*the* primary source" of legislation and not just "*a* primary source."[12] Eventually, in 1980, the amendment was pushed through by Sadat (in his "believing president" mode) and subsequently endorsed by public referendum. Now Islamists had constitutional sanction to advocate for their preferred policies, and that is exactly what they did. For secular parties, there would be mounting pressure to declare their commitment to the constitution and, by extension, to the implementation of sharia law.

The formal effort to synchronize Egyptian law, an odd patchwork of French and British codes, with Islamic law had the support of one of Egypt's most powerful men, Sufi Abu Talib, speaker of parliament and a close associate of President Sadat. On December 17, 1978, Abu Talib addressed parliament and announced the "formation of special committees with the responsibility for studying all legislative proposals relating to the application of Islamic law."[13] Five committees—covering litigation, the criminal code, social affairs, civil and trade regulations, and monetary and economic affairs—were established to provide recommendations on how to revise existing laws and codes to conform with sharia. Their brief was to study the practical application of Islamic law in other Muslim countries and summon legal scholars to provide expert advice. Several years of work later, Abu Talib addressed the assembly in July 1982:

> Our colleagues, the heads of the committees, will present to you a statement on each of the ongoing legislative initiatives. I should note here at the start that elevating Islamic law to the level of application and laying down its rules represents the return of not only the Egyptian people but the entire Arab and Islamic nation to its nature after being alienated [from its nature] for more than a century as a result of its subjection under laws foreign to it.[14]

In the same address, Abu Talib spoke of the need to close the gap between "what the Egyptian citizen believed and the laws that governed him" and explicitly mentioned the examples of alcohol, adultery, and usury.[15] No doubt some senior officials, including Abu Talib, felt strongly about the initiative on its merits, but this is also what it looked like when a government was trying to be responsive to popular sentiment, or what it took to be popular sentiment. Whenever activists and politicians made the case for Islamization, they would couch their appeals in populist terms. This, they insisted, is what ordinary Egyptians wanted and needed, and it was the government's job to channel and reflect these sentiments as much as it could.

It would be one thing if this were just mere rhetoric, but Abu Talib's committees had, in fact, painstakingly produced hundreds of pages of detailed legislation. A draft law on civil transactions was more than 1,000 articles long, one on tort reform included 513 articles, while legislation revising criminal punishments had 635. Draft legislation on the maritime code included 443 articles, while commercial code legislation came out to 776 articles.[16] Understandably, then, Abu Talib called it a "historic undertaking."[17] Mumtaz Nasar, a member of the litigation committee who became head of the parliamentary bloc of the ostensibly secular Wafd in 1984, congratulated Abu Talib on the progress being made. Speaking of his own committee's work, Nasar explained:

> The committee ensured that the project [to revise the law] had two sources, the first of them the Quran, the prophetic traditions, and the consensus of the scholars . . . and secondly [the authority of the president] in accordance with sharia law as it relates to the organization of the affairs of state . . . And the objective of this second source is the realization of the public interest on matters that do not have a specific textual injunction [in the Quran or prophetic traditions].[18]

After Mubarak replaced Abu Talib, much of the legislation, with the exception of sections of the maritime code, was tabled. Still, throughout the decade, there remained a visible faction in the ruling National Democratic Party (NDP) that favored the application of Abu Talib's proposals. In the NDP's 1986 party congress, for instance, the religion committee released 21 recommendations, all around the objective of "purification of existing laws in contradiction with provisions of the sharia."[19]

The Muslim Brotherhood and the Democratic Opening

The 1984 parliamentary elections were the first real test of Mubarak's professed commitment to reform. Despite lingering doubts about parliamentary participation, the Brotherhood saw an opportunity. After its leaders were granted amnesty in the early 1970s, the group had worked to rebuild its organizational structures and reacquaint itself with ordinary Egyptians, many of whom had little memory of the Brotherhood or what it stood for. By 1984, the Brotherhood hadn't quite recaptured past glories, but it had reconstituted itself as a force to be reckoned with. With parliament acquiring greater importance—or so it seemed—the Brotherhood thought it could translate its growing grassroots support into political influence.

This new chapter began with an electoral law that required parties to clear an electoral threshold of 8 percent, which wasn't a foregone conclusion even for the Wafd, then the country's leading opposition party. The Wafd needed a partner with a popular base, so it turned to the Brotherhood with a proposal for cooperation as a junior partner. Under the agreement, the Brotherhood would run candidates under the Wafd party list and form part of the Wafd parliamentary bloc, assuming the threshold was cleared.

With its surprise move to join forces with Egypt's oldest liberal party, it became easier to discern the group's priorities. One might expect that at such a high point of political openness—that with greater inclusion for the opposition in general and Islamists in particular—the Brotherhood would adopt a new approach, democratizing its discourse and moving away from a distinctly Islamist agenda. This, though, is not quite what happened.

This is not necessarily to say that Brotherhood leaders were hostile to democracy; they weren't. But they were yet to embrace it as a call to arms. Rather, their call was simple and predictable: a nearly single-minded pursuit of applying sharia law and promoting their own distinctive brand of morality. This made the alliance with the Wafd party controversial for both parties. While they shared an interest in ending emergency law and protecting political freedoms, this was obscured by the obvious gap between the parties' self-conceptions, and how, particularly, they viewed the place of Islamic law in Egyptian politics.

The Brotherhood went out of its way to emphasize that the alliance was not an ideological concession and by no means represented a change in its original position toward multipartyism. There was, after all, the legacy of founder Hassan al-Banna, who saw party politics as serving "the appetites of the rulers and the tyrannies of authority."[20] Brotherhood leaders insisted that their new course was born out of pragmatism and reminded their detractors that even Banna himself ran for parliament on two separate occasions.

As the Brotherhood's Salah Abu Ismail argued, "they didn't allow us to form a party on the basis of *aqidah* [creed] . . . and closed the door of *da'wa* [religious education]. We are not able to raise our voices on the pulpit or through our own political party, so what is left for us except to work through an existing political party?"[21] General Guide Tilmisani affirmed that "the Brothers have made clear more than once that they are not a party . . . they are an organization that calls for accepting God's law in all facets of life."[22] The Brotherhood's leaders were defensive, as were the Wafd, about the exact nature of the alliance, steering clear of the word "coalition" (*tahaluf*), instead opting to use the terms *ta'awun* (cooperation), *tanseeq* (coordination), or *tadamun* (solidarity). Fouad Seraj al-Din, the octogenarian leader of the Wafd, preferred the word *ta'atuf* (sympathy), while most others in the Wafd settled for *tadamun*.[23]

During the parliamentary session, the relationship between the two parties was tense and, at times, rather contentious. The problems began during the run-up to the 1984 elections when 15 Wafd members resigned, protesting the impending Islamization of their party, which they proudly saw as one of Egypt's last remaining bastions of secularism. For their part, Brotherhood members, from the beginning, lobbed accusations at the Wafd for failing to respect Islamic law.[24] The Wafd certainly tried, revamping its electoral program to address the Brotherhood's concerns. In its original 1977 program, there was only one passing mention of sharia as the "original" source of legislation. The 1984 program, in contrast, included an entire section devoted to the application of Islamic law, in which the Wafd stated that Islam was both "religion and state" and that sharia was the principal source of legislation. In addition, the program called for combating moral "deviation" in society, purifying the media of anything contradicting sharia and general morals, and emphasizing the media's role in actively guiding Egyptians toward a moral life.[25] There was also reference to *tathqif*, or the need to instill an Islamic consciousness among the population—an idea usually associated with the Brotherhood. If this is what Egypt's oldest secular party sounded like, then what passed for secularism in Egypt had been altered beyond recognition.

Its alliance with the Brotherhood was an important factor pushing the Wafd toward such a posture, but it was far from the only one. The party was not operating in a vacuum. The political and religious context in the country was changing. The Wafd, in turn, needed to change along with it and adapt to an Egypt where Islam and Islamic law—however one wished to define them—were becoming national preoccupations.

Islamizing its discourse was something the Wafd felt it had to do, and some of its leading figures seemed to have little problem leaning in this direction. The Brotherhood was only the junior partner in the alliance and was not in a position to force the Wafd's hand. Wafd leaders dominated platform preparations and would not have made changes unless they thought them necessary. Interestingly, much of the religious content of the 1984 program remained in the 1987 program, after the alliance with the Brotherhood had come to an end.[26]

Noha el-Mikawy, in her book *Building Consensus in Egypt's Transition Process*, argues that, in contrast to the polarization of Sadat's final years, a degree of consensus emerged in the 1980s between government and opposition as well as within the opposition itself. As Mikawy sees it, this was possible because of the Islamist opposition's willingness to compromise and accept the existing economic and political structure of the regime (even if it was rigged against them). Another sort of consensus was emerging too, but it was not the kind that would have reassured those who hoped democratization and moderation would go hand in hand. More democracy did *not* coincide with Islamists adopting a more democratic discourse or fundamentally rethinking their basic aims. Instead, multiparty competition helped produce a political environment oriented around not just the Islamization of society—this, after all, was happening anyway—but the Islamization of the country's legal system. The "sharia-ization" of Egyptian politics cut across ideological boundaries. Mohamed al-Taweel argues that from 1982 until at least the 1987 elections, there was a broad consensus favoring sharia legislation that covered nearly all of the Egyptian political elite, including "the president, senior government officials, religious scholars, legal experts, judges, and the legislative branch."[27]

Admittedly, in hindsight, Egypt's "democratic opening" was something of an illusion. However, from the perspective of the actors involved, there was a sense that something unprecedented was taking place. The Wafd, for instance, really did seem to believe that it would soon become Egypt's ruling party-in-waiting. Based on President Mubarak's own statements, this wasn't nearly as far-fetched as it might sound now. Back then, when opposition leaders could command a regular audience with the president, Wafd leader Fouad Seraj al-Din had a modest proposal for Mubarak. He suggested that he become a president "above politics," maintaining his distance from the ruling party. Mubarak reportedly responded that he liked the idea but would keep his membership in the NDP during the "transition."[28]

Meanwhile, the Brotherhood was aware that it remained vulnerable. The government could have easily blocked its alliance with the Wafd, but tolerance prevailed. Mubarak had little interest in making enemies of the Brotherhood, when there was little to suggest it posed an existential threat. And perhaps it made sense to lure the group into the open to better gauge its popular support. Either way, the openings under Mubarak, while limited in absolute terms, were a marked improvement over nearly everything that had come before. It wouldn't be a stretch to consider the mid-1980s the high point of political participation in the postwar era—at least until the 2011 uprising came along.

Because the "transition" that some had hoped for never came to pass and because the opening itself was eclipsed by the turn to repression of the early 1990s, Egypt's forgotten decade remains something of a curiosity. But in a region where autocracy seemed remarkably constant, the decade provides an important counterpoint. Since Egypt was not a democracy, opposition groups and ruling party officials were obviously not as responsive to popular demands as they otherwise might have been. But they had to be *somewhat* responsive, and to an extent they were.

The "Islamic Alliance" of 1987

After a series of meetings in the lead-up to the 1987 parliamentary elections, major opposition parties, along with the Brotherhood, agreed to field a unified list under the Wafd moniker. The heads of the parties were to attend a meeting at Fouad Seraj al-Din's house on February 14, 1987, to discuss drafting common principles. However, the night before, the Wafd announced its withdrawal from the coalition after Seraj al-Din lost a last-minute internal vote, 11 to 9, in the party's higher council.[29] The same night of the surprise announcement, the Labor party was holding a meeting. Brotherhood representatives were in attendance and suggested, in light of the Wafd's withdrawal, a more limited electoral alliance between themselves and Labor. It was agreed to the following day, with the Liberal party joining as a junior partner.

Ibrahim Shukri, chairman of the Labor party, was optimistic. "God wanted this, so it was," he said. They called it the "Islamic Alliance," reflecting the relative closeness of the parties and the greater ideological affinity they shared. Mustafa Mashour, the Brotherhood's deputy general guide, recounted: "After the Wafd raised the banner of applying sharia, we expected that they would live up to the commitment, but it quickly became clear from the beginning that Wafdists are Wafdists and Brothers are Brothers."[30] In 1987, it was different: the coalition was oriented around an explicitly Islamic focus, with application of sharia law at the top of the agenda. As General Guide Hamed Abu Nasr explained, "the cooperation this time has a sound basis . . . [All the parties] agreed on the importance of applying Islamic law and there is no difference on this issue."[31]

In this new alliance, the Brotherhood could keep its original focus intact. The electoral program it drafted with its coalition partners is unique among Brotherhood programs for its unabashed focus on Islamic law and public (and private) morality. The language used is surprising for its almost raw religiosity, employing terms not often heard in mainstream political discourse. It was precisely the kind of language that the Brotherhood would later take care to avoid for fear of alienating less conservative constituencies, liberal allies, and the international community.

At the start of the program, the alliance lays out its objective of a "complete system for governing and for every social activity."[32] It offers a critique of the economic and political status quo, but, for the alliance, Egypt's myriad problems ultimately had one source—the lack of religious observance in both public and private life. "Egypt faces one of the most difficult phases in all of its history," the program says, "and if we wanted to give this phase a name, we would call it the phase of 'the deterioration of values.' The reasons for the umma's economic, political, and social weakness comes back in the final analysis to the absence of noble morals and values."[33] Interestingly, it refers to the "hope" that existed in 1984 but "[what was hoped for] did not happen; God's law was not implemented."[34]

There is a whole section devoted to the application of Islamic law, something that would not be repeated in future programs. For the Islamic Alliance, there was no room for dissent on such a fundamental matter: "Implementation of sharia is a religious obligation and a necessity for the nation. This is not something that is up for discussion but rather it is incumbent upon every Muslim to fulfill God's commandments by governing by his law. For this reason, we call for the application of sharia to begin immediately in accordance with the constitution."[35] It will be, the program says, "a massive national undertaking that will require experts to devise how to apply Islamic law in a variety of realms."[36]

The word *tahrim* is used repeatedly, a religious term which means to make *haram*, or to forbid. The word is not one with any legal import because it refers to God's injunctions upon believers rather than legal injunctions on Egyptian citizens. Meanwhile, the plank on Copts does not even attempt to assert their equality as citizens (as later programs would).[37] At only 16 pages, the alliance's program is short and vague. The planks on democracy are boilerplate, calling for revision of the most egregious laws restricting political freedom but failing to offer any broader vision for, or interest in, promoting democratic reform in Egypt.

In comparison to the Brotherhood's more well-known and widely cited statements, position papers, and electoral programs from the 1990s and, later, those of 2004, 2005, and 2007, the gap in quality and sophistication is striking. However, taken on its own terms and in its own context, the 1987 program was not the narrow, uncompromising document it may now appear to be. At the time, it fell comfortably somewhere within Egypt's increasingly conservative mainstream. That the program may have been in tune with the mainstream did not mean it was in tune with the country's political elites. Opposition parties, particularly the leftist Tagammu, were keen to exploit the weaknesses it saw in the Brotherhood's approach, pointing to the program's vagueness. The retort of Mamoun al-Houdaiby was telling: "Before [Tagammu] demand a detailed program from us, they should demand that the correct foundation for the country be established. That foundation is Islam, and we make its application our first priority. After they do that, then they can ask for a detailed program."[38]

At times, the Brotherhood got more personal, accusing Tagammu and other leftists of atheism, or *ilhad*, for their opposition to sharia. "The philosophy of Tagammu rests," said Hamed Abu Nasr, "on a foundation of the denial of God and the idea that religion is the opiate of the people . . . and so it is impossible that the party will ever have a place among the Egyptian people."[39] When Islamists were attacked for a shaky commitment to pluralism, they made little effort to assert their democratic *bona fides*, perhaps because they didn't have many yet. As Hasanayn Tawfiq Ibrahim and Hoda Raghib Awad note, "the Brotherhood did not refute these attacks in a logical or consistent way as they did with other accusations and attacks. Rather, their responses were vague and murky, and appeared to confirm the accusations more than putting them to rest."[40]

The Muslim Brotherhood in Parliament, 1987–1990

The Brotherhood's prioritization of sharia did not appear to hurt its popularity; if anything, the opposite seemed closer to the truth. It ran an effective, professional campaign in the fall of 1987. The Islamic Alliance won 60 seats, the most of any opposition party or coalition since Egypt became a republic in 1952. Thirty-six of those seats went to the Brotherhood, a more than fourfold increase from its previous total. The Wafd won only 35 seats, losing its status as leader of the opposition. Meanwhile, the elections handed the ruling party its worst result ever—winning only 69 percent of the vote.

The elections confirmed what had already become obvious just by looking at Egyptian society. It had been unheard of to see young, educated women covering their hair, but, by the early 1980s, it was a common sight. Educational attainment was increasing exponentially, with millions of Egyptians acquiring high school diplomas and college degrees for the first time. More education did not lead to more "secularism," as many may have expected. Instead, it was political Islam that drew considerable strength from these changes. Over the 1970s, Islamists first made their presence felt in the universities, forming "Islamic groups," or *Gama'at Islamiya*, many of which clashed, sometimes violently, with their leftist opponents. Soon, they had taken over the student unions. In the 1980s, the Brotherhood won a series of elections in the professional syndicates. This was not the rise of the destitute and the disenfranchised: the Brotherhood's leaders and activists were disproportionately well educated, forming an increasingly confident counter-elite.

By the 1987 elections, it was becoming difficult to deny that the Islamists had arrived. After years of operating in the open, the electorate had become better acquainted with the Brotherhood and its program. Many Egyptians, in the early optimism of the religious revival, seemed to like what they saw. The call to implement sharia, far from being evidence of the Brotherhood's radicalism, was a vote getter, reflecting the emerging conservative consensus. With the results of the 1987 polls, their best showing yet, Islamists were emboldened, interpreting their growing share of the vote as a mandate for pushing Islamist policies. They did not necessarily overreach or impose their ideas on others—the Brotherhood, at its core, has always been a cautious organization—but they continued to view parliament as a means to the end of Islamizing Egypt.

In their study of the Brotherhood's political participation in the 1980s, Ibrahim and Awad write that "the call for applying Islamic law was the most important issue that the Brotherhood focused on in its parliamentary activities"; this ran the gamut from banning interest, restricting access to alcohol, closing nightclubs, keeping businesses closed on Friday, blocking immoral television programs, ensuring that government workers could leave work for prayer, and increasing religious programming on television as well as in the educational curriculum.[41] When government officials maintained that 90 percent of Egypt's laws were already in accordance with Islam, Mamoun al-Houdaiby was unconvinced. "God ordered us to rule by what he sent down," he said, "and not with what looks like what God sent down."[42]

An examination of the Brotherhood's parliamentary activities from 1987 to 1990 indicates a strong focus on sharia and moral issues, with 24 of 57 "questions" and 6 of 11 "interpellations" lodged by Brotherhood deputies falling into this category.[43] This was coupled with mounting concerns over the Ministry of Interior's abuse and torture of detainees. The Brotherhood's attacks on the government's conduct coincide with the appointment in 1986 of Zaki Badr as interior minister. Badr was notorious for his brutality against radical Islamists in Asyut, where he was previously stationed. His animus extended to the Muslim Brotherhood—at a 1990 rally he expressed his desire to completely wipe them out—and the group used its perch in parliament to undermine its new opponent.[44] That said, the attention on civil liberties was limited in scope—a natural reaction to the growing number of arrests—but did not extend beyond a parochial concern for the security of its own members.

The Muslim Brotherhood was still a niche party, albeit one with a growing, mass constituency. This, too, is how they saw themselves. As Mustafa Mashour put it, the Brotherhood is "a religious call before it is an association. The Brothers are God's call rather than Hassan al-Banna's call. They represent a call to Islam as it came to the Prophet Mohamed . . . No one should think that the Brotherhood is a limited group made up of a particular group of people. Rather, it is an Islamic current that covers every Muslim."[45] Meanwhile, Houdaiby saw parliament as a means to "promote awareness of God's laws through legislation . . . and work toward the application of God's law, in both letter and spirit, in various fields at the national level and in all the affairs of individuals and society."[46] Mashour elaborated:

It is not asked of members of parliament to offer their opinion regarding God's sharia, to revise it or determine its appropriateness, but what is asked of them is to execute God's law . . . and apply it fully without discussion . . . It is not permissible to pose the question to man of whether he agrees with its application or not, since God's sharia came down to man for him to apply it over Muslims, and it is incumbent upon Muslims to obey it . . . and he who refuses it or

thinks that it is not appropriate is considered a *murtad* (apostate) . . .
and if he does not repent, the punishment of excommunication can
be applied to him.[47]

Mashour's remarks—coming from such a senior Brotherhood figure—
are remarkable. He veers dangerously close to *takfir*, the practice of
making the blood of a Muslim licit. *Takfir* is the principle, if one can
call it that, that radicals use to justify their use of violence against other
Muslims. Their position on *takfir* is one of the key dividing lines between mainstream Islamists and their radical counterparts. That the
line, in the late 1980s, would occasionally become blurry is illustrative
of how far the Brotherhood still had to go. Indeed, it is difficult to overstate just how far removed this sort of exclusionary rhetoric is from the
much more measured, conciliatory discourse of the group in the 1990s
through the 2011 revolution.

None of this is to say that the Brotherhood, during this earlier period,
was bent on the destruction of pluralism and democracy. In the Egyptian context, none of the views cited above, with the notable exception
of the opinion on excommunication, would have been considered outside the mainstream; if anything, they were firmly within the emerging
consensus on the role of sharia in public life. In short, the Brotherhood
saw itself as the guardian of a project that, if not for its own spirited
advocacy, would be postponed indefinitely or simply forgotten. It was
an Islamist group and, as such, was concerned with Islamism. It was setting roots in society, winning a larger share of parliamentary seats, and
building strong coalitions with like-minded groups.

From an electoral standpoint, the Brotherhood's adoption of Islamic
law as a call to arms made sense, allowing it to expand its support in
society as well as energize its conservative base. A changing electorate interacted with an increasingly pluralistic party system, producing an environment conducive to Islamist ideas. A growing number of
parties were competing not only with the ruling party but also with
other opposition groups. With even ostensibly secular parties employing religious rhetoric and calling for sharia, a group like the Brotherhood needed to distinguish itself and maintain its position as the most
"authentic" Islamic voice. This kind of competition, or "outbidding,"
would have made it difficult for the Brotherhood to tack back to the

center and redefine itself. Another party, in this case the Wafd, was presenting itself as Egypt's pro-democracy force, and it is unlikely that the Brotherhood could have become a more convincing advocate in this regard without diluting its specifically Islamic appeal.

Lastly, it is worth noting the relative lack of importance of external factors during this period. In the early 1990s, the Bush and Clinton administrations would begin devoting more attention to political Islam. But in the 1980s, when the Soviet threat still loomed large, the Brotherhood did not need to worry about presenting a moderate face to Western journalists or policymakers. For the most part, they weren't watching—but perhaps more importantly, there wasn't much to watch. Egypt, while not yet a democracy, appeared to be slowly and quietly democratizing.

Jordan's Democratic "Experiment" Begins

Like Egypt's 1984 contest, Jordan's 1989 elections seemed to represent a shift away from the past but to an even larger degree. On the day of the vote, King Hussein spoke in grand terms: "This day is one of the most distinguished days in our lives. It is the day when, after a long absence, the sons and daughters of Jordan are exercising their full right to participate in drawing a new picture for the future."[48]

Political openings unthinkable 10 years before were now available to the country's Islamic movement. During the election campaign, Islamists distinguished themselves from the competition. With the exception of the Brotherhood's list, which represented only 4 percent of the total number of candidates,[49] there were minimal differences between those vying for office. "All candidates are for the Palestinian cause [and] support of the Intifada . . . They are for national unity and equal opportunities in jobs and education," the commentator Fahed Fanek observed.[50] Political parties were still banned, which made it difficult for the once-powerful leftists to organize coordinated campaigns. The Brotherhood, on the other hand, was able to run a coherent, professional campaign under the banner of "Islam is the solution." The Islamists stood apart from the crowd.

While its electoral program still left a number of questions unanswered, the Brotherhood's basic thrust was clear. "Our basic aim," explained spokesman Ziad Abu Ghanimeh during the campaign, "is to make the second article of the constitution, which says Islam is the state religion, true in fact and not only on paper."[51] Social issues predominated. In response to a question on future legislative initiatives, candidate Abdel Moneim Abu Zant touted his support for banning alcohol and making the headscarf mandatory for Muslim women.[52]

Though it was increasingly coming into vogue elsewhere, the Brotherhood did not seem particularly comfortable with the discourse of democracy. As the *Jordan Times* reported at the time, "the [Islamist] bloc calls for the adoption of Islamic shura—consultation—as a means for public participation, as opposed to Western-style democracy, a concept many Islamic scholars maintain is alien to Islam."[53] While not necessarily reflecting the official position of the organization, leading Brotherhood figures often displayed an ambivalence, and sometimes suspicion, toward democratic precepts. Youssef al-Azm, who would later serve as a cabinet minister in 1991, called democracy "a transitional stage in contemporary society which we develop [into] shura, to which we condone no alternative."[54] Meanwhile, the Brotherhood's Ahmad Nofal put it this way: "If we have a choice between democracy and dictatorship, we choose democracy. But if it's between Islam and democracy, we choose Islam."[55]

The Brotherhood in Parliament, 1989–1993

In the first freely contested elections since the 1950s, the Brotherhood had the opportunity to test whether its strategy of backing the monarchy—and being granted the space to spread its message in return—would finally pay political dividends. In discussions with close advisors, King Hussein predicted the Brotherhood would win only around 10 seats and felt that royal court chief Mudar Badran's estimate of 16 seats was "too much."[56] As it turned out, it was too little: 22 of the group's 26 candidates won. Despite running only 4 percent of the total number of candidates, the Brotherhood won 31 percent of the available seats.[57] In addition, independent Islamists won 12 seats, giving Islamists a loose bloc of 34 out of 80 seats. The results shocked the country's political elite. Badran, who stayed up all night with the king after the results were announced, recalls the tense discussions.[58] A number of former ministers were urging Hussein to cancel the elections and disband parliament. The king, fearful of the domestic and international backlash, brushed their suggestions aside. The experiment, at least for the time being, would continue.

As Brotherhood leader Ishaq Farhan later admitted, "[we] didn't really have a clear program or agenda." Although the group's 1989 electoral program may have been short on specifics, it left little doubt as to where Islamist priorities lay. The "first and most important duty," the program said, was to "exert every possible effort to revise all laws and regulations in Jordan so that they completely conform with the Islamic sharia."[59] Not surprisingly, the Brotherhood interpreted its newfound electoral success as a vote of confidence for its unabashedly Islamist agenda. One of the first tasks for the new parliament concerned the acceptable boundaries of political contestation. When the government proposed legislation abolishing the 1953 anti-communism statute, several Brotherhood members of parliament registered their opposition. Even Abdullah al-Akaileh, one of the Brotherhood's leading doves, argued that the legislation would contradict Article 2 of the constitution, which states that Islam is the state religion.[60] On social matters, Islamists seemed intent on imposing some of their more controversial views. The Brotherhood's parliamentary bloc, for example, proposed legislation to ban male hairdressers from working in women's beauty salons. Even though the law failed to pass, Islamists were able to successfully lobby the Ministry of Interior to issue the ban as an executive order. (A backlash ensued, forcing the government to rescind the decision just four weeks later.)[61]

Undeterred by initial setbacks, the most controversial set of decisions would come in the early months of 1991. After protracted negotiations, the Brotherhood joined the government of Prime Minister Mudar Badran on New Year's Day, accepting five ministries (the Ministry of Religious Affairs, Education, Health, Social Development, and Justice), while two independent Islamists who caucused with the Brotherhood took Transport and Agriculture. The positive aspects of their participation were quickly overshadowed by a series of provocative moves, particularly measures taken by Minister of Education Abdullah al-Akaileh and Minister of Social Development Youssef al-Azm to enforce sex segregation within their ministries. In response to media criticism, Islamist deputy Daoud Kojak argued that "if the majority of people were against coeducation and coeducation was allowed for a minority, then dictatorship of a minority over the majority would take place."[62] Now that religious conservatism was spreading throughout society, Islamists would increasingly couch their appeals in populist terms. It was no longer just that Islamist ideas were right, but that they reflected the will of the people as well. Gradually, the popular will and the Islamist will would become inextricably fused together, at least in the minds of Islamists themselves. This helped make democracy, at least in its more majoritarian forms, much more attractive to Jordan's Muslim Brotherhood. But it also led to missteps.

There was, for example, a ministerial decree issued by Akaileh that barred fathers from attending their daughters' sporting events, leading one disgruntled father to ask, "does he think that looking at legs can possibly be on our minds?"[63] The measure provoked outrage as thousands of parents organized meetings, distributed petitions, and lobbied the prime minister to intervene. This, however, was just one among many controversial decisions taken by Akaileh during his short tenure. Each morning, schoolchildren were made to recite a "victory prayer," which condemned Western influences and called on God to "bring the destruction [of the Zionists] through their own doing; may God encircle them, may God shame them, and bring us victory over them."[64] The ministry issued directives to schools warning of "Zionist" influence and calling on teachers to focus greater attention on the value of jihad.[65] Other measures included "banning male sports coaches from teaching sports to girls, limiting schools' freedom to close on Christian holidays, setting mid-term examinations in the week of the Christmas holidays, and attempting to ban certain books deemed incompatible with the kingdom's 'religious and moral ethics.'"[66]

While the new ministers were courting controversy, Brotherhood deputies were asserting their weight in parliament, but with limited success. During the first half of 1991, they proposed three pieces of legislation that focused on the application of Islamic law: a law banning coeducation in all primary and secondary schools, community colleges, and universities;[67] a law banning production and consumption of alcohol; and a law prohibiting interest.[68] All failed to pass.

After barely six months, the government fell. King Hussein replaced it with a "peace process" government. It would not be the last time that the demands of the international arena would take precedence over domestic democratization.

The National Charter

In the era of "democratization," there was an evident need to clarify the rules of the game. Democratization was welcome, of course, but what would it lead to?

King Hussein convened 60 leading figures from across the political spectrum, including leftists, liberals, Islamists, and tribal leaders. They were to devise a charter that would establish common principles binding the regime and opposition alike. The result was the National Charter, drafted in 1990 and ratified in 1991. What concerns us here is the role that Islamist members of the drafting committee played in discussions over the charter's content.

Here, the Brotherhood faced another important moment in the forging of a new politics, and its choice of emphasis is telling. The six Brotherhood members and four independent Islamists on the committee coordinated their approach, with Ishaq Farhan acting as their effective leader. Throughout the committee's discussions, which lasted nearly eight months, the Islamists were preoccupied with the role of Islam. Farhan stated early on that the top priority was the elevation of Islamic law from being *a* source of legislation to *the* source of legislation. As Russell Lucas notes, "Farhan saw the project of the Royal Committee as less of a political deal to restore pluralism than as a chance to affirm Jordan's Islamic identity."[69] As it turned out, the Islamist representatives settled for a compromise: it would be "*the principal* source of legislation."[70]

The discussions surrounding such an important document provided an unprecedented opportunity for the opposition to push for fundamental changes in the political structure, including redistribution of power away from the monarchy toward elected officials. But issues such as making the upper house of parliament accountable to voters (the king appoints all members of the Senate) or enshrining the principle of executive branch accountability (the king still appoints the prime minister, regardless of election results) were not brought up, in part because the committee members who were in the best position to do so—namely Islamists—chose not to.

Ultimately, the National Charter did not just set limits around political participation but set them on how far Jordan's fledgling democratic experiment could be expected to go. Democratization need not, after all, lead to democracy. Remembering how an assertive parliament had sought to usurp his powers in the past, King Hussein effectively used the charter to formalize a political "bargain": the regime would allow the opposition to form legal political parties and, in return, the parties would affirm the legitimacy and supremacy of the Hashemite monarchy and its vast institutional prerogatives. The charter delegitimized any future discussion of substantially reducing the king's powers—a necessary step for Jordan to evolve from an absolute monarchy to a constitutional one.

It was a lost opportunity. Instead of working with leftists and liberals to expand democratic space, the Brotherhood seemed more interested in limiting it. Islamists, notes Lucas, "used the Royal Committee to pursue their agenda against the secular opposition."[71] Echoing comments made by other Islamists, Farhan, for example, spoke out against the participation of secular, atheistic political parties.[72] During the committee deliberations, the Brotherhood released a four-page pamphlet titled "The National Charter: Its Basis as Viewed by the Muslim Brotherhood," which explained its stance on political pluralism: "The nation has reached a high level of awareness toward the role of [Islam in] its life [and] we view with disdain and disgust anyone who underestimates this fundamental aspect. We classify such people as outside the circle of the nation and we reject their belonging to it."[73]

The Founding of the Islamic Action Front

The changes ushered in by the return to parliamentary life shifted the Brotherhood's self-perception. Representing the largest bloc with more than a quarter of the seats, the organization was at the peak of its powers. The confluence of a democratic opening—and the realization that it was best positioned to take advantage of that opening—forced the Brotherhood to weigh the importance of parliamentary work against its traditional core functions of preaching, education, and social service provision. Sustaining such a diverse range of activities within one organization was daunting. Meanwhile, the regime was preparing to legalize political parties for the first time in decades. Anticipating the change, the idea of forming a party was raised soon after the 1989 elections, with actual preparations beginning in the middle of 1990.[74] After nearly two years of planning, the party was inaugurated in December 1992. The decision to form what would be called the Islamic Action Front (IAF) was not without dissenters. The hawks, led by Mohamed Abu Faris and Hammam Said, opposed the idea (although, ironically, both would later play prominent leadership roles in the IAF). They feared that the party would come to overshadow the movement.

The decision to form a political party has consequences. It means that the party will be at least somewhat distinct from the movement. Where one is governed by more explicit religious concerns as well as an overwhelming concern with self-preservation, the other is driven more by political imperatives. Regardless of what the party comes to be, the fact that it even exists is important. The Political Parties Law of 1992 required parties' renunciation of "all forms of . . . discrimination among citizens" and "adherence to the achievement of equal opportunity for all citizens to assume responsibility and participation [in the party]."[75] Where the Brotherhood, as a religious association, can discriminate based on religion or degree of religiosity, a party cannot impose any such limits on membership. Any Jordanian citizen can apply to be a party member, and, while still a rare occurrence, a small number of Christians have been IAF members.

The bylaws of the IAF, however, make clear that the party was not founded to further Jordan's democratization project or even to prioritize political reform in the country. The IAF, like the Brotherhood, seems preoccupied with threats, whether coming from "Zionists" across the border or from the perceived dilution of Islamic values at home. The preamble is revealing, laying out the party's rationale: "In recognition of the urgency of standing firm in the face of the civilizational threat to the umma—a threat that represents a dangerous phase in the ongoing colonial enterprise—[there is a need to] protect our civilization . . . and to strive to lead this umma with God's law."[76] After a list of other reasons, all having to do with either promoting Islam or opposing the Jewish presence in Palestine, the preamble concludes that "based on all of this, it became necessary to form the Islamic Action Front party."[77]

At this stage, the IAF seemed little more than a political expression of the Brotherhood's social and religious conservatism. The IAF was a niche party. Perhaps it didn't have to be anything more than that. The party, after all, was founded in response to specific changes in legislation. Not surprisingly, then, the IAF, although initially meant to be a broad front for all Islamists, failed to assert its independence from the Brotherhood. In the party's first months, a number of independent Islamists resigned after performing below expectations in internal elections for the party's Shura Council and executive bureau. Most leadership positions went to Brotherhood members.

While the founding of the party was an important milestone for the Islamic movement in Jordan, a party in and of itself neither necessitates nor produces moderation. Yet, at the same time, the fact that the Brotherhood's political activities were now taking place under the auspices of the IAF made the future adoption of a pro-democracy program more likely. The new division of labor meant that the IAF was less bound by the kind of controversial social policies advocated by the Brotherhood in 1990 and 1991. But these changes were still to come.

A Niche Party Still

For an Islamist group with a founding mission focused on Islamic law to reorient its message toward democratization, something in the political equation needed to change. That something had not happened yet. Another factor—the strength of a given Islamist group—should also be taken into account. At the outset of the National Charter talks, the Brotherhood was the preeminent political grouping in the country. Having performed well beyond expectations in the 1989 elections, it felt that its power would only increase, and for a time it did. When an Islamist party, or really any party for that matter, finds itself in a privileged political position, there is little incentive to push for structural changes in the system.

The Brotherhood would come to regret this calculation. The National Charter was particularly important for what it allowed the regime to do later. Its guarantees empowered the regime, effectively setting the stage for Jordan's turn to repression. The unqualified power the charter invested in the monarchy would be called upon in subsequent years to restrict and marginalize the Islamist opposition.

4

The Turn to Repression

THE SHIFT HAD BEEN slow yet unmistakable. Arab regimes, hoping to shore up their legitimacy and co-opt a rising opposition, tried their hand at political reform in the late 1980s and early 1990s. Some, like Algeria and Jordan, went further than most, seemingly on the brink of historic change. Others, like Egypt and Tunisia, cautiously opened up political space, holding competitive elections for the first time but within clear limits.

Islamist groups had spent the previous two decades preparing themselves for this moment, making the leap from minority group to mass movement. They largely stayed away from partisan politics, instead choosing to build local networks, providing much-needed social services, and spreading their message to a public that, at first, knew little about them. In elections across the region, they shocked regime elites. In Algeria, the shock was simply too much and too soon, as Islamists there stood on the precipice of a commanding victory. Regimes knew Islamists were gaining strength, but to this extent? In nearly every Arab country, Islamists were becoming leaders of the opposition. They weren't quite ready to take power, or even to fight for it, but they were a threat all the same. Some Arab regimes saw the threat as existential and acted accordingly.

The turn to repression became the defining feature of the 1990s. The gains of the previous decade would prove illusory, as regimes moved to neutralize and even eliminate the Islamist threat. These changes are critical to understanding the evolution of Islamist movements. In the previous chapter, we saw how Islamist groups tried to take advantage of small but significant political openings. But what happens when they close?

Egypt's Authoritarian Turn

By the late 1980s, the regime was growing alarmed by the Brotherhood's rising popularity. Already, with Zaki Badr's appointment as Minister of Interior, tensions were on the rise. President Mubarak seemed to shift back and forth, occasionally lending his support to Badr while other times distancing himself from Badr's controversial methods.[1]

In Egypt, the move to confront the Islamist challenge unfolded over several years. In some respects, 1990 serves as a point of demarcation. During the previous two parliamentary sessions, the Brotherhood had become an increasingly "normal" part of Egyptian politics. 1990, however, would mark the end of the group's presence in parliament for nearly a decade. That year, in May, the Supreme Constitutional Court declared the existing electoral law unconstitutional. Parliament was dissolved and new elections were called for the fall. The regime worked in secret to draft new electoral legislation, refusing to consult with civil society or opposition forces. The new law was a major step backward, with its flagrant gerrymandering and failure to provide for full judicial supervision of the polls.

These controversies came at a particularly tense time. The first Gulf War had just begun and, in October 1990, one month before the polls opened, Rifat Mahgoub, speaker of the house and one of the ruling party's most powerful figures, was assassinated by Islamic extremists. The government went on the offensive, using the incident to justify an extension of the hated emergency law, just as the opposition was making its abolition a central demand. After the new electoral law was passed over their objections, the Wafd, Labor, and Liberal parties along with the Muslim Brotherhood held a joint conference on October 20 to announce an election boycott. The Brotherhood was growing impatient. It thought its participation in parliament and willingness to play by the rules would change the regime's attitude, but in the end the group was still operating in legal limbo. Soon enough, the regime's attitude toward Islamists would indeed change, but not in the way the

Brotherhood had hoped. "It is fair to say," write Ibrahim and Awad, "that the [group's] decision to boycott was historic, marking the start of a new phase in the relationship between the Muslim Brotherhood and the regime."[2]

Most Egypt scholars agree that a qualitative change in the regime's treatment of Islamists took place in the early 1990s. A promising period of political openness and relative inclusion of Islamists was followed by a period of systematic exclusion. Hesham al-Awadi notes that "the relationship [between the regime and Islamists] went through two distinctive phases, where the first, from 1981 to 1990, was a period of accommodation and tolerance, and the second, from 1990 to 2000, was a period of confrontation and repression."[3] Mona el-Ghobashy points to 1992 as the "turning point in the government's approach to the Muslim Brothers, shifting from tenuous toleration to further legal and then physical repression."[4]

A variety of factors led the regime to reconsider its approach toward the Brotherhood. Most importantly, the organization became too powerful too quickly, increasingly asserting itself in a number of arenas, including foreign policy, one of the regime's points of greatest sensitivity. In addition to publicly voicing opposition to Egypt's participation in the Gulf War, the Brotherhood opposed the Madrid peace talks of 1991 and, through the Doctors Association, organized a mass rally of around 20,000-strong against peace with Israel.[5]

In September 1992, Brotherhood-affiliated candidates won a majority of seats on the board of the Lawyers Association—one of Egypt's last liberal strongholds—an event that provoked "shock and soul-searching among the nation's secular politicians and intellectuals."[6] The Islamists' surprise showing capped a string of victories in professional associations as well as universities. In Cairo University, once dominated by leftists, students running under the "Islamic trend" list won all 60 seats and all 72 seats in the engineering and medical faculties, respectively.[7]

The Brotherhood's control of the professional syndicates and student unions allowed it to manage programs and deliver services for members, in the process generating goodwill and support among Egyptians otherwise uninterested in Islamic activism. These efforts, apparently, went one step too far after the 1992 Cairo earthquake, when the Brotherhood provided relief services to victims, including food, clothes, and medical treatment. Embarrassed, the government lashed out at the Brotherhood, accusing it of using the disaster for political ends.[8]

The Mubarak regime belatedly came to see the Brotherhood for what it had become: a massive all-purpose organization, increasingly confident and more than willing (and apparently able) to act as a sort of government-in-waiting. The so-called Salsabil case of 1992 confirmed the regime's worst fears. Salsabil, founded in the early 1980s, was a computer company owned by leading Brotherhood figures, including the wealthy businessman Khairat al-Shater. Government officials accused Salsabil of being a front for illegal activities, using the case to push a number of charges against Brotherhood activists, including plotting to overthrow the regime.

Khaled Hamza, a Brotherhood figure who has worked closely with Shater, argues that the Salsabil case had a powerful effect on the Mubarak regime:

> What the security forces discovered surprised the authorities. Before the Salsabil case, the government had no idea that the Brotherhood had reached such a level of strength and capability. When it found documents outlining the group's willingness to open dialogue with the West, its effective use of modern communication, the complex nature of its organization, and the scope of its activities in all sectors of society, the regime realized the Brotherhood presented a real threat.[9]

Similarly, the Brotherhood's decision to hold internal elections in 1994, which will be discussed later in greater detail, gave the regime further grounds for concern. When more than 80 leading Brotherhood members were arrested in the crackdown of 1995, one of the government's accusations was that the group was holding elections, presumably a sign that an ostensibly illegal organization was acting as if it were legal.[10] A Brotherhood that was internally democratic meant that the government would have a more difficult time portraying it as backward, extremist, and autocratic.

Like elsewhere in the region, the Egyptian regime feared it was losing control—in part because it was. Facing what it saw as a mounting challenge to its own legitimacy, President Mubarak discarded the accommodation and tolerance of the past and took aggressive action to counter Islamist influence, both through legislation and outright repression. After 1990, mass arrests of Brotherhood members became commonplace, peaking in 1995, when 1,392 members and supporters were arrested in a three-week period ahead of parliamentary elections.[11] According to the Egyptian Organization for Human Rights, the number of political prisoners, many of them Brotherhood activists and supporters, jumped from 5,000 in 1990 to nearly 16,000 in 1995.[12]

Meanwhile, Law 97—the "anti-terrorism law"—was passed in July 1992, granting authorities extensive powers to detain political opponents. The main pretext was the gathering extremist insurgency in Upper Egypt, but the definition of "terrorism" became so broad as to include nearly anything the regime saw as a threat to its power.[13] Perhaps most problematic, such "crimes" now fell under the jurisdiction of State Security Courts, where the defendant's right to appeal was extremely limited. This, apparently, was not enough for the regime, which chose to transfer a growing number of cases against the Brotherhood to military courts, where the rights of defendants were even fewer and where judges were not actually judges but military officers.

By the early 1990s, the Brotherhood had come to play a leading role in most professional syndicates and associations. Here, too, the regime took action. In 1993, the ominously titled "Law to Guarantee Democracy Within the Professional Syndicates" effectively nullified the results of elections that had low voter turnout (which was often the case in syndicate elections). The regime also moved to assert its dominance over the religious and educational spheres, two areas where Islamists had long been influential. Egypt had become home to thousands of private mosques, often Islamist in orientation. In 1992, the government began the slow, arduous work of taking them over and bringing them under the control of the Ministry of Religious Endowments. By 1994, the ministry announced that 25,000 mosques had been "incorporated."[14] The schools were next. "The terrorists have been targeting [them] for years," explained Minister of Education Hussein Kamal Baha al-Din.[15] In 1994, over 20,000 teachers with allegedly Islamist sympathies were fired or transferred.[16]

The political situation deteriorated further. In what Ghobashy calls a "sweeping crackdown unseen since the 1950s," 82 leading Brotherhood figures were arrested in January 1995 on terrorism-related charges and tried in military courts.[17] In November, just before voters went to the polls, 54 of the accused were sentenced to prison terms, a verdict that was unprecedented in the post-Nasser era. In a perhaps unsurprising culmination of efforts to exclude Islamists from political life, only one Brotherhood candidate out of 170 ended up winning a parliamentary seat in the 1995 elections, while the NDP won 94 percent of seats, its highest ever total. The results were so obviously suspect that the Ministry of Interior did not even bother to release vote tallies.[18] The Court of Cassation ruled that nearly half of all the district results be invalidated. The judiciary was still at least somewhat independent, but so too was the regime. Where after past elections the government had heeded judicial rulings, this time they were simply ignored.

In sum, the years of 1990–5 saw a systematic escalation of regime policies against mainstream Islamists. The objective reality is obviously important, but so too are the perceptions of those who found themselves on the receiving end. By their own admission, Brotherhood officials felt that something fundamental had changed in the government's approach. Four internal Brotherhood documents published in the mid-1990s reflect an organization in crisis and fearing the worst.[19] In one document, titled "The Extended Crisis: The Relation of the Egyptian Regime with the Muslim Brotherhood," the authors saw an explicit shift from a policy of inclusion and tolerance to one of repression: "We can distinguish between two stages, the first of which was dominated by peaceful interaction, and the second by conflictual interaction. The first stage extended to the early months of 1990."[20]

The Brotherhood's Response to Repression

After the openings of the 1980s, the turn to repression that followed was sudden, largely catching the Muslim Brotherhood by surprise. How did the organization respond to the regime's efforts to exclude it from political life? Again, we might expect that the sharp increase in regime repression would produce a radical response or at least halt any movement toward moderation. But, instead, the turn to repression coincided with an aggressive strategy of moderation on the part of the Brotherhood.

Something else was happening at the start of the decade, and this is where we can begin telling the story of the Brotherhood's unlikely evolution. Extremist organizations, such as Gama'a Islamiya and al-Jihad, the group that spawned al-Qaeda's second-in-command Ayman al-Zawahiri, had had a presence in Egypt since the 1970s. But the level of violence increased dramatically in 1992. Between 1992 and 1997, there were 741 violent incidents compared to only 143 in the preceding 21-year period. An estimated 1,442 people were killed in clashes between militant groups and security forces.[21] As their conflict with the regime intensified, the militants became ever more brutal, resorting to acts of terror that claimed the lives of more and more innocents.

In light of these events, the Brotherhood came under increasing pressure to clarify its positions. Well aware of the risk of being lumped in with the extremists, it was quick to condemn the attacks and reassure skeptics that it had no sympathy for Gama'a Islamiya and its ilk. 1992 also marked the first in a series of strongly worded public statements in which the Brotherhood unequivocally condemned the violence in an attempt to distance itself from what had become a low-level insurgency. In a statement dated December 18, General Guide Hamed Abu Nasr affirmed that "violence and terrorism represent an exit from legality and from the correct Islamic understanding and lead to nothing except polarization and undermining of the stability of the umma and its security."[22] In November 1993, after an assassination attempt on Prime Minister Atef Sidqi, Abu Nasr declared that "this criminal act cannot be justified by God's injunctions, by law, by reason, or the common bonds of humanity."[23] Elsewhere, the Brotherhood accused the perpetrators of terrorist attacks as having no "conscience or religion."[24]

This was not enough for the regime, however, which mobilized the media to launch a full-fledged campaign accusing the group of supporting terrorism. Mubarak, who in the 1980s had been careful to distinguish between the Brotherhood and extremist groups, did an about-face, calling the former "an illegal organization that is behind most of the activities of the religious troublemakers."[25] The Brotherhood found itself in a precarious situation. As Khalil al-Anani points out, "everyone was on the side of the regime [during its fight against terrorism], including liberals and political elites," many of whom were growing alarmed by the rapid Islamization of society.[26] The journalist Mary Anne Weaver, in Cairo at the time, wrote in the *New Yorker* that "writers, directors, playwrights, and poets [find] themselves increasingly caught between the Islamists, on the one hand, and the government, on the other."[27] Many of them made their choice, judging mainstream Islamists the greater threat. "Some intellectuals," explains Anani, "asked the regime to suppress the Brotherhood as a payoff for supporting the regime in its battle with [violent] Islamists."[28]

Increasingly isolated, and concerned its message wasn't getting through, the Brotherhood issued further disavowals. The group released a short document in 1994 titled "Our Testimony," which reaffirmed its rejection of terrorism. "Some people," the statement complained, "deliberately and unfairly accuse the Muslim Brotherhood of taking part in acts of violence and of involvement in terrorism."[29] "We consider those who shed the blood of others or aid such bloodshed," the statement went on, "as wrongdoers and partners in sin."

As regime repression intensified, the Brotherhood found itself in increasing danger. The only option available was to continue making the case to domestic actors—legal opposition parties, political elites, and even potential sympathizers within the regime—as well as the international community that they were on the right side of the fight and, accordingly, that the regime's policies were excessive and unjustifiable. It made sense, then, for the Brotherhood to portray itself as a moderate alternative to extremist groups. It chose to underline this argument by releasing a series of declarative statements, laying out in detail the organization's positions on issues of controversy, including democracy, pluralism, the use of violence, and the rights of women and Christians.

Even though the organization had formally renounced violence in the 1970s, there remained a small but influential "Qutbist" wing—as one Brotherhood member described it to me—that saw nonviolent action only as a temporary tactical necessity.[30] The documents released in 1994 and 1995, however, were intended to put the matter to rest. Ghobashy calls these "the first glimmers of the [Brotherhood's] ideological revisions."[31] According to one Brotherhood official, the statements represented a "reassessment of the ideas of Hassan al-Banna."[32]

The Statements of 1994–5

The statement on "Shura in Islam and Party Pluralism in Muslim Society" and the statement on "The Muslim Woman in Muslim Society
and the Position Toward Her Participation" were issued by the Muslim
Brotherhood in a March 1994 pamphlet and deserve a closer look. In the
introduction, the authors explain that "these two statements provide a
summary of the most important jurisprudential foundations of the principles advocated by the Muslim Brotherhood."[33] The statement on shura
lays out the group's understanding of intellectual and political pluralism and affirms that the concept of shura—an Islamic term meaning
consultation—guarantees that the "umma is the source of authority."[34]
This is in clear contrast to radical Islamists and Salafis who advocate a
strict reading of divine sovereignty. The Brotherhood explains its support for political pluralism: "Difference of opinion deepens and diversi-
fies one's outlook, something which is necessary to discern the truth
and to reach that which is most beneficial, particularly if it is coupled
with tolerance and a multitude of avenues [for expression]."[35] It goes on
to conclude: "We see that acceptance of political party pluralism in the
Islamic society . . . includes acceptance of alternation of power between
associations and political parties through periodic elections."[36]

Meanwhile, the statement on women begins by noting that "women
are half of society" and proceeds to make religious arguments, using the
Quran and prophetic traditions, to justify an enhanced role for women
in public and political life.[37] It goes on to affirm the right of women to
vote in parliamentary elections and, moreover, that "in certain situations,
this participation becomes an obligation and necessity."[38] It then affirms
their right to stand as candidates in parliamentary elections, something
that, until then, the Brotherhood had never itself formally supported.

None of this, today, sounds particularly groundbreaking. However,
at the time, these documents represented the Brotherhood's first real attempt to expound on the intellectual foundations and principles guiding
its new pro-democracy approach. As Essam al-Erian explained to me in
2008: "Our position on political pluralism, women's rights, and the role
of Copts dates back to [the statements of] 1994, and these continue to be
the principal bases upon which we build."[39] Indeed, the Brotherhood's
later statements and positions, including the 2000 and 2005 electoral

programs, the 2004 reform initiative, and the 2007 political party platform all take the ideas contained in the 1994 documents several steps
further. Mahmoud Ghozlan, one of the lead authors of the 2007 platform, explains that "the drafting of the platform was, in the first place, a
result of the idea of political party pluralism . . . and it is an idea that has
its origins in 1994, or even before, but this was the document that really
started it. And from this time on, the Brotherhood made a number of
efforts to start a political party."[40] In this respect, the group's decision to
publish these statements in 1994 represents a critical turning point in its
political evolution.

Other documents published during this period push further in this
direction. *Points of General Agreement on the National Compact Initiative*, a pamphlet authored by the Brotherhood's Mamoun al-Houdaiby
in 1995, offers a list of 15 basic rights and principles for political reform.
Among other things, it "unequivocally confirms that the people are the
source of authority and that it is not permissible for any person, party,
organization, or association to claim the right to authority or stay in
power without the people's consent exercised through their free will."[41]
It affirms the Brotherhood's commitment to "freedom of personal
belief" and the "freedom of all Semitic religions to establish their own
religious rites." Houdaiby also calls for the unrestricted right to form
political parties, the right to free assembly, the right of every citizen to
be a member of parliament, the right to judicial appeal, and the depo-
liticization of the military. None of the 15 "principles" even so much as
mentions sharia law.

Perhaps more important than the content of these statements is the
context from which they emerged. As Ghobashy notes, "at the height
of the crackdown, the [Brotherhood] continued to produce incremen-
tally more detailed statements of their positions."[42] Indeed, as repression was increasing so too were the group's efforts to affirm moderate
policies and positions. There was a strategic logic to such an approach:
the Brotherhood was making the case that, in light of its moderation,
the regime's measures were even more unwarranted than they would
otherwise be.

The statements of 1994–5 represent a striking development not just in
tone and rhetoric but, more importantly, in the Brotherhood's overall
political strategy. They served to elevate pluralism and democracy in

the group's hierarchy of priorities while deemphasizing the application of sharia. That these were meant to be foundational texts—rather than, say, announcements of tactical shifts—meant that changing course, at some later point, would raise the question of why the Brotherhood was violating its own stated principles or, alternatively, how it got its principles wrong the first time around.

The Brotherhood was finding other ways to distinguish itself as well. In October 1994, members of the group's "middle generation"—younger leaders with a reformist bent—organized the Conference on Freedoms and Civil Society, which brought together over 500 political figures from across the ideological spectrum, including heads of the major opposition parties, syndicate leaders, and human rights activists. The Brotherhood participants proposed the idea of drafting a national compact, which would outline an agreement on basic rights and freedoms. According to the meeting minutes, the conference "[appealed] to different political and intellectual currents in Egypt with an urgent invitation to produce a national charter that reflects a national consensus among political forces on the desire for freedom, equality, and justice."[43] The Wafd's Ibrahim Abaza, the Brotherhood's Mamoun al-Houdaiby, Labor's Helmy Murad, and even Hussein Abdel Raziq of the staunchly anti-Islamist Tagammu party all pledged their support to the idea. While the effort ultimately failed, it represented one of the first real attempts to hammer out a consensus on basic rights.

The Internal Elections of 1994

Another event of interest—often overlooked—occurred just as regime repression was intensifying. Again, this was no accident; the decision to hold elections was devised in part as a response to repression.

For the first time in the post-Nasser period, the Brotherhood, in 1994, held internal elections for its Shura Council, effectively the organization's legislative branch. By holding elections, the Brotherhood, in Khaled Hamza's words, hoped to "forge internal renewal and to produce new leaders capable of effecting change."[44] In part, the decision was a matter of necessity—some Shura Council members were simply too old—but it also reflected broader strategic concerns. As

Hamza explains: "There were those in the Brotherhood who wanted to say, 'we are a modern organization, we are capable of change, we are able to govern, and we are willing to engage in dialogue with the West.'"[45]

But why in 1994? The government, with the help of liberal allies, was trying to paint the Brotherhood as extremist, undermining its reputation in the court of public opinion. "Before the internal elections," Hamza points out, "the regime had been talking about a dictatorial Brotherhood, a Brotherhood that upholds the principle of 'listen and obey'." Internal elections were a way of countering this perception. "The elections embarrassed the government and changed the stereotypical image of the Brotherhood that the government was promoting," says Hamza.[46]

The Brotherhood was intent on modernizing its organizational structures, part of the ongoing effort to distance the group from extremists. The movement's democratic discourse and its efforts to reach out to secular opposition parties were introducing a cognitive dissonance. According to one Brotherhood official, reform-minded members were putting pressure on the leadership, saying it's "not acceptable for you to publicly call for a democratic system and criticize the state for being autocratic because it rigs elections, while at the same time you yourselves don't hold elections."[47] The Brotherhood's public embrace of democratic ideas was reflecting, but also spurring, important shifts within the organization.

The timing of the elections—coming at such a high point of tension with the government—may appear odd at first. However, Khalil al-Anani notes that this isn't necessarily surprising for an organization that, as recently as October 2009, insisted on holding governorate-level elections in Menoufiya and Sharqiya during a particularly damaging period of repression.[48] "This is the point about the Brotherhood," explains Anani. "They don't show interest in internal issues unless they're under external pressure . . . [particularly] when the regime is trying to portray them as regressive and close-minded." He points out that "during the 1980s, the Brothers didn't feel threatened by the regime because it allowed them to participate openly through social and political activism, but once the regime started to attack and suppress them, [we start to see] internal voices calling for reform."[49]

The Case of the Wasat Party

In January 1996, a number of younger Brotherhood figures founded the Wasat party. With 74 official founding members—62 of them from the Brotherhood—the group formally applied for legal status. During the application process, the founders had a falling out with the Brotherhood's Guidance Bureau and tendered their resignations from the organization. They felt they had earned the right to a larger role in the group's decision-making process, a role the older guard was not ready to grant.

To a large degree, the split was about power and personalities. At the same time, there was no doubt that the Wasat party represented further movement toward an inclusive pro-democracy platform. After resigning from the Brotherhood, Wasat leaders went out of their way to distinguish themselves from their former organization. As Abu al-Ala Madi explained: "We are a political Islamic group whose doors are open to any person who believes in the Islamic [civilizational] project. We are very different from the Brotherhood, although most of us originally belonged to [it]."[50] Wickham notes that the Wasat program represented "a more subtle, but nonetheless significant, departure from the religious conservatism of the Muslim Brotherhood."[51] For the Wasat party, Christians were considered members of the umma while women had the right to assume any position in government, including head of state. In taking the party public, the Wasat founders were intent on presenting themselves as exponents of a kinder, gentler Islamism. Not surprisingly, Mamoun al-Houdaiby accused Wasat of playing to the media and "want[ing] to be in the news, at any price."[52] The media did, indeed, like it. The regime, however, did not.

Again, we are presented with the same puzzle as before: the Wasat party did not emerge in an atmosphere of openness and democratization, but rather the opposite. The party was founded on the heels of what was, up until then, the worst four-year period for the Brotherhood since the mihna, or ordeal, of the 1950s and 1960s. In this instance, repression appears to have helped produce a moderate outcome. For scholars who have written on Wasat, this is an interesting, if unsettling, finding. "On the face of it," Wickham observes, "the formation of the Wasat party under conditions of increased repression is surprising, not only because the incentives for moderation created by democratization elsewhere were absent but because repression might more logically trigger Islamist radicalization."[53] Joshua Stacher, meanwhile, remarks that "it would seem that the harsh nature of the government's 1995 security operation against the Muslim Brotherhood prior to legislative elections led to the moderation of some of the younger Brothers." But why? He hints at the answer: "A more moderate entity . . . might avoid the government's wrath."[54]

The assumption long held by Islamists, including the Wasat founders themselves, is that acts of moderation on their part will produce acts of moderation on the part of the regime. If a political party affirms its support for democracy and women's rights, deprioritizes sharia, and generally displays a "nonthreatening" posture, then, the thinking goes, the regime will have a harder time justifying a crackdown to domestic and international audiences, and perhaps even to itself.

Moreover, moderation is meant to appeal to key actors in the secular opposition, civil society, and the Coptic community, all of whom have long been suspicious of Islamist intentions. Most of Wasat's original founders were Brotherhood members, but it also included women and Christians. A group that can claim strong, reliable allies from across the political and ideological spectrum is more difficult to repress than a group that finds itself isolated. In Chapter 2, I referred to this as "moderation as protection."

Wickham sheds some light on how Wasat leaders, in their own words, perceived the relationship between repression and moderation:

> Interviews with Abu al-Ala Madi and Essam Sultan, two of the party's founders, suggest that the Wasat party initiative was indeed partly a strategic move by leaders in the Muslim Brotherhood to avoid repression. As Madi explained, the arrest of some of the Brotherhood's leading activists in 1995 confirmed that its secretive, insular "antisystem" form of organization had failed and that it was time for the Islamic movement to shed the handicap of illegality and secure the formal party status needed to participate in public life "like any normal party" . . . The achievement of legal status would offer the Islamists a number of strategic advantages, the first of which was a measure of immunity from state repression.[55]

The Wasat party is almost always portrayed as a Brotherhood off-shoot. While it did eventually break away, the reality is somewhat more complicated, as the quote above suggests. Initially, the Wasat party was meant to complement the Brotherhood rather than replace it. In 1994 and 1995, as the government crackdown was intensifying, interest in forming a legal party grew among Brotherhood activists and leaders. On January 9, 1996, Madi submitted an application to the NDP-dominated Parties Committee. The idea had been discussed at the highest levels of the organization. Mahdi Akef, a member of the Brotherhood's Guidance Bureau who would later become general guide, was a major supporter of the Wasat initiative.[56]

Early on, Brotherhood leaders spoke of Wasat in positive terms and indicated that it had the organization's sanction. More interesting are the reasons they gave for starting a party in the first place. General Guide Mustafa Mashour explained that "some of the *shabab* (younger people) in the Brotherhood came up with the idea of establishing a party so that we can operate in a legal manner, and this is the first time that the Brotherhood has intended to start a party since its founding in 1928."[57] Responding to another question, Mashour offered: "They are shabab who saw that the government was persisting in putting pressure on them, so they said: let us have a legal party through which we would be able to act."[58] Even as late as March 5, 1996, Mashour said: "We do not prevent the shabab from taking action. They said: we will establish a party since the government does not recognize the legality of the Muslim Brotherhood . . . The commitment of these shabab to the Brotherhood is self-evident and their actions are their prerogative and they do not intend to leave the Brotherhood. They saw that a party could be a means to conduct activities but that does not mean separation from the Brotherhood."[59]

The common thread in Mashour's explanations is the desire to acquire legal sanction, which would presumably allow Brotherhood members to evade limits imposed by the government. In short, Wasat was in large part a response to government repression. Regime measures had taken such a toll on the Brotherhood that leading members, including Abu al-Ala Madi, began to consider alternatives.

That said, the assumptions of Madi and his colleagues appear in hindsight to have been misguided. Instead of reducing regime repression, the Wasat initiative provoked it further. The government arrested several Wasat founders and referred them to military courts on the order of President Mubarak himself—"the first time in Egyptian history," Ghobashy notes drily, "that citizens were tried for petitioning to form a legal party."[60] Wasat's application for legal status was rejected. The Wasat founders, however, were not dissuaded. They spent the next two years restructuring the party and reapplied for legal status in 1998, this time with a different list of founders and a new and improved political platform. This time around, out of 93 founders, only 24 were former Brotherhood members.[61] Three were Christian and 19 were women.

In other words, Wasat chose to respond to regime efforts to exclude it by becoming even *more* moderate than it already was. But, again, its application was denied. Later, Wasat would face rejection for a third and fourth time. This leads to a confounding observation, one that we see in a number of other examples: as Islamists affirmed and reaffirmed their moderation, regimes became more repressive, even though Islamists may have originally expected—acting in good faith—that their gestures would be reciprocated in kind.

Jordan: The End of an Experiment

In Jordan, the Islamist and leftist opposition had an absolute majority in parliament from 1989 until 1993. 1991 was arguably the high point of democratization and the point at which the king could be expected to feel the most pressure to meet popular demands. The Brotherhood, then a junior partner in Mudar Badran's government, led public opposition against the Gulf War in a series of large-scale protests. It took advantage of rising anti-American sentiment, using the conflict to boost its profile. Despite the obvious international consequences of standing with his people and standing by Saddam's Iraq, King Hussein was boxed in. The lessons of the episode were clear. The fact that Jordan was now, it seemed, a young democracy—responsive to an increasingly assertive, and angry, electorate—constrained the king's already limited foreign policy options. To avoid sacrificing his agenda to popular sentiment in the future, he would need greater freedom to operate.

After the Gulf War ended with Iraq's defeat, Hussein found himself in a vulnerable position. There was the matter of Jordan's deteriorating economic situation, aggravated by the war. Addressing the European Parliament in September 1991, the king pleaded for aid.[62] Because of his support for Saddam, he had lost the backing of Saudi Arabia and Kuwait, Jordan's most generous donors. Increasingly isolated and concerned, as always, with survival, the regime began to move into the Western orbit. In a sign of things to come, the king participated in the Madrid peace conference in 1991. Just before Madrid, he had replaced the Badran–Brotherhood cabinet with a tamer government more open to negotiations with Israel, even if it was less representative. If there were, in fact, a tradeoff between foreign policy goals and democratic reform at home, then the king would have to make his choice. "Only peace," writes Markus Bouillon, would "fully [rehabilitate] Jordan in regional and international politics."[63]

Meanwhile, the Palestinians were charting their own course, culminating in the signing of the Oslo accords. Hussein, fearing that Jordan would be left behind, frantically moved to conclude a peace agreement with Israel. In return, he appeared to get what he wanted: debt relief of nearly a billion dollars, a tourism boom, and a generous American aid package making Jordan the world's second-largest per capita recipient of U.S. foreign assistance. This exchange, if one can call it that, represented a decisive shift. Two years prior, the demands of democracy necessitated moving closer to Iraq just as the rest of the region was moving away. Now, the opposite was occurring; moving closer to Israel necessitated effectively halting, and even reversing, Jordan's democratic "experiment."

The events of 1993 fundamentally altered Jordanian politics. Over the next 15 years, the Jordanian regime aggressively imposed restrictions on opposition activity. The previously cordial relationship between the regime and Islamists grew increasingly strained. The Brotherhood came to be seen as the greatest threat to what Hussein hoped would be his lasting achievement—a peace treaty with Israel and, by extension, the guarantee of Jordan's stability after his passing.

The Year Everything Changed

What was striking wasn't that there was a move back toward authoritarianism—such a thing is all too common—but, rather, that it came so quickly on the heels of a promising period of democratization. "Liberalization," writes Russell Lucas, "gave way to its opposite, de-liberalization."[64]

The events of 1993 represent a "turning point" in Jordan's political evolution, in reality certainly, but even more so in how they were perceived by Islamists. In public statements and documents, as well as in my own interviews with Muslim Brotherhood and IAF officials, 1993 is treated as the year that everything changed—and in many ways they're right.

It was that year that King Hussein unilaterally enacted the so-called one-vote electoral law, the primary objective of which was to limit Islamist power at the polls. With talk of a potential settlement with Israel, the king needed a pliant parliament to guarantee ratification. The previous elections had been conducted under a plurality block system where voters in a given district could cast a ballot for as many candidates as there were seats. For example, if a district had six seats, Jordanians could vote for up to six candidates, which helped well-organized groups like the Brotherhood that could call on the commitment and discipline of their supporters. In turn, smaller leftist groups and Christian candidates sought alliances with the Brotherhood. Both sides benefited.[65] Under the new law, the dynamics would change considerably. Now, in a district of six seats, each voter could cast a ballot for only one person rather than six. The system the regime constructed was, and still is, exceedingly rare. Today, the only other countries that use single nontransferable vote (SNTV) for national elections are Afghanistan, the Republic of Vanuatu, Kuwait (as of 2012), and, oddly enough, post-revolution Libya.[66] Brotherhood leaders whom I interviewed would constantly rail against the electoral system, saying that it had no parallel anywhere else in the world. As it turns out, they may have been exaggerating, but not by much.

The negative effects of SNTV are magnified in a country like Jordan, where tribal loyalties still hold sway. With only one vote, indigenous Jordanians are more likely to vote for a candidate from their tribe. There was also the problem of gerrymandering. Generally, tribal regions, long the backbone of the regime, were overrepresented, while the urban areas of Amman and Zarqa, the predominantly Palestinian strongholds of the Muslim Brotherhood, had considerably less representation.[67]

These changes threw the IAF into disarray and provoked a charged internal debate. Ibrahim al-Gharaibeh cites several of the arguments for participation that eventually won the day—that the Brotherhood would stand a better chance of blocking the peace treaty with Israel from within parliament; and that if the government's objective was to marginalize Islamists, then a boycott would play right into its hands. Perhaps more importantly, the Brotherhood "wished to avoid [confronting] the authorities to the point of *kasr al-'adham* [the breaking of bones]."[68] The tragedy of Algeria was not too distant, with civil war erupting there just the year before.

In the 1993 elections, only 16 of the IAF's 35 candidates won. Where the Brotherhood had won 85 percent of the seats it contested in 1989, the IAF win percentage was a mere 48 percent. Many incorrectly interpreted the result as evidence of Islamist decline. In reality, compared to 1989, the IAF's vote share actually increased slightly according to some estimates, which suggests that the electoral law accounted in large part for the drop in seats.[69] According to Gharaibeh, were it not for mistakes in electoral strategy, the IAF would have won at least 25 seats.[70] Similarly, Malik Mufti says that coordination problems cost it 11 seats.[71] In short, "one-vote" did precisely what it was supposed to do.

The electoral law of 1993 was important in and of itself as a statement of intent on the part of the regime, but it was just as important for what it would later enable. "One-vote" produced an overwhelmingly pro-regime parliament that, in turn, proceeded to pass legislation that further undermined the democratic process.

Shocked as Islamists were by the electoral law, they knew well what the government was trying to do. Initially, however, they felt it was something that could be managed. In time, Islamists would look back at the breach of 1993 and begin to understand that the electoral law was the first sign that Jordan's experiment with democracy was grinding to a halt. Whatever the merits, this was *their* perception, and how they perceived the events surrounding "one-vote" is crucial to understanding how they would craft their response to regime repression in the subsequent years.

On July 25, 1994, Jordan and Israel signed the Washington Declaration, moving the two countries one step closer to a formal peace. The following month, 24 preachers were suspended from giving sermons, presumably because they were using the pulpit to attack government policy.[72] Meanwhile, a purge of Islamist teachers from the public school system had begun earlier in the year.[73] The peace treaty was signed on October 26, and parliament predictably ratified it in a 55–23 vote. The regime had succeeded in clearing the way for normalization with Israel. Fearing instability at home, it had little tolerance for opposition in the months leading up to the treaty. And afterwards, the need to keep opposition groups in line only increased, as the treaty proved a prelude to a wholesale strategic realignment.

As part of its economic liberalization program under the direction of the International Monetary Fund, Jordan removed bread subsidies in August 1996, provoking riots in the southern town of Karak. In a national address, the king promised to face down protesters with an "iron first." Tanks could be seen on the streets of Karak, as the army imposed a curfew on the city. Meanwhile, Prime Minister Abdel Karim al-Kabariti was criticized for presiding over the worst human rights record of any government since 1989. According to the Arab Organization for Human Rights, the Kabariti government was responsible for "[carrying] out arbitrary arrests, physical and psychological torture of detainees, violation of freedom of expression, and abuse of legislation."[74] Despite such a record, the king publicly defended his prime minister— but only up to a point. When Kabariti expressed unease with the king's decision to visit families of the Israeli victims of a Jordanian soldier's shooting spree—and after Israeli Prime Minister Benjamin Netanyahu complained to the king—he was forced to resign.[75] Now that Hussein had a greater priority—namely realignment with the West—democratization became an inconvenience. At times, he seemed to take it personally: an attack on the peace treaty was an attack on him. In the last years of the king's life, this became the litmus test. Hussein increasingly micromanaged foreign policy, going through four prime ministers in the two years after the signing of the treaty.[76]

Not even the most prominent figures of the Jordanian establishment were spared. Ahmed Obeidat, the former prime minister, was forced to give up his seat in the Senate after he spoke out against the treaty. It is striking to see, during this period, just how much domestic conflicts—particularly the widening gulf between regime and opposition—were fundamentally about foreign policy.

The regime's authoritarian turn targeted primarily the Muslim Brotherhood and the IAF, which, in the regime's eyes, were the only political forces capable of derailing its economic and foreign policy objectives. Interestingly, this period of political deterioration, running from 1993 through 2007, coincided with several noteworthy developments. Jordan's mainstream Islamists, like their Egyptian counterparts, went through a significant shift. Having been deprived of democracy, they decided to fight for the little of it that was left.

Islamists adopted an increasingly pro-democracy discourse. Rather than just empty rhetoric, when the IAF spoke about democracy, it spoke about institutions, focusing on constitutional reform, separation of powers, parliamentary autonomy, cabinet selection, and judicial independence. The imposition of the electoral law also spurred greater Islamist cooperation with secular parties. For all their disagreements, opposition groups now had something real and tangible to bind them together. When "one-vote" was officially enacted, the IAF joined leaders from other parties in a press conference condemning the law, marking "one of the first instances of high-profile public cooperation with formal rivals around an issue of common concern."[77] Efforts to exclude the opposition had a unifying effect, bringing the disparate trends closer together. In response to a deteriorating political situation, their cooperation would intensify in the form of a new coalition. The IAF, along with 12 other mostly leftist and nationalist parties, formed the Higher Committee for the Coordination of National Opposition Parties (HCCNOP) in 1994. It is unlikely this increased degree of cooperation would have occurred without the shock of the electoral law and a general sense that the regime was going on the offensive. Increasingly vulnerable in the face of regime restrictions, the IAF needed to look for allies.

Unlike most opposition coalitions in the Arab world, the HCCNOP stood the test of time. For more than a dozen years, it met as often

as every week, boasting a set of regular, agreed-upon internal procedures, with leadership rotating every three months between the parties.[78] During each rotation, the chairing party would set the agenda
and represent the coalition in the press, which meant that, although the
IAF was larger than all the other parties combined, it formally led the
coalition only a small fraction of the time.

There were also important changes within the Islamic movement
itself. Under attack from the government and divided on how to respond, the Brotherhood and the IAF strengthened and institutionalized
internal democratic practices that effectively channeled such disagreements. In the past, certain Brotherhood leaders—usually those with
close relations to the royal court—would meet with the king and other
senior officials on an ad-hoc basis and then present a decision to the rest
of the group as a *fait accompli*. With internal debates becoming more
contentious, the need to respect a set of procedures that were binding
on all members became critical. At various points, when internal splits
threatened to tear the movement apart, the Brotherhood and the IAF's
increasingly democratic organizational structures successfully mediated
the divide. Both organizations, for instance, saw numerous rotations of
power between "hawk" and "dove" factions.

An Islamist Strategy Against Repression

But what did all of this mean? Simply because two parallel developments—regime repression and Islamist moderation—coincide with each
other does not necessarily indicate a causal relationship. In the coming
pages, I will try to chart how the two, in Jordan's case, were intimately
linked. Often, Islamist leaders and activists—in hundreds of hours of
interviews, discussions, and informal conversations I had with them—
gave voice to how they perceived government repression and how they
hoped to counter it. In these accounts, a narrative begins to emerge.

The Islamist perception of events is, in some respects, more important
than what actually happened. In the post-1993 period, Islamists altered
their tactics and strategies according to their own particular reading of
events. One could argue that the political deterioration of the 1990s and
2000s was not as bad as the Brotherhood thought. Even if this were the
case, it wouldn't matter—the Brotherhood *thought* it was.

In a long March 1995 letter to the prime minister, the Brotherhood laid out in detail its objections, citing four areas of concern: the growing number of politically motivated arrests, government interference in student union elections, the barring of preachers from giving sermons, and a return to the policies of martial law. Among these emergency law-era practices were "the blocking of citizens from holding government positions by the security services due to their political loyalties . . . and appointing them to positions only if they provide documents confirming their resignation [from political parties]." These developments, according to the Brotherhood, "[casted] doubt on the intentions of the government . . . and indicated a dangerous regression in the democratic process."[79]

Several months later, in a letter to the speaker of parliament, the IAF along with other opposition members of parliament called for a no-confidence vote against Minister of Justice Hesham al-Tal for "undermining judicial independence and attacking those individuals and organizations calling for . . . checks and balances between the three branches [of government]."[80] The call for separation of powers was beginning to figure prominently in Islamist demands: they were seeing firsthand just how fragile the democratization process was without such protections.

Jordan's Islamists, perhaps unique in this regard, came to grasp the importance of separation of powers not just for governments but for political parties as well, including their own. Nathan Brown has argued that the IAF "may be the most democratic party in the region in terms of its internal operations."[81] He may be right. The IAF has three main decision-making bodies, the Shura Council, the executive bureau, and the internal court, which loosely mirror the three branches of government: the executive, legislature, and judiciary. The 120-member Shura Council is effectively the party's legislative branch, setting policy and making major decisions, including whether to participate in elections. The nine-member executive bureau is tasked with the execution of policy and day-to-day management. The internal court interprets the bylaws of the organization and deals with the controversial matter of suspension of membership or expulsion. The internal court operates with considerable autonomy, having launched proceedings against some of the IAF's most senior figures, including Zaki Bani Irsheid, who was, for a time, the party's secretary-general and its top official. In Bani

Irsheid's case, he was "charged" with undermining his own party's candidates in the 2007 parliamentary elections, due to his disagreement over the Shura Council's decision to participate in the elections. Here, we can see how each "branch" of the IAF operated independently and, at times, at cross-purposes with the others.

The IAF also developed a fourth, irregular source of internal decision making—general referendum, or *al-istifta al-'am*. The results of this process, while not necessarily binding, tend to be respected by the organization's leadership. The general referendum allows every member to register his opinion on major issues facing the party. The process is usually initiated by the executive bureau, as it did in the lead-up to the 1997 elections, when the referendum returned a pro-boycott result, with 66 percent voting against participation.[82]

By the mid-1990s, arrests of IAF members were becoming a regular occurrence. These were not mass arrests in the hundreds or thousands like in Egypt, but they represented an unmistakable escalation by Jordanian standards. After all, the IAF was a legal opposition party, the largest bloc in parliament, and even took pride in its working relationship with senior government officials, including the king himself. In addition to arrests and the "legal repression" of electoral engineering and restricting civil society, the regime effectively barred Brotherhood members from holding senior positions in government and the public sector. Until 1993, the group had a significant presence in the Ministry of Education.[83] After 1993, however, it became difficult for Islamists to maintain their foothold, due to the regime's interest in producing a new generation of Jordanians attuned to the demands of peace with Israel. The government's decision to limit Islamist influence in the ministry and its growing reliance on Western consultants for curricula development was a major loss for the Brotherhood and evidence that the regime was willing to marginalize Islamists well beyond the strictly political arena.

Other, more troubling lines were being broached as well. For the first time in 1995, leading regime figures openly considered dissolving the Brotherhood. In one such meeting, Minister of Interior Salameh Hemad advocated the group's dissolution on the grounds it was practicing politics despite not being licensed as a political party. Fortunately for the Brotherhood, the suggestion did not go far. Deputy Prime Minister

Abdul Raouf Rawabdeh, himself a former Brotherhood member in the 1950s and 1960s, responded that "the Brotherhood operates here under the king's will, and dissolving it cannot happen unless it is by the king's will."[84]

The shifting fortunes of the Brotherhood forced the group to do something it hadn't done before—boycott the polls, which it did in 1997. The Brotherhood's statement explaining the decision provides some insights into the organization's mindset at the time. First, the statement offers a narrative of Jordan's political evolution. From 1989 through 1992, it says, a "democratic awakening" took hold of the country, contrasted with the period between 1993 and 1997, which "witnessed significant and critical deterioration" in the democratization process.[85] The Brotherhood goes on to argue that the three "pillars" of democracy—freedom of expression, free elections, and political party pluralism—had been destroyed by the government.[86]

This fear of democracy's collapse is cited as the reason for taking what the Brotherhood understood to be drastic action: "[We] believe the decision to boycott the 1997 parliamentary elections is necessary to establish democracy and protect the homeland." Moreover, it represents "an attempt to put a stop to the deterioration of democracy and to protect what remains of it and to restore what was usurped." The decision did not hinge at all on religious concerns or Islamic law, which was not mentioned anywhere in the document.

In the lead-up to the 1997 elections, the Muslim Brotherhood worked to build support for a common position with other opposition groups. Eight leftist and liberal parties joined the IAF and the Brotherhood in the boycott. Islamists also spearheaded a boycott petition that gained the signatures of liberal figures with impeccable establishment credentials, including Ahmed Obeidat and Taher al-Masri, both former prime ministers. Schwedler notes that "the range of individuals who signed the petition, some eighty in all . . . illustrates the extent to which a wide segment of the political spectrum had become frustrated with what they saw as a façade democracy."[87] The boycott coalition soon evolved into the "Conference for National Reform," whose goal was to facilitate coordination between members of the opposition during their exclusion from parliament.[88]

The turn to repression was pushing opposition groups closer together, but their increased cooperation seemed to have little effect; somehow it managed to get worse. As a result of the boycott, Jordan ended up with one of the most unrepresentative parliaments in its history. Moreover, parliament was dissolved in 2001, and King Abdullah ruled by fiat for two years, decreeing more than 210 temporary laws. By then, it seemed Jordan had become a full autocracy with virtually no checks and balances. The Freedom House index reflects this deterioration, with Jordan receiving a score of (6,5) in 2001, its worst result since the organization began tabulating country scores in 1972.[89]

In King Hussein's last days before succumbing to cancer, regime-opposition relations "had reached a nadir."[90] Many thought his half-British son Abdullah, educated at Oxford and Georgetown, might evince a greater interest in democratic reform, and initial interactions with the largely unknown monarch seemed to bode well. In the Brotherhood's first meeting with Abdullah after his father's passing, the young king told the group that the "relationship will be as it was or better."[91] As Brotherhood leaders left the meeting, he reportedly told them "you can see me anytime and without an appointment." But in a second meeting around six months later, the tone had changed. Samih Batikhi, the longtime domestic intelligence chief, launched a broadside against the Brotherhood in the king's presence, calling the group an "illegal organization" since it was licensed as a charitable organization but still practiced politics.[92] Batikhi used the word derogatory term *mahdhoura* (roughly translated as "illicit"). Voices were raised, and eventually the king spoke: "I have a festival to go to and you will be able to finish the discussion on your own. But it is on the Brotherhood to respect the law if they wish to exist."[93]

The honeymoon with King Abdullah did not last long. With the outbreak of the second Palestinian Intifada in September 2000, an increasingly nervous regime instituted a ban on public demonstrations. When the Brotherhood led a 20,000-strong protest march, security forces violently dispersed the crowd.[94] Similarly, the government cracked down harshly on protests marking the anniversary of Israel's creation in May 2001.[95] In response, Abdul Latif Arabiyat described the conduct of the government as unprecedented: "What happened today has never occurred here in Jordan . . . not even during the martial law era."[96]

The idea that more democracy leads to greater moderation and the inverse—that political exclusion makes radicalization more likely—are intuitive. Not surprisingly, then, Islamists, and those who observe them, feared that their exclusion from the parliamentary process, coupled with the regime's heavy-handedness, would either empower radicals or make moderates less moderate. After 1997, as the Brotherhood's Nael Masalha put it, "the government's siege on the Brotherhood only got worse." Referring to rank-and-file members, he told me that "when pressure increases on them, they remove themselves from the political arena and lose faith in peaceful activities."[97] Similarly, Ibrahim al-Gharaibeh had argued in 1997 that "the balance [had tipped] in favor of hardliners . . . Extremism on one side calls for extremism on the other."[98] But the fears of radicalization did not come to pass. Instead of radicalization, the Brotherhood and the IAF reaffirmed the moderate course they had set for themselves earlier in the decade. They, in effect, doubled down.

5

Learning to Lose

AS WE HAVE SEEN, repression, and the fear of it, pushed mainstream Islamists to fundamentally rethink their priorities. They thought that deemphasizing Islamic law and saying and doing the "right things" on democracy, pluralism, and women's and minority rights would put them in a stronger position. They sought allies from across the ideological and political spectrum. They democratized their organizational structures. No longer the niche parties they once were, they became leaders of the opposition with national platforms that, by now, went well beyond specifically Islamist concerns. If Arab regimes ever fell, however unlikely that seemed, it was Islamists who were best positioned to replace them.

Moderation is important, but it isn't enough: transitions to democracy require oppositions that are willing to assume power through, and after, elections. One study examining how competitive authoritarian regimes lose power identifies a strong, unified, and mobilized opposition coalition as the most significant factor.[1] But while they may have been strong, Islamist groups across the region were, with few exceptions, unwilling to take the fight to the regimes. And if they wouldn't, no one else could. Islamists were the ones who had the resources, the institutional networks, and the supporters in the hundreds of thousands. Yet they held back.

While Islamists had adopted more palatable policies, suggesting a readiness to assume the responsibilities of power, they had also become less confrontational. They seemed more willing to resign themselves to a (seemingly) stable status quo. It is not a stretch to say that Islamists—before the Arab Spring—made a habit of losing elections. The odd thing, though, was that they lost them on purpose. This phenomenon of "losing on purpose" can help us better understand the evolution of Islamist groups during the critical period of the 1990s and 2000s, when the process of Islamist moderation was unfolding.[2]

To the extent that repression "worked" by forcing Islamists to appreciate the importance of democracy, it worked in other ways too, and these would be just as consequential. It was ironic that just as Islamists were raising the banner of democratic change, they were making that same goal all the more difficult to achieve.

The Mismeasure of an Opposition

In an April 2010 article, Charles Kurzman and Ijlal Naqvi wrote that "the electoral performance of Islamic parties has generally been unimpressive."[3] After tallying 89 parliamentary contests over the previous 40 years, they found that "median Islamic party performance is 15.5 percent of votes and 15 percent of seats."[4] Accordingly, the United States and other Western powers should get over their Islamist paranoia, because even if there were free elections Islamists probably wouldn't win. But the authors assume that they were *trying* to win in the first place. In the Arab world, Islamist parties rarely contested the total number of parliamentary seats. Instead, they ran—and, in many countries, still run—"partial slates," usually operating well below 50 percent electoral strength. Some of the examples seem almost comical in retrospect, such as when Rachid Ghannouchi sent a letter to President Ben Ali saying that all he and his party wanted were, at most, 10 seats in parliament.[5]

Before the Arab uprisings began, there were six countries where the Islamist opposition actively contested elections on a regular basis—Egypt, Jordan, Kuwait, Bahrain, Morocco, and Yemen. Focusing on the last two election cycles, the average portion of seats contested was a mere 35.9 percent.[6] Limited contestation was coupled with remarkably high win percentages unheard of outside the Middle East. The Muslim Brotherhood in Egypt won 88 seats in 2005 while contesting only 160 out of a possible 444 seats. In 1989, the Jordanian Brotherhood won 22 seats out of the 26 it contested, while in 2006, al-Wefaq, Bahrain's largest Islamist opposition group, won 17 out of 18 seats (94 percent).

Islamists, as it turns out, were good at winning when they wanted to. To be sure, few parties are willing to win elections by any means necessary. However, most make temporary tactical compromises with the understanding that it will better position them for future victory. In contrast, Islamist parties went out of their way to *avoid* increasing their share of parliamentary seats. Not only that, they would often coordinate with regimes to ensure that they didn't exceed an accepted "threshold" of seats.

Jordan, as it happens, is a good example of this. The less contentious tenor of regime–opposition relations usually manifested itself right before elections. Some parliamentary seats are "protected" by the government, meaning that the IAF would choose not to contest them or would work with the authorities to defeat other opposition candidates. Ziad Abu Ghanimeh, the Brotherhood's official spokesman at the time, recounts Islamist participation in the 1993 election:

> Without the knowledge of many of the leaders of the Brotherhood and the IAF, there were secret meetings with the government . . . the agreement being that they would enter the elections and receive 16 seats, and the government would have a say on who the names were. In other words, they would choose who they wanted. . . . There was a deal.[7]

Later, on the eve of the polls, IAF leaders, in last-minute negotiations with regime representatives (which ultimately failed), agreed to "accept" only 12 parliamentary seats in exchange for the regime's withdrawal of the "one-vote" electoral law. Meanwhile, in 2007, the IAF ran only 22 candidates, the lowest number in the party's history. It adopted an odd campaign motto for a political party—*"al-musharika wa laisa al-mughaliba"*—which literally means "participating but not seeking a majority." In the lead-up to election day, IAF leaders reached an understanding with the government, agreeing to contest a reduced number of seats and avoid running explicitly pro-Hamas and antigovernment candidates.[8] In a series of interviews I conducted in 2008, senior IAF figures readily admitted that the reason for contesting such a small number of seats was to avoid offending the regime and to demonstrate that the party had no interest in escalating tensions.[9] One of them explained it this way: "I don't deny that there was coordination between some members of the opposition and the government. This is something natural in the interest of the country and I support this kind of coordination because the government is a critical part of the nation. We are all in the same boat."

The Moroccan case is similarly mystifying. Michael Willis was one of the first scholars to point to the peculiar electoral behavior of the Justice and Development Party (PJD), the country's main Islamist party. In 2002, the PJD ran in only 56 of 95 districts, well under what the major leftist and liberal parties were contesting. "The PJD's modesty about its electoral chances not only contrasted with the pre-election rhetoric of most political parties," writes Willis, "but also seemed to run counter to widespread predictions that the party was likely to perform well at the forthcoming elections."[10]

Despite running a limited slate, the PJD won 42 seats, while the Socialist Union of Popular Forces came first, winning 50 seats—and the opportunity to form a government. Interestingly, several newspapers claimed that the PJD had, in fact, ended up with over 50 seats but, in last-minute negotiations with the royal court, agreed to have the final tally changed. The PJD did not officially deny the allegations.[11] Later, in the 2003 municipal elections, the PJD reduced its coverage to only 16 percent of total districts, again raising the question of why Islamists, despite being capable of winning considerably more seats, chose not to.

The Taming of Islamists

Fear of repression is not unique to the Arab world. What is unique, however, is how Islamists respond to repression. As I discussed in Chapter 2, Islamist groups historically privileged self-preservation over political contestation. Their electoral success is dependent on the success of their charity, educational, and preaching activities, rather than the other way around. Since Islamist groups are largely blocked from the national broadcast and print media, the avenues for disseminating their message to voters are limited. Islamists compensate for this by attracting new supporters—and votes—through their grassroots outreach deep within local communities. Through their network of institutions, Islamists strengthen the perception that they have succeeded where the state has failed—that they care about helping ordinary people, provide high-quality services at affordable prices, and are less corrupt than their secular counterparts.

Starting in the late 1980s and peaking in the early 1990s, Islamists in Egypt and Jordan took control of most of the major professional associations. They began offering a host of state-like services, including low-cost health insurance plans, interest-free loans, and pension plans. Under Islamist leadership, the performance of the associations improved markedly. For example, through investments, commercial enterprises, and membership dues, deposits in Egypt's Engineers Association rose from 14 million pounds in 1985 to 170 million pounds just nine years later.[12] And in a country where insurance was nearly nonexistent, the Doctors Association launched a popular health insurance program for its members and their families, boasting participation rates of over 60 percent.[13] The perception that Islamists are in tune with society's needs is crucial to their chances at the ballot box, particularly in reaching non-Islamist voters not naturally drawn to the religious component of their message.

The fear of repression leads Islamists to deemphasize Islamic law and underscore their democratic *bona fides*, in the hope that this will give paranoid governments less reason to attack them. Doing so also attracts liberal and leftist support—as well as international sympathy—all of which can serve as a layer of protection, as discussed earlier. But the fear of repression leads Islamists to do something else in addition, and this is where two concepts—"moderation" and "nonconfrontation"—bleed together. These are two very different things, yet in the case of Islamist parties, they are related, with one seemingly triggering the other.

Fear of repression leads Islamist groups to appease the very governments that repress them, so they limit their electoral ambitions. They insist that they have no interest in taking power. Much is made of Islamists accepting the "rules of the game," but these rules are almost always blatantly unfair. In the process, Islamists are "tamed." The PJD, long considered a model of Islamist moderation, has been perhaps the most nonconfrontational of the region's Islamist parties. Holger

Albrecht and Eva Wegner use the phrase "anticipatory obedience" to describe the PJD's strategy. As they note, "from the very beginning of inclusion, the leadership of the [PJD] has aimed to reassure the palace that it would play by its rules. Indeed, the party's readiness to help legitimize the regime is remarkable."[14]

In many cases, the rules of the game are imposed by regimes and opposition groups can do little else but complain. Yet the odd thing about the PJD is its complicity in creating the unfair political arrangements in the first place. The PJD actually supported the government's electoral reforms in 2002 and took credit for being among the first to advocate a proportional list system.[15] However, this particular system made it nearly impossible for any one party to win anything close to a majority. Here, again, was a peculiar act of electoral castration—an opposition party advocating changes to the electoral system that effectively negated its chances of securing a clear victory at the ballot box.

Meanwhile, in Kuwait, leaders of the Islamic Constitutional Movement (ICM)—the political arm of Kuwait's Muslim Brotherhood—had been pushing for electoral reform and, after the 2006 elections, they got it. The total number of districts was reduced from 25 to five. As the best-organized and most ideologically coherent political grouping, the ICM stood to benefit most from the larger districts. However, despite what seemed like a more favorable electoral context, it reduced its coverage in 2009 from 22 to 16 percent of the total seats in parliament.

The odd electoral arrangements of the Arab world can only explain so much. While electoral systems—what Giovanni Sartori called "the most specific manipulable instrument of politics"[16]—can limit the seats Islamists win, they cannot limit the number of seats they contest. Moreover, as Sartori's comment suggests, regimes throughout the world have long used electoral engineering to perpetuate their power. Unfair electoral systems are not a permanent fact. They can be altered through opposition pressure and popular mobilization.

The Ghosts of Algeria

Not only did Islamists have unique relationships with their own governments, but they had them with foreign powers as well, particularly the United States. It is difficult to think of another ideological movement that became—for lack of a better word—obsessed with what the outside world thought about it. The world wasn't ready for Islamists, or so it seemed. The Algerian debacle of 1991–2 was an instructive example, and one that Islamists have not forgotten, of how Western powers can "block" the election of Islamist parties.

Besides being a tragedy—more than one hundred thousand were killed in a long, bloody civil war—Algeria became a definitive moment in the Islamist narrative. For every year that Islamist parties were repressed and rounded up, Algeria would accumulate greater meaning. They had come so close, but the chance had come and gone. For another two decades, until the Arab Spring, the rest of the world was reduced to unending speculation about what Islamists wanted, what they would do in power, and whether they were really, in fact, democrats.

As the IAF's Ishaq Farhan put it in 1996, "our phobia is Algeria."[17] So they went out of their way to reassure governments that not only would they play by the rules, but also that they would not seek power or even so much as think about it. Jordan's Islamists—with their motto of "participation not domination"—were good about staying on message. The few times that they slipped and spoke publicly about the mere possibility of winning an election (for a parliament that, in any case, had limited powers), there was considerable outcry. When Azzam Hneidi, head of the IAF parliamentary bloc, told *al-Hayat* newspaper in 2006 that the party was "mature enough to take over government responsibility," many accused the Islamic movement of attempted insurrection.[18] Hneidi's crime was saying that his party aimed to do what political parties, by definition, are supposed to do—win a majority and form a government. What in any other context would be considered normal and rather banal was, in Jordan, perceived as "undemocratic" and "radical." As one government official explained: "They have to . . . agree to be part of the political scene like any other legal party. They have to respect the law, the constitution, and the higher interest of Jordan, which has strong ties with Washington and diplomatic relations with Tel Aviv."[19] Implicit in the official's comment is the assumption— largely correct—that the rise of Islamists to power, particularly in a strategically vital country like Jordan, would lead to tensions with the United States and Israel.

Islamists would often speak of the "American veto." The assumption was always there that, somehow, the international community would be waiting in the background, stopping them from claiming what was rightfully theirs. Hamas's surprise victory in the 2006 Palestinian elections—and the international community's response—only served to confirm what they already suspected. During the height of Mubarak's repression in 2008, Essam al-Erian explained it to me this way: "Even if you come to power through democratic means, you are facing an international community that doesn't accept Islamist representation. This is a problem. I think this will continue to present an obstacle for us until there is real acknowledgement of the situation."[20]

Islamists were fighting on two fronts—first against their own regimes and then their international backers. In hindsight, Islamist groups probably overestimated America's importance as well as the extent of its opposition to political Islam. But this was how they perceived it, and it shaped their behavior, reinforcing their cautious, deferential approach to Arab regimes.

Before the Revolutions

Throughout the 2000s, mainstream Islamist groups across the region went further than they ever had before in an attempt to woo the international community. Increasingly, Western analysts came around. They realized something important had changed and started calling them "democrats." Islamists becoming democrats, however, wasn't necessarily good for democracy. On the one hand, they continued to modernize their political platforms, doubling down on the ideological revisions of the previous decade. But, on the other hand, moderation and nonconfrontation increasingly seemed to go together. Brotherhood affiliates in Egypt, Jordan, Algeria, and Kuwait and Brotherhood-inspired groups like the PJD and Yemen's Islah had been criticized from both right and left for not being "opposition" in the truest sense of the word. They had, in effect, sold out in return for the most dubious of promises. It was one thing to be "loyal opposition" in a democracy but quite another to be loyal to a system that was undemocratic by design.

The inherent gradualism of Islamist movements is an important part of the story. Even at the height of repression, they managed to retain a stoic calm in the face of considerable odds. They believed they were right, and, as a result, history (and presumably God) was on their side. They could wait it out. In the meantime, they spent the decade establishing their democratic *bona fides* and reaching out to the secular groups that had long been suspicious of them. They continued to democratize their internal structures, holding elections at various levels of their organizations. The goal, at least in part, was to send an unmistakable message to audiences at home as well as abroad: Islamists were sober, responsible actors on the regional and world stage. They were no longer outcasts to be shunned or ignored. Whatever one thought of them, they were permanent fixtures in their societies, and they were popular to boot. In short, they had to be engaged. If Arab countries were ever to democratize, Islamists would inevitably play a major, perhaps even dominant role. It was just a matter of the right moment, and when exactly it would come.

If moderation was embraced in the hope that it might forestall repression, then it made sense that Islamists would tame their political ambitions if that, too, would forestall repression. So they did both, with one reinforcing the other.[21]

Mubarak's Last Years

In the final years of Mubarak's rule, the Muslim Brotherhood had worked itself into a corner. Sure, they had made democracy their call to arms—but what were they willing to actually do about it? The group's traditional caution, coupled with its fear of repression, undermined its ability to push for tangible democratic change. This paradox—a function of the contradictions inherent in Islamist activism—is worth exploring in greater depth.

The decade, to be sure, did not begin well. The attacks of September 11 introduced an unexpected shock, one that would force Islamists to further refine their political strategy. America's "war on terror" emboldened the Mubarak regime in its own war against the Islamist opposition. According to Freedom House, "international fear of terrorism following the September 11 terrorist attacks in the United States gave the government of Hosni Mubarak reason to increase its suppression of domestic opposition in 2001."[22] 2002 saw a quick return to the strategy of arresting Brotherhood activists and trying them outside the judicial system. A military tribunal, for example, sentenced 16 Brotherhood members to three to five years in prison.[23]

The 2002 Associations Law was another significant setback. In a report analyzing the legislation, Human Rights Watch concluded that "overall, it [creates] a legal regime that gives the state excessive latitude to dissolve, reject, or slowly choke any organizational financially, should it wish to do so."[24] Grounds for dissolution included "threatening national unity" and "violating public order or morals."[25] Article 11 of the legislation prohibited organizations from engaging in "the exercise of any political activity . . . and exercising any unionist activity."

In 2004, despite tentative efforts to placate Western demands for reform, the Mubarak regime "launched the most sweeping crackdown on the Muslim Brotherhood since the mid-1990s."[26] Neither was Western attention enough of a concern to even make a show of holding minimally plausible elections for the upper house of parliament; ruling party candidates won 87 out of 88 contested seats. And as might have been expected, indiscriminate crackdowns on Islamists seemed exempt from Western criticism. While the regime began to tread more carefully in its interactions with secular activists, it persisted in using its arsenal of repression against the Brotherhood.

While many tend to think of 2005 as the year in which Islamists won an unprecedented 88 seats in parliament, it was also the year in which the Brotherhood withstood the largest number of arrests in years. Not wanting to be upstaged by the secular-leaning Kefaya movement, which was gaining international attention for its spirited street protests, the Muslim Brotherhood staged its first ever pro-democracy protest on March 27, 2005, calling for political and constitutional reform. By May, the organization had staged 23 demonstrations—an average of one every three days—in 15 governorates, with some bringing out as many as 15,000 people. On May 4, the Brotherhood staged a coordinated nationwide protest in 10 governorates, with an estimated 50,000 to 70,000 protestors.[27] In the course of less than two months, the total participation of Brotherhood members neared 140,000.[28] It was the largest pro-democracy mobilization Egypt had seen in decades.

Such a show of strength came at a cost: around 4,000 Brotherhood members were arrested.[29] Yet, with few exceptions, the international community was silent. Paying a high price, the Brotherhood was reminded of the challenges they would continue to face. This, at the height of the first "Arab Spring," is what happened when the world was watching. What about when it wasn't?

It wasn't like the Brotherhood to put so many of its members in harm's way. Historically, the group had always been reticent to fully mobilize its masses, knowing the costs could be considerable. This time, however, the Brotherhood was coming under pressure from its younger members to join, and perhaps even lead, the budding pro-democracy movement. The international community, and particularly the Bush administration, was putting more pressure on Mubarak to respect the rights of the opposition. There seemed to be an opening, in part due to U.S. efforts, as Brotherhood officials would later acknowledge.

These were not protests about Islamic law: Brotherhood members were told not to raise Qurans and to stay on message. Instead, the demonstrations were about national, democratic demands. But the Mubarak regime didn't care whether the protest was about Islamic law or constitutional reform. If anything, the latter was more threatening, because it brought the Brotherhood closer to the demands of liberal and leftist forces, raising the specter of a more unified opposition. When the regime cracked down, there was no international outcry to speak of.

In the subsequent months and years, Brotherhood officials would repeatedly complain about double standards: the United States was willing to suspend loan agreements with Egypt over the arrest of one secular activist, Saad Eddin Ibrahim, but a systematic campaign against the Brotherhood—with thousands of arrests—garnered no such response. The world *still* wasn't ready, it seemed. (The Brotherhood would not return to the streets *en masse* until nearly six years later, on January 28, 2011.)

And it only got worse. In the first round of the 2005 parliamentary elections, the Brotherhood was permitted to show its strength. After it performed unexpectedly well, winning 88 seats, the usual repressive measures resumed, ushering in a sustained crackdown from 2006 onwards that some considered the "most widespread campaign against the group since the 1960s."[30]

In such a context, the same question can be posed as before: how did the Brotherhood respond, and why? The group's 2004 "reform initiative," released to much fanfare during the Bush administration's democracy push, stands as a landmark in the Brotherhood's political evolution.[31] It reflects a shifting of priorities and the slow but unmistakable realization that, in an existential struggle with an increasingly authoritarian regime, the fight that mattered most was the one for democratic reform. The initiative represents an effort to elevate the cause of democracy in Egyptian politics and bring other political forces around a shared vision for change.

Early on in the document, the Brotherhood explains the rationale for its release: "Political reform is needed since it is a starting point for reform in all other aspects of life, [yet the state of reform] has witnessed a speedy degradation in Egypt and the Arab and Islamic world to the point where it has hit rock bottom." As the group saw it, the continued political deterioration required a more vigorous response from the opposition. In other words, the less willing the regime is to push for reform, the more willing its competitors must be. In the introduction to the reform initiative, the Brotherhood's General Guide Mahdi Akef makes the link between government repression and the group's decision to prioritize democracy even more explicit:

> When the Egyptian government's refusal to respond to the national demands proposed by the Brotherhood and other powers . . . became apparent to us, and since the pace of reform undergone by successive governments has been very slow to the point that the reform process over the past decade has been—to a striking degree—delayed, we decided to present this initiative.

This captures, in the Brotherhood's own words, the causal process of cognitive change—the experience of authoritarianism, particularly when preceded by a period of democratic opening, elevates the importance of democracy for those who have been deprived of it.

In the section on political reform, the group affirms its "commitment to a republican, constitutional, democratic system of government within a framework of Islamic principles"—a new formulation it hadn't used before. However, because of the regime's full-blown authoritarianism, the task at hand is "too large to be handled by . . . any one political power on its own." The Brotherhood makes a pitch for unity to Egypt's notoriously fractious opposition:

> [We] are of the view that the necessities of the time call for all political forces—as well as intellectual and cultural elites and all those concerned with public life—to come together around a broad framework based on the essential pillars of society, and to cooperate on issues of agreement—and they are many—and to engage in dialogue regarding areas of disagreement—and they are few—in the service of the nation's best interests.

The Brotherhood then calls on political forces in Egypt to support the reform initiative as a basis for a national charter anchored around the "full recognition that the people are the source of authority," "freedom of personal belief," and the unrestricted right to form political parties. In addition, the initiative devotes considerable attention to the distribution of power and the role of institutions. For the first time, the Brotherhood declares its preference for a parliamentary system, in which "the party that receives the most votes in free and fair elections is the one responsible for forming a government." Meanwhile, the head of state plays a mostly ceremonial role, "making [the president] a symbol for all Egyptians by ensuring he does not preside over any political party and that he be completely removed from any executive responsibility for governing."

Throughout the document, the Brotherhood expresses its desire to limit executive power and restrict the reach of an all-encompassing state. In the section on reforming al-Azhar University—the Arab world's preeminent center of Sunni Islamic scholarship—the group makes two recommendations for returning the oldest center of Islamic learning to its past state of independence, free of the government interference that became the norm under President Nasser. First, the Grand Imam of al-Azhar, rather than being appointed, would be elected by a Higher

Scholars Committee, which itself would be elected by the general body of al-Azhar scholars. Secondly, the administration of *waqfs*, or religious endowments, would be removed from the purview of the state and no longer bound by the state budget. In effect, such changes would be tantamount to the democratization of Egypt's religious institutions, which would be separated from the tight and, in the Brotherhood's view, destructive embrace of the modern Egyptian state.

Just as important is what the reform initiative does not say. Interestingly, not even one reference to the application of sharia law, or *tatbiq al-sharia*, can be found in the initiative's pages. There is a discernible move toward a more general, and presumably less controversial, promotion of religious values in society. The document, for example, affirms the "freedom to explain the nature and principles of Islam, most importantly the fact that it is comprehensive in dealing with all aspects of life." The section on education and scientific research calls for "solidifying religious values, moral principles, noble comport, and loyalty to the nation," while the section on social reform calls for the "realization of God-consciousness and religiosity in society."

The reform initiative, despite the international context in which it was conceived, could not simply be dismissed as a veiled message to the United States or a cynical public relations stunt. A decade earlier, there were concerns that the more conservative local branches of the Brotherhood downplayed the 1994 statements on women and pluralism, dismissing them as "just for the media."[32] This time around, despite internal dissent, including from within the Guidance Bureau, there was a strong, coordinated effort to build support for the reform initiative at all levels of the organization.[33] The program was distributed in all the various Brotherhood-affiliated organizations and institutions. According to Khaled Hamza, each Brother with full membership privileges was given a copy of the initiative and was expected to study and familiarize himself with the contents. Members of each branch or *shu'ba*[34] (consisting of 40 to 50 individuals) were expected to discuss the initiative upon its release.[35] For example, Hamza himself spoke to various *shu'bas* regarding the reform program and its contents, leading discussion and answering questions from members.

Meanwhile, the Brotherhood's 2005 electoral platform built on the reform initiative, providing a more detailed discussion of the group's approach to economic and political reform.[36] It was, at the time, the most sophisticated document the Brotherhood had produced. The program offers a substantive critique of existing political structures and proposes a broad set of recommendations aimed not necessarily at changing policies, but at modifying the institutional setup of the state.

Much of these proposals are concerned with establishing a workable system of checks and balances and ensuring the autonomy of local government. If there is a theme that runs throughout, it is that the executive branch has too much power, which it abuses at will. Accordingly, competing centers of power—municipalities, professional syndicates, and once-powerful religious institutions such as al-Azhar—must be strengthened in order to provide effective checks on executive authority.

The section on "financial and administrative decentralization" is among the longest and best reflects the group's apparent fixation on empowering elected local bodies to counterbalance (unelected) central authorities. Under the Brotherhood's plan, national ministries are limited to devising broad policies and strategies, while municipal governments are responsible for execution. Localities are empowered to collect taxes and fees within their own geographical jurisdiction without requiring the approval of the central government. They are also responsible for collecting zakat funds for poverty alleviation.[37] If any funds remain, only then are they to be transferred to the treasury. Finally, to ensure the independence of municipal leaders, their salaries are to be paid through a private funding mechanism.

On a more basic level, the Brotherhood attempts at the program's outset to explain its understanding of the relationship between sharia, Islam, and democracy. As in the 2004 initiative, they have little to say about the implementation of Islamic law. A different kind of vocabulary is used. The program is "based on a reference from which our method of change stems, and that is the Islamic reference (*marji'iya islamiya*) and the democratic mechanisms of the modern civil state (*dawla madaniya*)." The "Islamic method," as the Brotherhood understands it, "gives emphasis to the principle of consultation, which respects the will of citizens when choosing their representatives in all institutions of society—whether legislative and executive branches, syndicates, or associations—and emphasizes to their right to hold their representatives accountable as well as withdrawing confidence from them." As for the sharia, it "represents a way for establishing progress, development, and reform as well as defining the lawful and unlawful in legislation and social interactions. All of this connects politics with morals and makes our means noble and, consequently, our ends noble too."

The two terms—"Islamic reference" and "civil state"—were new additions to Islamist discourse. The notion of a "civil state" suggested that the Brotherhood was willing to concede a sort of implicit separation between the sacred and the political:

> Since Islam rejects clerical rule, the state in Islam is a civil one in which the people, being the source of authority, determine its systems and institutions. This is a human judgment which changes and improves within the fixed principles of sharia . . . Concerning the authority of the ruler, it is according to the social contract between the governor and the governed. The social contract is established by the people, thereby improving the civic institutions of the state . . . So the nation has the right to appoint the ruler, control him, and depose him if necessary, as he is a civil governor in all respects.

Taken together, the 2004 reform initiative and the 2005 electoral program—along with efforts to democratize their organizational structures—reflected an evolving strategy. As in 1994, the Brotherhood's public focus on reform came to both reflect and mirror internal demands for accountability. After postponing internal elections scheduled for 1999 due to security reasons, the group held elections in 2004 and 2005, this time introducing the vote at every level of the organization. For the first time, each *shu'ba* (branch), *mantaqa* (region), and *muhafadha* (governorate) would have its own elected council, including a *mas'oul* (chair) and *na'ib mas'oul* (deputy chair). To enact these changes, the Brotherhood's bylaws were amended in 2004 at the initiative of the newly elected general guide, Mahdi Akef.

Egypt's Islamists were positioning themselves as leaders of an emergent democratic opposition. And they increasingly tried to lead efforts to unify the country's notoriously fractious opposition groups. In June 2005, the Brotherhood announced the formation of the National Alliance for Reform and invited the country's major parties to join.[38] The

Labor party's Magdi Hussein set the tone when he said "there should be one goal for this alliance—toppling Mubarak and his family rule."[39] In the past, the Brotherhood would offer lukewarm support to similar coalition-building efforts initiated by secular parties. This time, however, they were more interested in playing a leadership role. Ultimately, the alliance—like most in Egypt—failed to gain traction, but it seemed like an encouraging step.

In the lead-up to the November 2005 parliamentary elections, there was a second attempt to unify the opposition. The United National Front for Change (UNFC) was perhaps the first opposition alliance to include such a wide range of parties and groups, including the Wafd, Tagammu, Wasat, the leftist Karama party, Kefaya, and the Muslim Brotherhood. The UNFC put forward a unified electoral slate of nearly 180 candidates, although the Brotherhood ran its own list, due in part to its already having undergone preparations to finalize its 160-candidate list (as well as due to the lopsided power imbalance). Still, the Brotherhood coordinated with the UNFC list and withdrew nearly 25 of its own candidates to avoid splitting the opposition vote. The increased cooperation—and a shared realization that the Mubarak regime was worse than nearly all possible alternatives—led to an unprecedented optimism within opposition ranks. According to Anani, 2005 marked a high point in cooperation between the Brotherhood and non-Islamist groups and parties.[40]

Hopes for the United Front were quickly dashed, however, when fewer than 10 of its candidates won seats, performing well below even the lowest expectations. By blocking the UNFC from real representation, the regime managed to drive a wedge between the Brotherhood, which won 88 seats, and the rest of the opposition. That said, initiatives such as the UNFC and the National Alliance for Reform were steps in a positive direction and suggested that opposition groups were growing more interested in focusing their efforts on an unpopular, repressive regime rather than on each other.

Jordan Under King Abdullah

In Jordan, too, the promise of early democratic openings faded beyond recognition. Jordan never quite reached Egypt's level of repression, but, on its own terms, the country's descent into autocracy was just as striking. Jordan's Islamists did not compare their country to Egypt; they compared it to what it was and what it still claimed to be. Some scholars like Mansour Moaddel used to speak of "Jordanian exceptionalism" and he even wrote a book about it.[41] Jordan was supposed to be different: it was one of the first countries to legalize Islamist parties and include the Muslim Brotherhood in government. It had registered the highest-ever Freedom House scores for an Arab country.

But, by 2001, it was difficult to find any real bright spots. The attacks of September 11, the regime's dissolution of parliament, and the postponement of the 2001 elections all factored into what Nael Masalha called "a siege on the Brotherhood."[42] There were two years of rule by fiat. In October 2001, the penal code was amended to forbid publication of "false or libelous information that undermines national unity or the country's reputation."[43] As a result, activists and journalists could be tried in State Security Courts for promoting "deviation from what is right" or organizing strikes and sit-ins. Meanwhile, a new public gatherings law banned gatherings that did not have prior government approval and permitted officials to use force against protestors. The 2001 State Security Court Law granted the prime minister the authority to refer cases to security courts and extended the time of detention without charge from 48 hours to seven days. Government interference was also taking its toll on the judicial branch, particularly after the forced retirement of the president of the Court of Cassation in 1998.[44] In November 2002, the judiciary moved to dissolve the Engineers Association, the most powerful of Jordan's professional syndicates.

It was in such a context that the Brotherhood and IAF were faced with the difficult choice of whether to participate in the 2003 parliamentary elections. All the factors cited for boycotting in 1997 either remained or had worsened. At the same time, some Brotherhood leaders took this as evidence that their self-imposed exile from parliament had not helped matters. The political situation was deteriorating further, and, recognizing what was at stake, the vast majority of the Brotherhood's ranks came out in support of reentering the political process. So the IAF began to prepare a new electoral platform for the first time in nearly 10 years. Much had changed in the span of the previous decade, and, not surprisingly, so too did the party's program.

The 2003 Electoral Program and 2005 Reform Initiative

The introduction to the 1993 electoral program had focused on Islamic law while failing to mention the word "democracy" even once. The first sentence of the program explained that the IAF "is an Islamic party that [invites to the path] of Islam and works for the promotion of the Islamic life and the application of the rules of the Islamic sharia."[45] It then proceeded to offer a warning of "the dangers of the [Western] civilizational onslaught" and the "threat of the Jewish presence."[46] Of course these topics—Islamic law and the liberation of Palestine—had been the two main components of the Jordanian Brotherhood's message for decades.

The 2003 program begins on a different note. The introduction—subtitled "why we participate in parliamentary elections"—states that "the Islamic Action Front party considers its presence in parliament as one of the political means to the realization of the sentiment 'Islam is the solution' and a means of building the nation's strength." Clarifying what this might mean, the party pledges to "facilitate a climate that helps in realizing the objectives of the people in regards to freedom, shura, and democracy, and protecting the rights of the people on the basis that they are the source of authority."[47] The program is presented "in the context of democratic regression in our country," again underlining the link between regime attacks on democracy and the Brotherhood's prioritization of it.[48]

The most significant mention of the application of Islamic law, early on, is on page six, where it is highlighted as one of the party's main goals. According to the program, "re-assessing those laws which contradict the sharia" can be accomplished through 12 measures, including for example: "Enacting constitutional reforms that provide an opening for comprehensive development and the strengthening and safeguarding of the democratic process"; "putting into practice the article of the constitution that states that the people are the source of authority"; "working toward instituting a new electoral law to replace the one-vote electoral law"; and "establishing the principle of alternation of power in practice and following sound practices in the formation of cabinets."[49] Only one of the 12 measures listed—a proposed prohibition on usury—is explicitly "Islamic." It is telling that a section supposedly focused on how to further Islamic law is actually about promoting democratic reform.

Influenced by their Egyptian counterparts—as well as by the brief openings of the first Arab Spring—Jordan's Islamists released their own "reform initiative" in 2005. Released under the joint auspices of the IAF and the Muslim Brotherhood, the initiative represents the most far-reaching and comprehensive expression of the Islamic movement's changing orientation. The document was a product of an era, forged in a time of crisis both at home and abroad. The program refers to the 2000 Palestinian Intifada and post-9/11 American hegemony but ties it back to the domestic. The last five years, the authors write, were marked by "the failure of ruling Arab regimes to establish a new democratic reality in their countries and exercise their weight in the international arena in the service of the umma."[50] Moreover, the Brotherhood recognizes the influence of the Bush administration's "Broader Middle East Initiative" in the development of its own reform program. In one section, it even discusses the Bush initiative while countering that its own effort repre-sents the true voice of reform.[51] The Brotherhood's initiative affirms the importance of comprehensive reform while emphasizing that it cannot be "imposed from the outside."[52]

Like the 2003 electoral platform before it, the reform initiative is concerned with institutional and constitutional reform, particularly by "preventing executive hegemony over other branches." The Senate—whose members are appointed by the king—had long given the mon-archy a direct means with which to block legislation. For the first time, the Brotherhood addressed this publicly, saying that the body should either be abolished or elected by popular vote "as is done in most demo-cratic systems."[53] In the hope of strengthening parliament's influence, the program proposes that parliament be in session no less than eight months of the year and that parliamentary immunity be respected.[54] To strengthen the judicial branch, the Brotherhood reaffirms its support for the establishment of a supreme court with the autonomy and author-ity to provide clear guidelines for the exercise of executive power.[55] One might expect that an Islamist party would consider the judiciary critical to the effort to apply Islamic legislation, but, out of eight planks in the section, only one makes any mention of Islamic law—a stock reference to ensuring that laws do not contradict sharia.[56]

Generally, the program's references to Islamic law are vague and sub-sumed under universal principles, as when it says "our intellectual and political understanding of reform depends on the creed of the umma and the major objectives of the sharia (*maqasid al-sharia*) in protecting the person, the mind, religion, wealth, honor, and the establishment of justice."[57] If Islamic law is about anything, it (now) appears to be about freedom: "Indeed, the Islamic sharia and its lofty objectives— the preservation of the life of the person and his faith, his mind, freedom, money, and honor—make freedom the protector and guarantor of equality, considering that freedom is among the most distinguished of human characteristics."[58]

Nearly as interesting as the program's content is the context in which it came to be. The reform initiative was published on the heels of intensifying repression. After some initial optimism in the wake of the IAF's return to parliament in 2003, the regime resumed its efforts to restrict Islamist activity. With the continued failure of political parties to gain traction in society, Jordan's professional associations, mostly led by Brotherhood members, had become the center of opposition to the regime's pro-American foreign policy. Since engineers, lawyers, and journalists were required by law to be members of an association to practice their profession, the associations had a large membership upon which to draw. For those who did not feel comfortable joining the IAF, the associations presented a meaningful space for political participation as well as cross-ideological cooperation with Islamist colleagues. And for these same reasons they were becoming an intolerable annoyance for the Jordanian regime.

Unsurprisingly, disagreements over the Israeli–Palestinian conflict were the cause of the growing tension. Hoping to further solidify Jordan's reputation as a moderate, pro-Western nation, the regime had little patience for anti-Israel agitation. In January 2005, Interior Minister Samir Habashneh caught civil society off guard with a series of unexpectedly harsh statements, demanding that associations "completely halt" all political activities.[59] In early March, Prime Minister Faisal Fayez's government presented a draft professional associations law to parliament that would authorize the Audit Bureau to monitor each association's funds to ensure they were being spent only on internal activities.[60] If there was any doubt over the government's intentions, Habashneh explained that the legislation aimed to eliminate the "prevalence of one current" within the associations.[61]

Making an already volatile situation even more tense, the government proposed a new political parties law that would prohibit the use of mosques, professional associations, and sports clubs for political party activities, ban recruiting and campaigning at educational institutions, and bar activities that harmed Jordan's relations with other countries. After months of acrimony between the regime and the opposition, and even between the regime and normally supportive members of parliament, King Abdullah gave a scathing televised address, attacking the entirety of Jordan's political class. He reserved his harshest criticism for the political "salons" in "certain parts of the capital" and accused his opponents of allying with "foreign forces [. . . to] intimidate our homeland."[62] But the increasingly authoritarian bent of the regime did not appear to produce any noticeable radicalization on the part of the opposition. Rather, Islamists—again—doubled down on their pro-reform advocacy.

From 2005 to 2007, the confrontation between the regime and Islamists reached another peak. Jordan had its own September 11th on November 9, 2005, just a month after the release of the Brotherhood's reform initiative, which was quickly forgotten as a result. The Amman hotel bombings killed more than 60 Jordanians. As Freedom House reports, "[King] Abdullah replaced his security advisers, dissolved the Senate, and appointed a new prime minister, Marouf al-Bakhit, along with a new cabinet . . . Political reform was stalled with the renewed focus on security."[63] Antiterrorism legislation was once again rushed through, limiting judicial review and expanding the power of military courts. The effect of Hamas's election victory in January 2006 ensured that Bakhit's government would take few chances in the lead-up to Jordan's own closely watched parliamentary elections.

A key flashpoint was the death in June 2006 of Abu Musab al-Zarqawi, leader of al-Qaeda in Iraq and mastermind of the Amman bombings. Zarqawi, as his name suggests, was from Zarqa, the second-largest city in Jordan, and hailed from a prominent East Bank tribe. Four IAF parliamentarians attended his wake, paying condolences to the family. One of them, Mohamed Abu Faris, called Zarqawi a "martyr" on an Al Jazeera television program. The four were charged with "fueling national discord and inciting sectarianism" (11 non-Islamist members of parliament also attended the wake but were not charged).[64]

The following month, on July 5, 2006, with the Zarqawi affair far from over, the government formally launched its attack on the Islamic Center Society, the Brotherhood's charity arm (whose activities were discussed in Chapter 2), alleging financial "violations and reservations."[65] The following week, the ICS board was dissolved and a new one appointed in its place. This, too, signaled a new escalation: it was the first time the regime had ever taken any kind of serious action against the Brotherhood's charity activities, long one of the "red lines" in the relationship between the regime and Islamists.

In the hope of avoiding further escalation, a number of meetings were held between Brotherhood officials and the regime. For their part, the Brotherhood and the IAF issued a joint statement in which they condemned all forms of extremism, stated that no group has a monopoly on defining the principles of the nation, and underscored their support for ideological and political pluralism. The statement was released on the same day that the public prosecutor's office announced it was pursuing legal action against the ICS. It is interesting that the Brotherhood chose to respond to such an unprecedented provocation by further highlighting the moderate, nonconfrontational approach it had carved out for itself in the years prior. On July 11, the group went even further, releasing a statement in support of the "Amman declaration"— the monarchy's signature initiative to bring together leading Islamic scholars to condemn extremism and terrorism.[66] These "clarifications" from the Islamic movement were controversial not necessarily for their content but for their deference to the regime.

Moderation Leads to Repression?

In the above statements, we can see how "moderation"—committing (and recommitting) to democracy and political pluralism—went hand in hand with an avowedly nonconfrontational approach. The Brotherhood went out of its way to appear as nonthreatening as possible. The same instinct to compromise on ideology, or compromise with their colleagues in the liberal opposition, led to a willingness to compromise with the regime.

This deferential strategy, however, does not appear to have worked, as the regime continued criminal proceedings against three of the four

IAF deputies who attended Zarqawi's wake. Something similar happened to the Wasat party in Egypt, as we saw in the previous chapter. Wasat chose to respond to regime efforts to exclude it by trying to find new ways to highlight its moderation. But Wasat founders continued to be harassed, persecuted, and arrested. Their application for legal status was not denied twice or even three times, but four times.

Time and time again, in Egypt and Jordan, this pattern seemed to hold. One might expect that with Islamists making ideological concessions and demonstrating a strong desire for compromise, regimes would respond in kind. As Stathis Kalyvas notes, "rational challengers will have an incentive that, once in power, they will behave moderately and will even guarantee the incumbents' material interests."[67]

The idea here is simple. For regimes to accept democratization, they need to be reassured that their opponents are not seeking total victory. In the cases of Egypt and Jordan, however, opposition moderation did not produce regime moderation. The confounding reality is that moderation is precisely what autocrats find so threatening. A "moderate" party is a more viable substitute for the regime. Such a party has a better chance of attracting liberal and leftist supporters, in the process forging a common front against authoritarianism. Just as important, the more moderate Islamists are, the more palatable they become to Western policymakers and the more insistent the calls for the U.S. and Europe to engage with them. Arab regimes long depended on presenting themselves as the reliable alternative to dangerous Islamists, who were waiting in the wings, ready to take over and subvert the regional order. In this sense, it made sense to suppress Islamists but not to eliminate them entirely. After all, as Noah Feldman writes, "preserving the conditions that justify repression is good practical policy for the autocrats."[68] It was easier for them to portray Islamists as a threat when they spoke of imposing Islamic law and keeping women locked up at home. It became more difficult when they spent much of the 2000s talking about human rights and political freedoms.

This results in an odd feedback loop: the opposition moderates and the regime represses (a dynamic Jason Brownlee aptly terms "unrequited temperance"[69]). In response, the opposition moderates even more. The regime, feeling threatened, represses—and so on and so forth. Broadly speaking, this is what seems to have happened in the Egyptian and Jordanian cases.

But why would Islamist groups continue along a course of moderation (and nonconfrontation) when it failed to produce its intended objective? Islamists, interestingly, point to this as evidence that their commitment to nonviolence and democracy is "strategic" and not contingent on particular circumstances. This is an argument for the "stickiness" of moderation, that once certain commitments are made and publicly adopted, it becomes difficult to renege on them.

But moderation is also sticky for another reason: while moderation may fail to produce a change in regime behavior, it remains better than the alternative. Wasat founders and IAF leaders alike wagered that their commitment to moderate policies would attract support for their parties, which, in turn, would make it more difficult for the regime to block their progress. They were not necessarily wrong to think this; that they failed perhaps says more about the regimes than it does of them.

Are Islamists an Obstacle to Democracy?

On the eve of revolution, it seemed that Islamist groups were stuck. When I met with Mohamed Morsi in 2010—before he could even imagine he'd be president in two years (and then be ousted in a coup just a year later)—he insisted that the Brotherhood had no interest in power. He wasn't even comfortable using the word "opposition" to describe the group. There didn't appear to be a plan or a vision for how to deal with the problem of repression. Even during the 18-day uprising, Morsi, switching to English at a press conference just days before Mubarak fell, spoke of a "wait and see" approach.[70]

The one success that Islamists could claim was that Western governments were giving them another look and taking them seriously as potential partners in power. The other "success" was that, in Egypt, Jordan, and across the region, mainstream Islamist groups had, at the very least, survived. For groups that had suffered from persecution for decades, this was no small feat.

Over those decades, they had accumulated considerable political capital and public goodwill, creating states-within-states in the process. Despite their promising efforts at moderation, however, Islamists failed to play the role that true opposition parties are expected and—for democracy to come to be—required to play. Their deference to regimes and the status quo made it difficult to envision Islamist groups taking significant risks—whether through civil disobedience or mass protest—to weaken Arab autocrats' hold on power.[71]

Elsewhere, nonviolent resistance has amassed an impressive record of success against authoritarian regimes. When regimes use brute force against peaceful protesters, it provokes international awareness and condemnation. As Maria Stephan and Erica Chenoweth note: "Externally, the international community is more likely to denounce and sanction states for repressing nonviolent campaigns than it is to violent campaigns."[72] But there's a catch: international outrage is harder to come by when it is Islamists who are being repressed. In the two decades leading up to the Arab Spring, there were no instances of anti-Islamist repression in the Arab world that elicited significant international outrage.[73]

Well aware of these realities, Islamist groups had little incentive to aggressively confront Arab dictators. Even when they formed alliances with liberal and leftist groups, their own members would invariably make up the bulk of any protest action, with the smaller secular parties providing only token representation. It was easier, then, to opt for caution and to avoid overt confrontation with regimes.

After the tragedy of Algeria, not one mainstream Islamist group launched a decisive bid for power in the Arab world. In this respect, Islamist exceptionalism helped to account for Arab exceptionalism—the region's once-stubborn and singular resistance to democratization.[74] To be sure, Western governments were getting better at distinguishing the Egyptian Muslim Brotherhood from Hamas, and for that matter al-Qaeda, but that did not mean that any significant shift in foreign policy was forthcoming. The United States was not about to support revolution in countries like Egypt and Jordan that were vital to American interests in the region.

For a brief moment, it looked like it couldn't get much worse, yet the United States, under the Obama administration, showed little interest in prioritizing democracy. In late 2010, three close American allies—Egypt, Jordan, and Bahrain—all held elections. The Brotherhood in Egypt, cautious as ever, reduced its electoral coverage to 135 seats.[75]

The regime did not seem to appreciate this sign of goodwill. Due to unprecedented fraud, the Brotherhood was reduced from 88 seats in the previous parliament to zero. In the first round, the ruling National Democratic Party won 209 out of 211 seats, straining the credulity of even those most sympathetic to the regime.

In Jordan, the Muslim Brotherhood boycotted the elections altogether (and they would do so again in 2013). Remarkably, the resulting parliament had no formal opposition representation. In Bahrain, the situation seemed better but only marginally so. Its October 2010 elections were reasonably free. Turnout was 67 percent and the Islamist opposition won a large share of the seats. But rather than suggesting a bold, if unlikely, democratic experiment, the elections reflected a new and troubling trend: the free but unfair—and rather meaningless—election.[76] Bahrain, too, was at a breaking point.

The international response was predictably quiet. As Islamists were growing comfortable with losing elections—or not contesting them in the first place—and with much of the world similarly comfortable watching them lose, Arab democracy seemed to drift further out of reach.

6

Chronicle of a Coup Foretold

AT THE OUTSET OF the revolution, Egypt's Muslim Brotherhood was caught off guard. They were also afraid. On February 9, 2011, I made my way to Tahrir Square in the early afternoon. By then the square had been transformed into something like a carnival, with food and beverage carts, different corners for speakers, and an array of political displays and demonstrations. While the mood had changed dramatically from just a week before—when regime supporters attacked protesters during the "Battle of the Camel," leaving at least 11 dead—there was still a profound sense of uncertainty. How would it end? What if Mubarak refused to leave?

From the square, I made my way down the street that housed the American University of Cairo. It looked like a war zone, with barricades and trash strewn on the sidewalks. All the restaurants were boarded up. There was only one coffee shop open. Cilantro—a sort of Egyptian version of Starbucks—had just reopened. It was a good place—really the only place—to meet with activists like Abdel Rahman Ayyash. They would step away from Tahrir Square, walk to Cilantro, and meet with journalists, each other, or researchers such as myself. Ayyash, then a prominent Brotherhood activist and only 20 years old, exuded a kind of nervous excitement. He was confident but worried, particularly when it came to the Brotherhood's role. "If it's ever perceived that this revolution is an Islamic one," he said, "the U.S. and others will be able to justify a crackdown."[1]

For this reason, the Brotherhood purposely downplayed its participation in the protests. But behind the scenes, it played a pivotal support role in the square, providing food and medical services to protesters, protecting them from regime thugs, and generally keeping order.[2] Brotherhood officials instructed their followers to avoid using ideological slogans. The group, as always, was cautious, fearing that even a hint of Islamism in the square would undermine opposition unity and provide the regime an opening to discredit the revolution, including in the eyes of the international community.

After decades of U.S.-backed autocracy, the Brotherhood had thoroughly internalized the "American veto." Just two days before Mubarak fell, the Brotherhood's Abdel Moneim Abul Futouh penned an op-ed in the *Washington Post*. He seemed convinced that U.S. policymakers could be persuaded to support the revolution as well as the Brotherhood's democratic aspirations. Abul Futouh's op-ed—simultaneously overestimating America's influence, decrying it, and believing that, somehow, it could be used for good—was representative of the genre. "We want to set the record straight so that any Middle East policy decisions made in Washington are based on facts," Abul Futouh wrote. "With a little altruism, the United States should not hesitate to reassess its interests in the region, especially if it genuinely champions democracy."[3]

Fearing repression and hoping to neutralize American backing for the old regime, the Brotherhood highlighted the moderate policies it had painstakingly developed the previous two decades. The concern—some would say obsession—with what the United States thought was illustrative. The Brotherhood craved legitimacy not only at home but abroad. The group's leaders had a mantra in those early days of uncertainty—repeated over and over to anyone who would listen: they would not run a presidential candidate. They would contest only one third of the seats in parliament. They would not seek a parliamentary majority. They would work to build consensus among all of Egypt's political forces.

This was not an act, as some would latter suggest. This was the moderate, reconstructed Brotherhood, which had spent years smoothing over the hard edges of its political program. Islamists had not moderated because of democracy, but before it. It was the experience of repression that had forced Islamists to moderate. And now that regime repression was reaching its end, Islamists found themselves in a political environment that they had never, in all of 83 years of existence, encountered before. There was no precedent, memory, or model upon which to draw.

And so the Brotherhood issued a procession of statements in an attempt to reassure their skeptics, of which there were many. "We don't want to leave one dictatorship just to enter another, religious one," the Brotherhood's Hamdi Hassan insisted. "That's why the Brotherhood clearly announced that it won't run for the presidency and won't try to take the majority in parliament."[4] Khairat al-Shater, the group's brilliant but domineering strategist, was feeling particularly magnanimous: "Egypt will not return to the days of one-party rule. The Brotherhood will help strengthen other parties."[5]

For a time, they actually backed up the rhetoric. The idea, early on, was to create a broad national front, led by the Brotherhood, which would contest the upcoming parliamentary elections. As early as March 2011, just one month after the revolution, the Brotherhood along with several secular parties, including the liberal Wafd party and leftist Karama, "agreed in principle to enter the election with an open, national list."[6]

The Brotherhood wasn't quite acting like a self-interested political party might be expected to. Parties normally seek power, even in delicate transitional situations like Egypt's. But, here, Islamists were offering what seemed like preemptive concessions. They were saying, in effect, that they were too strong and the others too weak, and that they would prop up their competitors to level the playing field. As leading Brotherhood figure Mohamed al-Beltagy explained it, "everyone must act so we can reach the point where we become like the rest of the countries in the world, with three or four strong parties." Not only that, the Brotherhood, just like it had been before, was willing to lose on purpose, at least at first. "We will not forever remain in the position of not seeking power, the majority or the presidency," Beltagy said, "this is a temporary position until the time there are forces that can compete."[7]

Just after Mubarak fell, Brotherhood officials spoke of contesting one third of the parliamentary seats. By April, the numbers were changing: the Brotherhood would now contest up to a half of the seats, but they insisted that was as high as they would go. It was still early days, and the Brotherhood was stuck in old patterns of participation.

They were paranoid about provoking opposition at home and abroad. Was the world ready for Islamists? They weren't so sure. "The people won't accept an Islamist president," Essam al-Erian, deputy leader of the Freedom and Justice Party, told me in May of that year. "They feel that anyone Islamist will provoke antagonism from the U.S. and Europe—and this is sensible."[8] It made sense, then, to take things one step at a time, an approach well in keeping with the group's traditionally unhurried attitude to political change.

Brotherhood leaders had good reason to worry about the role the United States would play. The Obama administration would later come under attack from both Republicans and, oddly enough, Egyptian liberals for becoming too cozy with the Brotherhood (or worse). Early on, however, the United States was keeping its distance from Egypt's largest and most powerful opposition group. Erian roundly criticized the American stance. "It was a fatal mistake to be hesitating from the start," he said, "and they are still hesitating now."[9] Remarkably, the Obama administration had no high-level contacts with the Brotherhood until October 2011, eight months after Mubarak fell. Even then, Anne Patterson, America's ambassador in Cairo, was not quite ready to take the step herself: "I'm not personally comfortable with it enough yet," she said. When a journalist asked her why, she replied awkwardly, "well, I'm just not comfortable."[10]

In revolutionary contexts, Islamist groups generally prefer to stay on the sidelines, letting others, usually secular figures and parties, lead the way in order to secure international legitimacy. In Syria, although the Muslim Brotherhood was the single most influential party in the Syrian National Council, the body would be headed first by Paris-based secular academic Burhan Ghalioun and then George Sabra, a Christian. Later, the same could be said of the Syrian Opposition Coalition, formally led by centrist and secular figures like Moaz al-Khatib and Suhair al-Attasi. In both cases, the Brotherhood was accused of playing a shadowy role behind the scenes, but that was how they liked it: the less attention, the better. In Egypt, one can go back before the revolution to find any number of examples. The liberal Nobel laureate Mohamed ElBaradei—later to emerge as one of the Brotherhood's chief antagonists—enjoyed a close, cooperative relationship with the group throughout 2010, during Mubarak's last days. The Brotherhood actively backed ElBaradei's petition of seven reform demands and mobilized its considerable organizational machine to collect signatures for the initiative. Even after the revolution, the Brotherhood considered the possibility of supporting ElBaradei for president as late as April 2012.

Indeed, for months, Brotherhood leaders affirmed time and time again their decision not to field a presidential candidate from their own ranks. Again, this was in keeping with their pre-revolution mindset of gradualism and deference to the status quo. The watchwords were "consensus," "dialogue," and "unity." For the parliamentary elections, the Brotherhood and its newly formed Freedom and Justice Party (FJP) launched the "Democratic Alliance," the centerpiece of its efforts to essentially allow weaker parties to ride the coattails of its electoral success. At its peak, the alliance claimed as many as 35 political parties. Most of Egypt's major parties from across the political spectrum—leftist, liberal, and Salafi—counted themselves as members. Far from an alliance just on paper, cooperation between the parties was intended be on three levels: the formation of a committee to work on a new election law; another to coordinate a joint electoral list; and the third to draft a common set of principles and objectives for member parties.[11]

As it turned out, these efforts, as significant as they appeared to be, were not the start of a bold new era of revolutionary cooperation, but rather the last, dying gasps of the spirit of cooperation that had prevailed in Tahrir Square just months before. Repression is what brought Egypt's fractious opposition closer together in the last days of the Mubarak regime. In Tahrir, during those 18 days, repression—and the threat of even greater repression—reached unprecedented levels (I remember the day when a Muslim Brotherhood official called me on the phone and broke down in tears, as he told me that the regime was about to perpetrate a massacre in the dead of night).

Repression, as we saw in previous chapters, has a way of making ideological debates seem irrelevant. In 2010, the Brotherhood and ElBaradei—a classic liberal if there ever was one—joined forces. As one Brotherhood official told me at the time, "every single member—without exception—is working to gather signatures for ElBaradei."[12] At the height of the petition campaign, the head of each usra[13] would ask members daily how many signatures they had collected. This wasn't just the usual, vague talk of working together. By the fall of 2010, ElBaradei's reform petition had reached one million signatures, a remarkable figure considering that each signatory had to include his Egyptian ID number (a risky move in an autocracy). The Brotherhood's backing was decisive—before it joined the effort, the petition had only around 100,000 signatures.

It is no accident that this degree of cooperation came at the height of regime repression and amidst fears that it would only get worse. The Brotherhood, in particular, feared that those coming after Mubarak—including his son Gamal and the "neo-liberal" clique around him—would be even more authoritarian than the father, threatening the group's existence. ElBaradei, meanwhile, had his own message for anyone who was willing to listen. He forcefully defended the Brotherhood's right to participate in politics, making the case that they had changed and moderated over time. The Muslim Brotherhood could be trusted. In a memorable interview in the early days of the revolution, ElBaradei took to CNN. The host of the program, Fareed Zakaria, asked, "are you confident that a post-Mubarak Egypt will not give rise to some kind of Islamic fundamentalist force?" "I'm quite confident of that, Fareed," ElBaradei replied. "The Muslim Brotherhood has nothing to do with the Iranian model; it has nothing to do with extremism."[14]

A Split in the Opposition

If repression brought them together, removing the repression would presumably push them apart. The cracks in the façade became apparent almost immediately. The March 19, 2011 referendum, ratifying a set of amendments to the old constitution, was arguably one of the Egyptian transition's many "original sins," pitting Islamists and non-Islamists against each other for the first time. Liberals and leftists who were at an obvious electoral disadvantage favored postponing elections and focusing instead on drafting a new constitution (by a panel of experts and civil society representatives). This coalesced into what became known as the "Constitution First" movement.

As the Brotherhood and other Islamists threw their weight behind a "yes" vote—citing the need to end military rule and set a clear path to stability—debates that were really about the sequencing of the transition became, at least publicly, about religion. Accusations abounded of

Islamist actors using religious rhetoric to rally support and marginalize their opponents. A vote against the amendments was portrayed by Islamists as endangering the place of sharia in the constitution. Some Salafis went further, telling their supporters that a "yes" vote was a religious duty.[15] As the political divide entrenched itself, it became increasingly difficult to tell the difference between a procedural objection and a substantive one.

The question of holding elections or writing a constitution first became one of the key fault lines of Egyptian politics, and one that would grow more important over the course of a troubled transition. Power and ideology had become fused together. Fearing that they would lose badly in free elections, liberals demanded more time to prepare and organize. Liberals—and non-Islamists more generally—were in a particularly weak position, and this only heightened their sense of siege in the face of ascendant Islamist forces. Almost in parallel, Islamists were shedding their apparent magnanimity. By the summer of 2011, there was a noticeable shift in the Brotherhood's tone. The paranoia of old, always in the background, was creeping back in. In public statements, the group started to emphasize what they called the subversion of the "popular will." The shift coincided with the Brotherhood's souring relationship with the Supreme Council of the Armed Forces (SCAF).

The problem with regime-managed transitions is that the regime can't always be trusted to actually give up power. Beginning in June 2011, close to the original deadline for a handover to civilian rule, the military began floating the idea of "supra-constitutional" principles as well as guidelines for selecting members of the constituent assembly. The Brotherhood saw this as an attack on the future jurisdiction of the elected parliament. As they saw it, the country's elected representatives should have "full freedom in selecting this constituent body for drafting the constitution."[16] The military had two objectives: first, to protect their own prerogatives—immunity and autonomy—in any future constitution, and, second, to divide the opposition and gain liberal support as a pressure point against the Brotherhood. The supra-constitutional principles would include not only guarantees for the military, but also protections on rights and freedoms that many liberals were demanding.

The gathering controversy over the constitution pushed the Muslim Brotherhood and Salafis to hold their first large-scale protest since the revolution, on July 29, 2011, a day that would become etched in memory—for liberals at least—as "Kandahar Friday." The goal of the protest was to "affirm the authority of the people and their right to establish their own constitution without any group trying to impose its own prescription."[17] But that message got lost in the overt Islamist slogans and symbols, with Salafis demanding the implementation of sharia law. The result was a media fiasco for the Brotherhood, which tried to distance itself from the Salafis.[18] But the polarization, regardless of what the Brotherhood thought or wanted, had become further entrenched.

Brotherhood officials continued to insist that they had no fundamental disagreements with other political parties. Their problem, they said, wasn't so much the content of the supra-constitutional proposals but rather the principle that something could be imposed through "nondemocratic means."[19] In August, the Brotherhood warned of replicating the Turkish model, where the military "play[s] the role of the protector of the constitution and the guardian of the civil state."[20] In a preview of a debate that would dominate Egyptian politics for the next several years, the Brotherhood's language sharpened, as it took to accusing the minority (read: liberals) of circumventing the will of the majority.

Meanwhile, the much-touted Democratic Alliance gradually lost most of its members largely due to disagreements over each party's share of candidates. Some liberal and leftist parties stayed on, but they were small and lacked any real constituency of their own. The alliance, the centerpiece of the Brotherhood's outreach to non-Islamists, had become a shell of its former self. Meanwhile, a group of liberal parties coalesced in the form of the "Egyptian Bloc," with the explicit goal of countering Islamist dominance of the political scene.

In September 2011, the military overreached when it clumsily rolled out the infamous "Selmi Document." The document, ostensibly spearheaded by Deputy Prime Minister Ali al-Selmi, formally outlined supra-constitutional principles that would protect the army's outsized role in society and politics. This, for the Brotherhood, provided confirmation that a loose alliance of the military, liberals, the judiciary, and other elements of the "deep state" were out to deny the group its rightful role. On November 18, in a show of force, the Brotherhood and the Salafis brought tens of thousands of their supporters to Tahrir Square. Some youth activists and revolutionary groups also participated, and the crisis started when they stayed on and set up tents later that night after the Brotherhood left. The following morning, with little warning, the army moved to disperse the small group of peaceful protesters still encamped in the square.

The clashes of Mohamed Mahmoud—named after a street leading out of Tahrir Square—had begun. The military's brazen brutality, seemingly unprovoked, swelled the ranks of the protesters. By the time it was over, fierce street battles had claimed the lives of at least 40 Egyptians.

Islamists stayed on the sidelines, fearing that the instability—which they felt the army had intentionally provoked—would be used to delay or cancel parliamentary elections. Many liberals, who disagreed with the very idea of early elections in the first place, supported their postponement. They accused the Brotherhood of being so obsessed with elections that it would turn a blind eye to the killing of protesters. And they were at least partly right. So close to what they felt would be an historic victory, the Brotherhood increasingly feared it would be taken away from them. There were no guarantees, and they had come this close before, including of course in Algeria. Brotherhood leaders, never comfortable with revolutionary action in the first place, argued it was time to shift the battle to the halls of parliament, conveniently the very place they would be strongest.

During the Mohamed Mahmoud clashes, I spoke to Dina Zakaria, a senior official in the Freedom and Justice Party. When we met, she had a pained look on her face, and I could tell she was struggling with the Brotherhood's decision to stay away from the protests. "I thought to myself, how can we abandon the people in the square?" she said. "I can't bear to see people still being killed." She continued: "But at the same time does this movement stay in the street, or should it be expressed through institutions? I think the right choice is through institutions."[21] Some in the Brotherhood, like Mohamed al-Beltagy, publicly disagreed with the group's stance. He went to the square to express solidarity with the protesters but was soon shouted down by several of them. Fearing a confrontation, his supporters quickly ushered him out. The problem was one of legitimacy. "There are some forces saying Tahrir does not represent the people. And in an official and legal sense, they're right," he told me. "What we need is someone to represent the people in this battle of wills with the army."[22]

It was an old debate—revolutionary versus democratic legitimacy—and one that would repeatedly threaten to derail Egypt's transition. For a society that had seemingly become conditioned to mass protests and inflated crowd estimates, would enough Egyptians be content with the boring, slow, and often inconclusive aspects of procedural democracy?

Parliamentary elections did take place on time. They were free, fair, and—to the surprise of many—peaceful. On election day, the clashes of Mohamed Mahmoud seemed distant. The Brotherhood had gotten what they wanted, but the old fears lingered. In the days leading up to the polls, some Brotherhood activists I spoke to worried that they might do *too* well. They were worried about how the military and the international community might respond to an Islamist landslide. After all, just a few months earlier, Saad al-Katatni, the FJP's secretary-general, had sought to reassure the Brotherhood's critics, predicting that parliamentary seats would be evenly split between Islamists and non-Islamists.[23] The Salafis, though, were a bit of a wild card. They were political novices with virtually no experience running election campaigns. But they, like the Brotherhood, had something their opponents did not—grassroots networks and deep support throughout the country, particularly outside the major cities. The "Islamic Alliance," which included the Nour party and two smaller Salafi parties, won around 28 percent of the vote and 25 percent of the seats. Altogether, Islamist parties secured nearly 75 percent of the seats, which exceeded even their wildest expectations. The Brotherhood and the Nour party were triumphant, pointing to a clear popular mandate. The results, however, demoralized the non-Islamist opposition, further entrenching the Islamist–liberal divide in Egyptian society.

For Cairo's secular elite, it was like waking up to a different country. They knew, of course, that the Brotherhood would do well. But the notion of Islamists, including hardline Salafis, winning almost three quarters of the vote was difficult to digest and even more difficult to understand. Liberals were at a profound disadvantage in democratic politics. If there were any doubts about that before, they were now put to rest.

In the new parliament, Salafi representatives were quick to embroil themselves in a number of controversies, one of which went viral. Seemingly out of nowhere, a Salafi member of parliament from the Asala party interrupted the parliamentary session and started announcing the call to prayer. The Brotherhood's Saad al-Katatni, now speaker of parliament, attempted to shout him down, telling him that there was a mosque not too far away if he couldn't wait.[24] But the Salafi representative wouldn't stop, leading to several tense minutes of Katatni trying to defuse the situation. For many liberals watching on television, this was the first time they saw Salafis in action. How could 28 percent of their fellow Egyptians have voted for these extremists, they wondered? Instead of being proud of their country's first democratically elected parliament, they felt embarrassed.

The Brotherhood went into parliament with high hopes. The group planned to use its perch in parliament to challenge the ruling military council. In those early, heady days, the Brotherhood, confident and claiming vindication, believed it could transform Egypt into a parliamentary democracy. Those were the days when Brotherhood candidates would cite Israel as a model for a strong parliament and a weak, ceremonial president.[25]

Brotherhood members had put so much time, energy, and resources into the fight for parliament, thinking it would be a turning point for both themselves and the country. What they hadn't bet on was a military council that had little interest in respecting the Islamist-dominated parliament, which it increasingly saw as a threat to its own interests.

A full month before the third and final round of the parliamentary elections, SCAF member General Mukhtar al-Mulla had given an extended briefing to a group of mostly American journalists. He effectively dismissed the initial election results and made it clear that the military would still be in charge. They would not let the Islamists take control over either the constitution-drafting process or the government, regardless of electoral outcomes. "Whatever the majority in the People's Assembly, they are very welcome," Mulla said, "because they won't have the ability to impose anything that the people don't want."[26] Despite the integrity of the election results, he added, they were not necessarily representative of the Egyptian people, and therefore it wouldn't be fair for one current to dominate the country's politics. "Do you think that the Egyptians elected someone to threaten his interest and economy and security and relations with [the] international community?" General Mulla asked. "Of course not."

The military and the Muslim Brotherhood had apparently very different notions of what the elections meant. After the polls had closed, the Brotherhood announced its interest in forming a coalition government headed by one of its own members, with Khairat al-Shater floated as a possibility.[27] For the Brotherhood, it was simple: the parliamentary majority should be responsible for forming the next government.

In the weeks following their victory, the Brotherhood talked tough, drawing strength from the "popular will" and claiming democratic mandates they did not necessarily have. The Brotherhood's Essam al-Erian warned the military that times had changed: "No institution or establishment is above the state. Parliament is the supreme authority of the country with control over all others."[28] Legally and constitutionally, however, the Brotherhood was on shaky ground. Egypt was not in fact a parliamentary democracy and the army, still the de facto executive authority, was not about to let it become one.

Islamists Versus the Army

After the high point of free, competitive elections—Egypt's first since the 1940s—the transition could have perhaps regained its momentum, but instead the seeds were planted for a slow but unmistakable deterioration in the country's political life. The Brotherhood's worst fears were confirmed: the military, along with some in the opposition, would not let them enjoy the fruits of victory. At the start of the new session, on February 1, 2012, protesters gathered outside the parliamentary building, preventing the newly minted representatives from getting inside. The Brotherhood released a strongly worded statement attacking those who "think the legitimacy of the square is greater than that of parliament." "Even if all their demands are met," the statement read, "they will find reasons to bring up problems . . . and block the path of democracy and the revolution, until there is a parliament that they like."[29]

This was supposed to be the Brotherhood's reward for more than eight decades of patience and resolve in the face of untold persecution. But, as they saw it, a basic problem remained: their opponents—whether liberals, the military, or the old regime—would stop at nothing to block them from exercising power.

In the subsequent months, as the Islamist-led parliament gradually became aware of the very real limits to its authority, it aggressively confronted the army-appointed government of Mubarak-era Prime Minister Kamal al-Ganzouri, hoping to bring it down. But beyond a limited reshuffle, the military refused to give way. In the same vein, the group's attempt to dictate the formation of a constituent assembly also ended in failure—after the judiciary issued a ruling dissolving the body.

Parliament was often frustrated in its attempts to push through reforms. While its members busily drafted legislation on a range of issues, the fact that laws had to be approved by SCAF meant that they often amounted to baby steps, in revolutionary terms. Examples included a new police law that focused more on improving the working conditions of officers than weeding out malpractice, and a law on military trials that removed the president's ability to send civilians to military courts but "maintained the right of the military judiciary to determine its own jurisdiction."[30] Perhaps most egregious from the Brotherhood's perspective was the law on exclusion of senior Mubarak-era officials. Despite being passed by parliament and approved by SCAF, the new law met opposition in the courts and was unable to prevent Ahmed Shafiq—Mubarak's last prime minister—from running in presidential elections. "For the first time in Egypt's history a People's Assembly is elected in fair and fraud-free elections. It issues a law which is then trampled all over by an administrative body that doesn't like the law and so gave the law a holiday," railed an exasperated Mohamed al-Beltagy.[31]

Soon enough, the Brotherhood came to a conclusion that would have a number of intended, and unintended, consequences for Egypt's troubled transition: they decided, after considerable debate and internal dissent, to reverse their position on running a candidate for president.

One reason, already discussed above, was the failure of parliament to play the role they hoped it would. Another reason, which cuts to the heart of the kind of organization the Brotherhood is, was the need to maintain internal cohesion. Egypt's revolution was a threat as much as it was an opportunity for an organization that had grown accustomed to the unifying power of repression. Without a clear enemy— the Mubarak regime—the task of ensuring organizational discipline was becoming more difficult, so it had to be enforced. First, the

Brotherhood's leadership forbade its members from joining any other party but its own. Those who joined other parties or started their own were suspended or expelled. For the Brotherhood, it was a simple matter of respecting the institution of which they were a part and to which they had pledged their lives. It was, after all, the group's policymaking body, the Shura Council, that had voted to prohibit members from joining other parties. "All decisions are taken as an organization, with shura [consultation], with democracy," Essam al-Erian told me at the time. "[The youth] are appreciated but they are appreciated in the context of the organization, not outside of it."[32] Dissent was allowed before a final decision was made, but not after.

Indeed, from the standpoint of organizational unity, the controversial decision to run a presidential candidate was not so surprising. In the early months of 2012, the group had tried to find a sympathetic consensus candidate whom they could support. They couldn't. In the resulting vacuum, Abdel Moneim Abul Futouh, the prominent Brotherhood figure who was expelled from the group in June 2011, had become an unlikely frontrunner, gaining support from a diverse group of liberals, leftists, Muslim Brotherhood youth, and even Salafis. Despite his origins and long service in the movement—or rather because of them—Abul Futouh emerged as a serious and even existential threat to the Brotherhood's organization, or the *tanzim* as it is known in Arabic.

To understand the group's overwrought paranoia, we can think of its leaders as institutionalists. Individuals within the Brotherhood derive their influence not primarily from their own political talents but from the fact they are part of a *gama'a*, or group, one that is presumably greater than the sum of its parts. In the past, whenever prominent figures broke off from the organization to start new parties, they failed. Without the Brotherhood's grassroots support and infrastructure, they found themselves relegated to the political margins (see for example al-Wasat, founded in 1996, and the Egyptian Current Party, founded in 2011). This was why Abul Futouh represented such a threat: he was attacking the idea that success can only come through the strict confines of the tanzim.

Abul Futouh threatened them from the left, and the Salafis, meanwhile, threatened them from the right. The fiery, charismatic Hazem Salah Abu Ismail, appearing seemingly out of nowhere, rose to the top

tier of presidential contenders.[33] Abu Ismail had also been a Brotherhood member before becoming Egypt's leading purveyor of "revolutionary Salafism."[34] What was the point of sitting out the presidential
race, Brotherhood officials wondered, if another Islamist—a more radical one—might actually win and challenge the Brotherhood's grip on
the Islamic movement? One of the Brotherhood's rationales for sitting
out the election was that an Islamist as Egypt's head of state would provoke foreign powers weary of Islamist rule. But that rationale no longer
seemed to hold with two other Islamists as frontrunners.

And so the Brotherhood—realizing that parliament, by itself, would
not be enough and fearing the rise of their erstwhile compatriot and
a Salafi hardliner to boot—entered the race at the last moment. Their
first choice, Khairat al-Shater, whom some called Egypt's most powerful man, was disqualified from running due to a legal technicality. This,
for them, seemed to confirm—again—that the military and its allies
were seeking to block their rise by any means necessary. The Brotherhood had a second, much weaker candidate—Mohamed Morsi—who
quickly replaced Shater as the group's standard-bearer.

The Brotherhood insisted they were reluctant contenders. Their reversal was indeed just that, they admitted, but it was the result of shifting
circumstances that neither they nor anyone else could have predicted.
Though burdened with a weak candidate and with only two months
to campaign, the group's members fanned across the country, promoting Morsi's so-called Renaissance Project (which, before it, was Shater's
Renaissance Project). In one coordinated show of strength, they held 24
simultaneous mass rallies across the country in a single day.

At one of those rallies, I asked a young Brotherhood activist if he
was enthusiastic about Morsi. He smiled and then laughed. Some other
Brotherhood youth were supporting Abul Futouh, but he wasn't. "This
is about the preservation of the Brotherhood," he told me matter-of-
factly.[35] The Brotherhood's loyalists were treating it as an existential
moment, in part because it was. A Morsi defeat—particularly at the
hands of Abul Futouh—might spur a major internal split. Perhaps more
than any of the other candidates, Abul Futouh was dangerous. Charismatic and with his own distinct sources of legitimacy, the 62-year-
old doctor fell out with the Brotherhood's conservative leadership for
a variety of reasons, among them his desire to keep the group out of

partisan politics. As president, he would undermine the group's once-firm grip over Egyptian Islamism. And if Abul Futouh managed to create a movement or party behind his presidency, it would force the Brotherhood into a perpetual state of defense. It didn't help that Abul Futouh was threatening to treat the still-secretive Brotherhood like any other nongovernmental organization, requiring it to disclose its sources of funding.

For the Brotherhood, then, this was not about the candidate, Mohamed Morsi; it was about the future of an organization that had grown accustomed to finding enemies and fearing the worst. In times of repression, a pronounced paranoia may have made sense, but less so during a democratic opening. But, for them, the democratic opening itself was far from certain. Some of their fears were imagined. Some, however, were real and they would accumulate, one after the other, in the subsequent months and years.

Morsi ended up winning by a narrow margin in the presidential runoff with 51.7 percent of the vote. But SCAF held out on announcing the results for several days, stoking speculation that they would rig the vote and hand the election to Ahmed Shafiq. They didn't. But they had seemingly prepared themselves all the same. In early June, SCAF—in a flurry of activity over the course of just one week—reinstated martial law, stripped the presidency of many of its powers, and, most importantly, dissolved the country's democratically elected parliament. Later, in August 2012, the Brotherhood would claim that they had intelligence that the army was planning to stage a coup against the elected president. Fearing that the army might make its move at the end of the month, Morsi launched his own civilian "counter-coup," forcing top military leaders into retirement. On August 11, one day before Morsi acted, the privately owned *al-Dustour* newspaper published an editorial—taking up the entire front page in big bold and red letters—calling for a popular military coup. The words make for an eerie read in light of what would later come to pass: "Saving Egypt from the coming destruction will not occur without the union of the army and the people . . . If this does not happen in the coming days, then Egypt will fall and be destroyed . . . Taking to the streets in peaceful protest is imperative and a national duty until the army responds and announces its support for the people."[36]

The editorial came in the context of a frightening upsurge in polarization. One extreme example was Tawfik Okasha, the sensationalist owner of the television station Al Fara'een, calling for violence against the Brotherhood and Mohamed Morsi, saying, "I make your blood permissible as well." Meanwhile, a million-man "second revolution" calling for the "dissolution" of the Brotherhood was scheduled to take place on August 24. As Hesham Sallam writes, "these trends, coupled with the developments that followed, signal that some military leaders may have been prodding their allies among opinion shapers and friendly media outlets to promote the image of popular support for a coup d'etat against the Brotherhood."[37]

For the Muslim Brotherhood and other Islamist parties across the region, another Algeria was, and is, always around the corner. Winning one election after another is no guarantee of political survival, just like it wasn't in 1991. They believed that the conflict with their opponents was, at its core, about the latter's fear of democratic elections.The Brotherhood was, in a sense, vindicated by the coup that ousted the first freely elected president—and the fact that nearly all prominent liberals backed it. But it was also, in part, a self-fulfilling prophecy: in expecting the worst, you act in ways that make your feared outcome all the more likely. Indeed, Morsi and the Brotherhood's most provocative moves seemed to be animated by an endless reservoir of distrust and dismissiveness toward their opponents.

This became clear during Morsi's next battle, this time with a judicial establishment dominated by Mubarak appointees. On November 22, 2012, Morsi announced a constitutional decree, granting himself expansive powers and immunizing presidential decrees from judicial review, a move that for many liberals constituted a point of no return.

The Brotherhood once again saw existential threats on the horizon—one after another. Looming in the near future were court rulings that would dissolve both the constituent assembly and the upper house of parliament. Brotherhood and FJP officials told me at the time that they knew from sympathetic judges that rulings revoking Morsi's August 12 move against the army and even possibly annulling the presidential election law were in the cards. Another Brotherhood official went so far as to suggest that, if they didn't act preemptively now, the closing of Brotherhood offices could be next in a new campaign of repression, followed by the dissolution of the organization itself. To be sure, the Brotherhood was well aware of just how bad Morsi's decree looked. As one senior FJP official admitted: "Yes, the decree isn't democratic and it's not what you would expect after a revolution," but he claimed there was simply no other choice.[38] The message was clear: the Brotherhood was fighting (again) for its very survival; the normal rules simply didn't apply. One Brotherhood official I spoke to likened Morsi's November 22 decree to "shock therapy that runs the risk of leaving the patient dead."[39]

Islamists in Opposition; Islamists in Power

An Islamist movement in opposition and an Islamist party in power are two very different things. When Brotherhood officials were promising not to run a presidential candidate in March 2011 (and as late as February 2012), they were still stuck in old patterns of behavior. In authoritarian settings, Islamists learn how to lose, and they get used to it. Because of their long time horizon, this is something they are willing to accept. In the absence of a meaningful political process, Islamist movements can still pursue their original, core functions. They can continue expanding their reach deep into society, preparing themselves for the day that politics will open up, as it inevitably will.

In much of the region, including Egypt, Jordan, Bahrain, Yemen, and Morocco, Islamists in opposition did not face an existential threat. As part of their understandings with ruling regimes, they would have the space to advance their social and educational goals. They would be permitted limited representation in parliament. In return, they would refrain from revolutionary, antisystem activity. Until 2011, the bargain, with all its ebbs and flows, remained in place. Even in Egypt, the most repressive among them, the Brotherhood never once reneged on its side of the bargain.

Opposition is something you can get used to, particularly if the alternative—power and its temptations—threatens to alter the very nature of the movement. Repression, in addition to its moderating effects, also has a unifying effect, both between opposition groups and within them. It is always easier to stay together when you face a common enemy. In repressive contexts, defection makes less sense, since government restrictions make it difficult to establish new political parties.

Even when parties are granted legal status, the challenge of reaching a wider audience, with all the limitations and restrictions of authoritarian regimes, becomes nearly insurmountable. Dissenters, then, have an incentive to stay within the fold, and in part for this reason Islamist movements across the region have succeeded in containing various competing currents within their organizations. However, the temptation to defect grows in democratizing contexts, as Egypt's transition period attested. The freedom that comes with meaningful political openings transforms the role of organizations like the Brotherhood within the broader society.

In autocracies, any kind of activism—political, religious, or otherwise—is fraught with peril. There is the risk of harassment, arrest, and, perhaps more perniciously, the denial of access to government services, college placements, and employment opportunities, particularly in the public sector. For most Egyptians or Jordanians, incarceration is simply something they cannot afford. Who can be counted on to provide food, shelter, and education to their children while they serve a prison term? Islamist movements, with their organizational discipline and intense bonds between members, lower the cost of activism by providing a buffer against repression. When a Brotherhood member is arrested, the organization steps in and ensures the family is taken care of. The organization may also help provide a lawyer and take care of legal fees.

Moreover, in the absence of a spirit of volunteerism—a problem particularly acute in autocracies—Islamist groups offer a number of activities that provide their members with a deeper sense of community and belonging. As previously mentioned, each Brotherhood member is part of an usra, or "family," which meets weekly to study religious texts, where the bonds of friendship and loyalty are strengthened.[40] In short, the Brotherhood provides a set of institutionalized channels for religious work, educational pursuits, and political action.

However, the freedom that comes with democratic openings makes a group like the Brotherhood both less unique and less essential. There are, for the first time, viable options outside of the movement. The mushrooming of civil society actors, political parties, and religious organizations (including Salafi ones) means each Egyptian can pick and choose instead of relying on one tightly wound network like the Brotherhood for an array of services.

When I met with one dissenting Brotherhood member, who held a leadership position in one of the governorates, he complained that the organization was losing its way. "There's been about a year where they don't really do anything but politics," Mustafa Kamshish told me in May 2012. "All these elections—for the professional syndicates, student unions, and parliament—the rank-and-file are all consumed by this. So the other activities have stalled."[41]

But if this was where the Brotherhood was going, then what was the point? "The biggest thing the Brotherhood had to offer was the social umbrella it provided its members, which no one else could provide," Kamshish said. Now, however, the Brotherhood seemed at risk of losing the one thing that made it so attractive. If the politics continued to overwhelm the other functions of the organization, then would-be members would look for alternatives, and in a more open society those alternatives would proliferate.

Conservative Revolutionaries

Everything about a group like the Muslim Brotherhood was designed for making the most of small (but significant) openings under autocratic regimes. Brotherhood affiliates and Brotherhood-inspired movements across the region believed in change, but not the revolutionary kind. It is difficult to remember it now, but before January 2011 "revolution" was simply not part of the opposition's vocabulary in most of the Arab world. It was difficult to envision what a mass uprising might look like. Regimes had grown stubborn and more repressive, rather than the opposite. The best-case scenario was a long, arduous Moroccan-style regime-led transition. Islamists wouldn't have to face the pressures of governing right away. They would learn gradually and on the job, as part of coalition or national unity governments.

And so when the revolution came, Brotherhood leaders in Egypt were far from prepared and, at least initially, they were afraid. If the revolution backfired and the regime managed to hold on to power, it was Islamists who would bear the brunt of the crackdowns that would no doubt follow. They would be blamed by the regime for putting their own organizational interests over Egypt's stability. And all the social and organizational gains they had made over the past few decades would come under threat.

Even if the revolution succeeded, the temptations of power brought other risks. The longtime Islamist ambivalence toward power was about fearing repression, preserving the organization, and avoiding crippling internal divisions. Playing a role in parliament, or even leading it, was one thing, but holding positions in the executive branch—and taking responsibility for compromises and controversies—was another matter. It may have bothered their critics, but the Brotherhood's vagueness on, say, tax policy and subsidy reform was a virtue for a mass organization with different functions and different constituencies.

When it comes to movements like the Muslim Brotherhood, members join for a variety of reasons. As one Brotherhood official would often remind me, some members want to "use the group to get into heaven." Others are more interested in political action and parliamentary work. Some are interested in the group's message of social justice, while some Islamist businessmen saw the organization as a vehicle for neoliberal business ventures. With such disparate elements, and differing conceptions of the role of religion in public life, it was easier to avoid answering the difficult questions. On foreign policy, the tensions were perhaps even more apparent. Some, like Abul Futouh, went on the record as early as 2006 accepting a two-state solution.[42] Others warned that giving up on the resistance would be tantamount to a betrayal of the Brotherhood's original anticolonialism. In 2006, one Brotherhood official, Ali Abdel Fattah, criticized some of his more pragmatic colleagues and threatened to leave the organization if it ever recognized Israel's right to exist.[43]

In Jordan, the problem of Israel has been even more complicated. Successive Jordanian prime ministers invited the IAF to join the government in the 1990s (as well as more recently). Yet "hawks" opposed any participation in the executive branch as long as the government maintained the peace treaty with Israel. For the IAF, whose members are mostly of Palestinian origin, Israel is not just a foreign policy issue but a domestic one as well.

In short, taking part in government compels Islamist parties to take definitive positions on controversial issues, which is something they would rather avoid. At best, delving into such issues alienates supporters and, at worst, precipitates internal splits. Until the Arab Spring, and even after it, there have been few actual experiences of democratically elected Islamist parties in power for a significant period of time. In Jordan in 1991, Turkey in the mid-1990s, and Gaza in the late 2000s, the gap between ideals and practice, between ambition and reality, was large, perhaps too large. Islamist parties were forced to make uncomfortable decisions. Turkey's Welfare party, for example, had consistently denounced Turkey's military alliance with Israel and advocated a more pro-Islamic foreign policy posture. "We shall never become lackeys of the Christians. We shall establish an Islamic union," declared the party's leader, Necmettin Erbakan, in 1994, while still in opposition.[44] But during his brief stint as prime minister, with the military's threatening gaze over him, Erbakan was forced to ratify a series of trade and military agreements with Israel. Meanwhile, in Jordan, there were the inevitable examples of overreach. During its brief six-month stint in which it controlled five ministries, the Brotherhood was criticized for what it didn't do and also for what it did, such as efforts to enforce sex segregation in the ministries of social development and education.

For the Jordanian Brotherhood's doves, 1991 remains a symbol of unfulfilled potential, a bitter reminder of more than two decades of exile in the opposition. For the group's hawks, however, the experience of 1991 would be remembered as an unacceptable compromise. There was no point, in their view, to accept token ministries, to have enough power to be criticized but not enough to actually change anything. The organization's most prominent hawk, Mohamed Abu Faris, published a book titled *Participation in the Cabinet under Un-Islamic Regimes*, where he runs through the many reasons for abstaining from government. First, ministers in un-Islamic regimes must be willing to bind themselves to constitutions that are based on un-Islamic sources of law. Second, ministers are responsible for executing existing laws, many of which "make permissible what is forbidden."[45] Third, participation in government associates Islamists with unpopular policies. Lastly, participation legitimizes the government and improves its reputation in the eyes of the population.[46]

Abu Faris argues that governments seek Islamist participation not to advance Islamic goals, but rather the opposite: to either neutralize Islamists or embarrass them.[47] In addition, bringing Islamists into government is a way to sow division within their ranks, something the very existence of Abu Faris's book appears to affirm. Abu Faris's objections would foreshadow many of the challenges that Islamists would face in the wake of the Arab uprisings. As Abu Faris saw it, Islamists should avoid the temptations of power until they are truly prepared—and until society is truly prepared to accept them. The Islamic project needed to be anchored by a clear theological understanding of the Islamic state, and that, in turn, would require a public that was both ready and willing for what was to come. Until then, preaching, religious education, and keeping the regime honest were the Islamic movement's appropriate roles.

Even in opposition, elaborating on policy specifics can be a risky proposition. As we saw earlier, the Brotherhood in Egypt, hoping to deflect criticisms of vague sloganeering, released a succession of increasingly detailed programs. This got them into some trouble in 2007 when they released their political party platform, their longest and most detailed yet. The document, running at around 120 pages, came under attack for showing the Brotherhood's "true colors." Two issues in particular courted controversy: a stipulation that neither women nor Christians could hold the position of head of state and a proposal for a religious advisory council to review legislation. The former was not a reversal at all and was actually the group's longstanding position, as expressed in the 1994 statement on women. But since then, the group hadn't, for whatever reason, thought to include it in their electoral programs.

The clauses distracted from the rest of the program, which was very much in keeping with the pro-democracy focus of the 2004 reform initiative and 2005 electoral platform. As Mustafa al-Naggar reasoned in 2008 (before he left the Brotherhood): "If you took out those few lines, it would be an amazing program; it would be like any program of a liberal party."[48] But that, for some, was a big if.

A Fear of Being Destroyed

Islamist movements have had different ways of interpreting Algeria. One interpretation—the one that counseled caution and patience—reigned supreme for Egypt's Muslim Brotherhood before the 2011 revolution and in the early months after Mubarak's fall. The fear of provoking the military, the old regime, and the international community led the group to tread carefully and make a series of pledges that they would later renege on and regret. It was odd for a party to make so many preemptive concessions so early on in a transition. Then again, Islamist parties were a unique proposition; their rise would almost inevitably arouse opposition, some of it based on what they did and some of it based simply on who they were. The Brotherhood was still acting as if it was an opposition party facing off against a potentially repressive regime. The Democratic Alliance, today a relic of a distant past, was central to the Brotherhood's efforts to portray itself as a magnanimous actor intent on sharing power.

But the political dynamics shifted more quickly than they—and almost everyone else—expected. First, there was the increasingly obvious weakness of liberal parties. Brotherhood leaders had always been dismissive of what they called "cardboard parties." However, they, and many others, assumed that a real political opening would allow liberals and leftists to gain ground. Yet non-Islamist parties, as fractious as ever, struggled to gain traction. So-called liberal parties had trouble defining what liberalism meant in the Egyptian context and even avoided using the word. Instead, they defined themselves in opposition to Islamists, playing to the Brotherhood's strengths. Perhaps most problematically, liberal and leftist parties struggled to mount effective campaigns, particularly in far-flung rural areas where they had little organizational presence. Even in Cairo, they seemed unprepared. As one Brotherhood figure told me on the eve of the 2011 parliamentary elections, "I'm disappointed. No one seems to be campaigning. There's no one in the street but the Brotherhood."[49]

Still, even if they remained weak, Egyptians who were uncomfortable with the Brotherhood would have no choice but to consider non-Islamist alternatives—or so the thinking went. But such hopes were thwarted by the dramatic rise of Salafis, who despite their longtime opposition to democracy, quickly joined the democratic process and soon secured a stunning second-place finish in the elections.

In addition to the weakness of liberal parties, there was an impressively robust rearguard effort from old regime elements. Nathan Brown captured it well in an article suggestively titled "Just Because Mohamed Morsi is Paranoid Doesn't Mean He Doesn't Have Enemies."[50] In the

tense months of late 2012, it was difficult to know which of the Brotherhood's fears were real and which were imaginary, products of a hard-to-
dislodge persecution complex. But *some* were real. The two main parties
in question were the military and the judiciary, effectively the most
resilient pillars of the old regime (along with a bloated security sector).
Morsi was able to temporarily sideline the military on August 12, 2012
with a decree that was welcomed by most of Egypt's revolutionaries. Few
could deny that SCAF, whether through malevolence or sheer incom-
petence, had mismanaged the transition beyond recognition, poisoning
the country's politics in the process. The judiciary, purported protector
of the rule of law, was a different matter. With its share of Mubarak
loyalists, the judicial establishment was clearly politicized, but it had
also developed a reputation for occasional bouts of independence. After
the revolution, the Supreme Constitutional Court took it upon itself to
check the Brotherhood's ambitions, which it saw as a threat to its own
prerogatives. Leading figures on the bench, such as the Islamists' bête
noire Tahani al-Gebali, worked closely with the military to help them
dissolve the elected parliament and reassert control of the constitution-
drafting process. Gebali was forthcoming about her motives. "I knew
the elections would bring a majority from the movements of political
Islam," she told the *New York Times*.[51]

Meanwhile, Ahmed al-Zend, head of the country's leading judicial
association, accused the Brotherhood of "[carrying out] a systematic
plan meticulously designed to destroy [the] country."[52] He went so far
as to suggest that the association's members would have done more to
block Islamists' rise to power if they had known the Brotherhood and
Salafis would do so well in the elections. During a televised address
in June 2012, he expressed his reluctance to supervise the presidential
runoff, pitting Ahmed Shafiq and Mohamed Morsi, fearing that the
latter might win. He also openly declared the judiciary's politicization:
"We won't leave matters for those who can't manage them, with the
excuse that we're not people of politics. No, we are people of politics."[53]

In many respects, the judiciary proved the more formidable adversary.
The judges represented rule of law and separation of powers, important
components of any successful democracy. After the military was seemingly sidelined in August 2012, they stood as the primary check on the
Brotherhood's power. What the judiciary did, however undemocratic,

was "legal." When the opposition called on the Brotherhood to respect the rule of law, they may have had a point. But the Brotherhood also had a point when they accused the judiciary of bringing Egypt closer to the brink.

The anti-Islamist hysteria intensified that summer, capped by the rise of Mohamed Morsi as Egypt's first democratically elected president. It was odd to see liberals gathering to protest Secretary of State Hillary Clinton's July 2012 visit to Cairo. They felt that the United States was interfering in Egypt's domestic affairs, but for unusual reasons. Former presidential candidate Abul-Ezz al-Hariri claimed that the Obama administration was backing the Brotherhood so it could use the establishment of Egyptian theocracy as a pretext for an Iraq-style invasion. Emad Gad of the Social Democratic Party asserted that the United States was "working with purpose and diligence in order to enable the forces of political Islam to control the institutions of the Egyptian state."[54]

These accusations formed a narrative that became increasingly commonplace during the presidential runoffs—that the United States was actively backing the Muslim Brotherhood's candidate, Mohamed Morsi. Before the final election results were announced on June 24, a coalition of leading liberal parties held a press conference condemning the Obama administration for its interference in the elections. "We refuse that the reason someone wins is because he is backed by the Americans," said Osama Ghazali Harb of the Democratic Front Party. As Egyptian politics descended into acrimony and polarization, a growing number of liberal politicians and parties celebrated the dissolution of parliament, backed Mubarak ally Ahmed Shafiq for the presidency, and supported an interventionist role for the SCAF in Egyptian politics. Fear and panic over the Brotherhood's seemingly unstoppable rise seemed to overwhelm nearly everything else.

This, of course, did not mean that *everyone* was out to get the Brotherhood, but that was increasingly how the Brotherhood and its allies acted, to their and the country's detriment. The November 22nd decree was perhaps Morsi and the Brotherhood's most damaging move, if not in intent then in effect. There was, however, little to suggest that the decision—which gave Morsi unprecedented, if temporary, powers—was part of some furtively held plan to seize the state and impose Islamic autocracy. Rather, the same sense of destiny that led them toward caution before the revolution, as well as just after it, was now leading them in the opposite direction. What united them in both cases was a fear of being destroyed. They had come close before only to see their gains snatched away. They wouldn't let it happen again. And so they made the particularly fateful decision to contest the presidency. With what seemed like a great victory in hand, they decided to move against the military. But then the judiciary struck, threatening to undo their electoral victories. It had already dissolved Egypt's first democratically elected parliament and now threatened to dissolve the constituent assembly. So Morsi and the Brotherhood moved there too. Throughout it all, they insisted that each move was both temporary and necessary. Because they faced an existential threat, the normal rules of politics would have to be suspended. But for how long and at what cost? And when they had time to think about it, there was a lingering question: to what end?

7

Illiberal Democrats

THE TRANSITION SIMPLY DIDN'T go as planned. A series of unexpected events forced Egypt's Islamists to alter their approach. The environment was changing—more quickly than they could have ever imagined—and so too were they. The advent of electoral democracy introduced a new set of pressures into an unstable political arena.

As we saw in previous chapters, the repressive constraints of the old regime had kept Islamists in check. There was only so far they could go and so much they could do. They limited their ambitions accordingly. Regime repression had distorted the original mission of the Brotherhood, pushing the group to be not just more moderate but also more cautious than it would have otherwise been.

The normative, philosophical matters of the nature of the nation-state were beside the point when there was simply no chance of holding power, certainly not anytime soon and perhaps not for decades. Ideas traditionally associated with political Islam—such as banning alcohol or usury—seemed irrelevant and even petty.

Political realities reinforced the Brotherhood's tendency to play the long game and think of politics as consisting of stages (*siyasit al-marahil*). Something in one stage might not be appropriate for another. In the stage of opposition, they could afford to postpone the contentious ideological debates that they, in any case, had little interest in engaging in for fear of provoking internal dissent.

But when regime change finally came and they graduated to the next stage—one that entailed thinking seriously about power and governance—they were, slowly but insistently, pulled to the right. This shift to a more recognizably "Islamist" politics could have been expected to take years, not months, but two factors accelerated the process, pushing Islamists to discard some of their longstanding caution. As discussed earlier, liberal and leftist forces remained exceptionally weak throughout the early phase of the transition. Meanwhile, young revolutionaries were either unable or unwilling to make the jump from street action to party politics. Egypt's secular elites may have been ubiquitous in the print and television media but much less so on the ground, particularly outside the urban centers of Cairo and Alexandria. Unlike the Brotherhood, they had limited experience running campaigns and getting out the vote. Even when they did knock on doors, their message seemed muddled. As polarization grew, they turned to an explicitly anti-Islamist discourse. Islamists, for their part, were all too willing to fight political battles on religious turf.

The weakness of non-Islamists also contributed to the remarkable rise of Salafi parties. Well before the revolution, Brotherhood leaders would warn their American interlocutors that the alternatives to Islamists were not liberals but rather other, more conservative Islamists. For their part, Salafi groups had typically been content to focus on preaching. Few on the outside seemed to care or pay much attention, but what Stephane Lacroix calls a "quiet revolution" was taking place, as Salafi religious discourse moved from the fringes to the mainstream.[1] Over the course of the 2000s, Salafi television channels grew increasingly popular, becoming some of the most watched in the country. In one of the few studies of Salafis in pre-revolution Egypt, Nathan Field and Ahmed Hammam argue that the popularity of Salafi media outlets reflected "a logical shift towards more puritanical interpretations of religion, across broad segments of society."[2]

The rise of the Salafis coincided with the Muslim Brotherhood's "elections-first" strategy of using the little that was left of the democratic process to keep the pressure on the Mubarak regime. The Brotherhood, an organization like any other with finite resources, was shifting attention away from preaching and education toward electoral politics. The group's members were being asked to assume a constant state of mobilization for elections at the local, national, and syndicate levels. The Brotherhood was as politicized as it had ever been, and this wasn't to everyone's liking. For those seeking "purity," the Salafis offered a less compromised alternative. As Field and Hammam argued at the time, "there is a sentiment in Egypt that the Brotherhood is wasting its time participating in an ineffective Egyptian parliament and has lost a sense of priorities."[3]

When Western analysts and policymakers spoke of weakening the Brotherhood's seemingly firm grip on opposition politics, the response was a knowing one: "Be careful what you wish for."

Salafis After the Revolution

The Salafis were a small but significant presence in Tahrir Square. This was the first sign of the coming Salafi thrust into politics. Since they believed in "divine sovereignty"—in other words, that God is the sole lawgiver—Salafi groups had generally stayed away from parliamentary politics. But it wasn't simply a theological objection. They felt there was little use participating in a system that was rigged against them. The kind of Islamization that they hoped for simply wasn't possible under the old regime. But it was possible now. With the political arena wide open, Salafis sensed an opportunity to push for sharia and move toward their goal of establishing a real Islamic state and not just the watered-down version they accused the Brotherhood of supporting. Several Salafi groups, each representing various trends, formed political parties, the most important of which was the Nour party, the political arm of the Alexandria-based Salafi Call, the country's largest Salafi movement. Early on, Salafi preachers sounded ambitious notes. Mohamed Abdel Maqsoud, for instance, told an Egyptian newspaper in May 2011, "the Brotherhood said they would run for one-third of parliamentary seats, why shouldn't Salafis run for the rest?"[4]

They knew that they were strong. Those outside the Salafi movement were much more skeptical. Salafis were political novices, they pointed out, not knowing the first thing about how to run in—and win—elections. The Brotherhood had been doing this sort of thing for nearly four decades, transforming it into a science. Not surprisingly, then, Brotherhood officials spoke of Salafis with the patronizing tone of older brothers. Their little brothers were always causing trouble, saying

intemperate things and otherwise making Islamists look bad in the eyes
of the public.

The Salafis, though, knew better. I met with Mohamed Nour, a
senior official and spokesman in the Nour party, days before the first
round of parliamentary elections in November 2011. He was sitting
in Tahrir Square next to a pitched tent, cross-legged with an admir-
ing crowd of about 20 young men. He was talking about religion,
work, and success, interspersed with quotes from Dale Carnegie's
How to Win Friends and Influence People. (Nour was the sort of
Salafi who, iPad in hand, would talk of Steve Jobs as an inspiration.) He was surprisingly relaxed, considering that the polls were
coming up in just a couple days. He told me matter-of-factly that
the Nour party's coalition—which included Gama'a Islamiya, still
on the State Department's terrorist list, and the smaller Cairo-based
Asala party—was expecting anywhere between 20 to 30 percent of
the vote.

In a country as socially stratified as Egypt, it was difficult to tell
what was actually happening. There was a part of the country, which
had largely benefitted from the Mubarak regime's neoliberal economics,
that had chosen to look away. And, soon enough, they saw a country
where nearly 30 percent of their fellow Egyptians had voted for ultraconservative Salafis who, apparently, wanted to impose their own aus-
tere version of Islam on everyone else. This, they thought, was not what
Egyptians had fought for during those 18 days.

The rise of the Salafis was important for other reasons. In a region
where public opinion polling was not particularly reliable, elections
served a similar purpose of gauging where the popular mood was at
a given moment. It was difficult to know whether ordinary Egyptians were voting for Salafis because they agreed with their hardline
religious views, or because they saw Salafis as uncorrupted populists
in touch with the poor and disenfranchised. Either way, they voted
for Salafis knowing that they were deeply religious, conservative,
even puritanical. The Salafis, after all, made no secret of who they
were, what they stood for, and what they hoped to accomplish in due
time. Their victory both confirmed and reinforced a trend that had
long been in the making: Egypt had become increasingly Islamized

and even "Salafized." Salafi ideas had shed their exoticism; they were becoming normal facts of life in a changing Egypt.

A Shifting Political Spectrum

It is difficult to overstate the effect that the political emergence of Salafis had on Egypt. As the country's second largest electoral force, they now had an outsized influence on the future course of Egyptian politics. They managed to inject religion into nearly every political debate. And the more they made their presence felt, the more their liberal opponents responded in kind, further entrenching the Islamist–liberal divide.

The very presence of Salafis effectively shifted the entire political spectrum to the right. The Brotherhood no longer had a monopoly on the votes of the Islamist faithful. The relationship between the Brotherhood and Salafis became particularly tense during the 2011 parliamentary elections. As Lacroix writes, "it was as if each group took the election to be a zero-sum game. Every vote gained by the Salafis would have to be taken from the [Brotherhood], and vice-versa."[5] Where the Brotherhood had made too many deals and too many compromises, Salafis portrayed themselves as the purer Islamic alternatives. They had never been part of the corrupt system under Mubarak, and this was central to their electoral appeal. As one Nour party official put it: "We are from the people, we were on their side constantly during the Mubarak days, we have developed intimate knowledge of their problems . . . while the Brotherhood were wasting their time [with] useless institutional politics."[6] For those who truly wanted an "Islamic state," and all that entailed, the new Salafi parties were an attractive option.

Religious conservatism, even of the most uncompromising sort, had gone mainstream, and this was a reality the Brotherhood could not ignore. The Brotherhood, as always, was pragmatic, but pragmatism can cut both ways. In some contexts, the desire to maximize votes pulls ideological actors to the center. Other times, it may push them to adopt more conservative positions that they would otherwise avoid. Democracy opens the door to the proliferation of Islamist parties, which outbid each other over who can be more "Islamic." Because democracy is, in part, about responsiveness, Islamist groups simply cannot afford to alienate conservative constituencies that would like to see more Islam in the public sphere, rather than less.

The process of outbidding can intensify in democratic settings, particularly in fragmented parliamentary systems and even in two and three-party systems like those of the United States and United Kingdom, where the center-right is pulled further to the right. In the Muslim world, the case of Malaysia offers a window into the sort of unhealthy dynamic that can evolve. In his fascinating book *Piety and Politics*, Joseph Chinyong Liow paints a picture of a seemingly endless cycle of Islamization and counter-Islamization between the ostensibly secular ruling party, the United Malays National Organization, and the Islamist Pan-Malaysian Islamic Party. As Liow writes,

> Thanks to the Islamization race between the two, mainstream Malaysian national politics was soon dominated by issues such as the Islamic state, sharia law and the implementation of hudud punishments, polygamy, religious education, the construction of mosques and religious schools, and the definition of "proper" and "correct" Islam. From an outsider's point of view, it appeared as if Malaysian politics had been dominated solely by religion, and particularly Islam, alone.[7]

This is all the more striking considering that Malaysia is much more ethnically and religiously diverse than most Arab countries, with Muslims representing only around 60 percent of the population. In the course of what Liow calls "piety-trumping," Islamization becomes "very difficult to manage, let alone reverse, as the line between instrumentalism and ideology becomes increasingly blurred and the process begins to assume a life of its own."[8]

The Brotherhood's Base

Before the revolution, the Brotherhood's pro-democracy agenda met with indifference or skepticism among the rank-and-file. But in a repressive environment, the Islamist base was willing to give the leadership wide latitude to do whatever was necessary to survive, even if that meant diluting their Islamism. Over time, the group's leaders developed more "moderate" ideas that many of their supporters would not have been comfortable with. According to the survey of Brotherhood activists in Egypt conducted by Khalil al-Anani in 2006, which I discussed in Chapter 2, only 27 percent of respondents supported the right of Copts to hold the position of prime minister, while just 40 percent believed women should be members of parliament, both of which were at odds with the group's official public positions.[9]

Such discrepancies were not limited to the Brotherhood's base. According to numerous polls, the Brotherhood's illiberalism, including on women, Christians, personal freedoms, and sharia law, is widely shared by the broader population. Earlier, I cited a 2011 Pew poll which found that 80 percent of respondents favored stoning adulterers while 70 percent supported cutting off the hands of thieves—positions that accord more closely with the views of ultraconservative Salafis.[10] Meanwhile, in an April 2011 poll, only 18 percent of Egyptian respondents said they would "support a woman president."[11] On the controversial issue of clerical oversight of legislation, 69 percent of Egyptians said that "religious leaders should advise those in authority with writing national legislation" (with another 14 percent saying they "should have full authority to write national legislation").[12] Finally, it is worth mentioning one particularly striking result from a Pew survey conducted in March and April 2012, well after the rise of the Brotherhood and Salafis had provoked fears of Islamist overreach: Egyptians said they preferred the "model of religion in government" of Saudi Arabia over that of Turkey (61 to 17 percent).[13]

While it is true that ruling Islamists, particularly in Egypt, invited considerable anger and opposition, with their popularity ebbing in even former strongholds, there is little to suggest that this was due to their religious conservatism. Rather, many of the criticisms of the Brotherhood revolved around the group's secretive decision-making process, its tendency to put organizational self-interest above nearly everything else, and the authoritarian tendencies of President Morsi. On the mass level, there was a basic frustration with the Morsi government's failure to address the country's economic woes. For liberal elites, however, it went well beyond this. They feared the Brotherhood not only for what it had done, but for what it might do in the future. And this is why the Brotherhood or even milder Islamists like Ennahda will always provoke a certain degree of fevered opposition regardless of their actual policies and positions. "On matters of economic policy and social expenditures you can always split the difference," the political scientist Dankwart Rustow once wrote, decades before the Arab revolutions.[14] How, though, do you split the difference on religion? At stake in most Arab countries are a set of still-unresolved questions of identity, of how society is ordered, and how people live their lives. This, unfortunately, is the stuff of raw, existential battles.

How to Move to the Right

In times of crisis, the temptation to veer to the right becomes nearly irresistible. To be sure, the Brotherhood never shed its pretensions toward moderation and portraying itself as a mature, responsible actor. But the vagaries of electoral politics meant that it had to rally its base, play up its Islamism, and court, however reluctantly at first, Salafi groups.

Ironically, it was precisely at the height of the 2012 presidential contest that the Brotherhood, closing ranks, fell back on religiously charged mobilization. It was less important to look "responsible" when you needed to win—and the Brotherhood needed to win. In a deeply religious society, where the symbols of the divine are everywhere and where even the irreligious use Islamically infused language, the religious all too easily became political. It was difficult to know whether politics was being instrumentalized for religion or if religion was being instrumentalized for politics. The fact that the two had blurred together so completely was itself suggestive.

With Egypt as polarized as ever, the Brotherhood paid less attention to reaching out to liberals and leftists, focusing instead on exciting its base and securing the Salafi vote. Once again showing its nimble pragmatism, the group, which had spent a considerable amount of time deemphasizing sharia law, re-Islamized its message. Hearkening back to the rhetoric of the 1980s, Khairat al-Shater, the Brotherhood's original candidate for president, affirmed that the application of sharia was his ultimate objective and that he would form a committee of scholars to help parliament achieve that goal.[15] Shater was speaking to the Islamic Legitimate Body for Rights and Reform—a Salafi-leaning council of religious scholars. It was his first event as a presidential candidate. (He met with the council for a second time the following week.)

Shater aggressively courted Salafi organizations, hoping to win their endorsement. The backing of the Salafi Call and the Nour party, now two of the country's most powerful organizations, with the ability to mobilize hundreds of thousands of supporters, would be critical. With the only Salafi candidate in the race, the preacher Hazem Abu Ismail, likely to be disqualified for having an American mother, Shater was already the most "Islamist" candidate. In a two-round election, it made little sense to make a real play for liberals and leftists. Shater, no matter what he tried to do, was unlikely to be more successful in courting liberals and leftists than the actual liberal and leftist candidates in the race. On the other hand, the Salafi vote and the Islamist vote more broadly was very much up for grabs, as various Salafi organizations gave former Brotherhood figure Abdel Moneim Abul Futouh a closer look. The case that the Brotherhood had to make was a simple one: that Shater was the only candidate who could be counted on to take the implementation of sharia law seriously.

After Shater was disqualified, Mohamed Morsi—derided in the Egyptian media as the "spare tire" candidate—took up the mantle. A weaker, less convincing candidate, Morsi doubled down on Shater's back-to-basics message. In his first television interview, Morsi said, "this is the old 'Islam is the solution' platform. It has been developed and crystallized so that God could bless society with it."[16] Similarly, at his first campaign event, he declared: "Some want to stop our march to an Islamic future, where the grace of God's laws will be implemented . . . Our Salafi brothers, [and Gama'a Islamiya], we are united in our aims and Islamic vision."[17] Morsi succinctly summed up his message: "Needless to say, currently, [I am] the only contender who offers a clearly Islamic project."[18]

Despite his best efforts, the Salafi Call, the Nour party, and Gama'a Islamiya decided to endorse Brotherhood defector Abul Futouh instead. This, however, only intensified the outbidding. The Brotherhood and its supporters hailed Morsi as the only true Islamist in the race, hoping to split the Salafi camp (indeed, prominent Salafi clerics and smaller Salafi parties, such as Asala, endorsed Morsi). Morsi surrogate Safwat Hegazy, a firebrand preacher, campaigned for Morsi across the country, all the while attacking Salafis for being afraid to implement sharia.[19]

Seeing Abul Futouh as a major threat, the Brotherhood and its Salafi allies attacked him in numerous public statements. They unearthed old statements from Salafi Call preachers attacking Abul Futouh for his liberalism, pointing to controversial remarks that public atheism falls under protected speech. One such Brotherhood statement adopts a mocking tone throughout: "Isn't this what you wrote with your own hands dear brothers? . . . And now you choose to back him for the most important office in the country." The statement, penned by the Brotherhood's Mahmoud Ghozlan, is a telling example of Islamist "outbidding," with each side under pressure to prove its *bona fides*. Addressing Salafis, Ghozlan asks, "are we the ones giving up our principles for political gain?"[20]

In a tight contest, the difference came down to who could turn out more of their supporters to the polls. And, here, the Brotherhood had the advantage of a network of more than 600 al-Azhar and Salafi preachers, who held meetings and seminars across Egypt to educate citizens on the Brotherhood's Renaissance Project.[21] It was unclear just to what extent mosques were used for campaign purposes in violation of the law. Abdel Rahman al-Barr, a member of the Brotherhood's Guidance Bureau, insisted that "mosques are only for praying" but that preachers could "familiarize people with the relationship between the candidates and the voters, without mentioning the names of particular candidates."[22]

This didn't mean the Brotherhood had become any less pragmatic, just that pragmatism was not the same thing as moderation. And when the situation called for it, Morsi and the Brotherhood could just as easily shift back to a more conciliatory tone. In the second round of elections, Morsi, having by now secured Salafi support, needed to reach out to prominent liberals and leftists who were sitting on the fence, unwilling to vote for Mubarak's last prime minister Ahmed Shafiq but skeptical of Morsi's intentions. In an effort to peel off swing voters, Morsi made a number of pledges at what became known as the "Fairmont meeting," assuring them he would appoint an independent prime minister and a largely technocratic government. He would distance himself from the Brotherhood and appoint a Christian or woman as vice president. Morsi and the Brotherhood agreed to govern in the spirit of consensus. But it didn't last: the already wide gap between Islamists and liberals could not simply be papered over. The gap, after all, was based on something deeper, less tangible, and all the more difficult to address.

Do Islamists Have an Alternative Project?

As we saw in previous chapters, power and ideology had become fused together, contributing to Egypt's growing polarization. In academic and policy circles, there has been a marked shift toward assessing Islamists' behavior by looking at how they respond to political constraints. While this shift is welcome—consider the absurdity of reading the Quran to understand the Brotherhood's actions—there is sometimes a tendency to dismiss the importance of ideology. Ideology matters, although the extent of ideological commitment is inevitably constrained by domestic and international factors, whether it be regime repression, resilient institutions (the so-called deep state), or the desire of Islamists to be seen as responsible actors on the world stage.

In the short term, Islamist parties in power can go only so far. In transitional periods, their focus is on stability and staying in power, not on applying Islamic law or creating the mythical Islamic state. But, over time, constraining factors are likely to become less relevant or disappear altogether. What happens when Islamists become more secure in power and the fear of being destroyed subsides?

Islamists are Islamists for a reason. They have a distinct ideological project, even if they themselves struggle to articulate exactly what it entails. In Egypt, the Brotherhood had been developing the Renaissance Project, which was intended as a sort of blueprint for Islamist would-be technocrats. While some of the project's ideas on institutional reform, economic development, and urban renewal are impressive, they shouldn't be taken as the end point of what Islamists are trying to do. Which brings us back to a vexing question: what do Islamists really want and what do Islamists *really* believe?

Addressing these sorts of questions is challenging, in part because Islamists have spent so little time trying to answer them. For reasons discussed earlier, mainstream Islamists spent much of the 1990s and 2000s touting their newfound democratic credentials. In the struggle against repressive regimes, all that really mattered—or all that seemed to matter at the time—was getting to democracy. Everything else was a distraction. Nothing else was possible without clearing that first, essential hurdle, and there was no knowing just how long that would take. As Mustafa al-Naggar, then still with the Brotherhood, put it, "you can't apply sharia in a society that doesn't have freedom."[23]

The positions the Brotherhood adopted in the 2000s were premised on the assumption of being and staying in opposition. It may seem foolish in hindsight, but it is worth emphasizing that revolution wasn't considered an option. Even if the Mubarak regime somehow loosened its grip on power, the move toward even semicompetitive democracy would take years if not decades. Once there was a real democratic transition, then the Brotherhood could think through more carefully the relationship between Islam, democracy, and the nation-state. They could learn from the challenges of governance gradually, without the stifling pressure of being responsible for the economic recovery of an entire country. Politics wouldn't need to be all-consuming. The Brotherhood, a religious movement, would not need to become synonymous with the controversial decisions of politicians. Even as late as May 2011, three months after Mubarak fell, Brotherhood leaders were talking about a five-year period of transition, where the focus would be on building the foundations of a healthy democracy.[24] This, though, is not quite the way it turned out.

Before the uprisings of 2011, Islamist political wings were subservient to what remained, at the core, broad-based social movements. Political parties learned to lose because the broader movements couldn't afford to win. After the revolts, this dynamic was turned on its head. Increasingly, the aims of gradual Islamization through education, preaching, and social outreach were subsumed by an almost single-minded devotion to electoral politics.

Indeed, Islamists had mastered the art of getting out the vote and winning elections, but they were not at all prepared for the task that followed. The Brotherhood, more than anyone else, could draw upon the skill and talents of tens of thousands of professionals in engineering, law, medicine, business, construction, and other sectors. They had experience running disciplined and effective organizations, at least on a smaller scale. Yet governing a country as unwieldy as Egypt was an entirely different matter. Some of the problems they encountered were inevitable. A new Islamist elite, with no actual governing experience, was asked to run corrupt government institutions that were generally hostile to the Brotherhood. But another problem was more basic and represented both a failure of leadership and a failure of imagination.

The Search for Political Theology

When mainstream Islamists talk about politics, it is striking just how little theology figures into the discussion. For a movement ostensibly devoted to Islamization, Islamists had precious little to say in the lead-up to the Arab uprisings about the intellectual framework that would guide their approach to governing or, more fundamentally, their particular conception of the nation-state.

Islamists, as one might expect, do not begin from the starting point of liberal democracy. This presents a problem for groups that have been intent on presenting themselves in the most moderate light possible. Islamic political theory, in even its mildest "moderate" versions, diverges considerably from liberal democratic theory as most Westerners would understand it. Not only does this create tension with the international community, but it also introduces a polarizing domestic debate that Islamists do not necessarily want to have. But in avoiding that discussion, Islamist groups may have only postponed the inevitable.

Islamists can try to hide behind their majoritarianism, claiming that Egyptians, Tunisians, or Libyans prefer a state that is *not* ideologically neutral, a state that takes it upon itself to protect and promote religion. This descent into majoritarianism absolves Islamists from clarifying their preferred role for religion. They can simply point to an elected parliament and say: this is what the people want, this is democracy. Even those like Rachid Ghannouchi or Abdel Moneim Abul Futouh who have articulated a distinctly noncoercive "liberal Islamism" rely on a majoritarian assumption to square the circle between their Islamism and their supposed liberalism.

When I sat down with Abul Futouh for the first time in the summer of 2006, I wanted to understand his philosophy of government. He repeatedly emphasized that the people, represented by a freely elected parliament, are the source of authority. Abul Futouh was confident that once Egyptian society was free, the best ideas would rise to the top.

There was little need, then, to regulate society from the top down. On their own, without government getting too much in the way, Egyptians would do the right thing. And this would inevitably be to Islam's benefit. "What happens in a free society?" Abul Futouh told me. "I hold conferences and spread my ideas through newspapers and television to try to bring public opinion closer to me . . . We have confidence in what we believe."[25]

Abul Futouh's message has analogues elsewhere in the region, most notably in Tunisia, where the Ennahda party came to power in 2011 by tapping into a religious mainstream that had lost faith in the secular project of past decades. Rachid Ghannouchi, the leader of Ennahda as well as its primary ideologue, is one of the few Islamist figures in the region who has written extensively on the problem of Islam and liberal democracy. Central to Ghannouchi's political philosophy, as explained in his most comprehensive work *Public Liberties in the Islamic State*, is the notion of vicegerency, or *istikhlaf*. Popular sovereignty is possible because the people, as vicegerents, have accepted their role as protectors of God's law. Through the democratic process, the people and their elected representatives give shape and meaning to sharia according to their particular context. In a sense, the sharia is whatever the people want it to be, but under one condition: that they accept vicegerency and that they act, in good faith, to respect and reflect God's will and his law.

Ghannouchi insists that this should happen without coercion. The divine constraint on popular sovereignty is "a self-limitation after this umma—or a majority of it—has accepted Allah as its lord and Islam as its religion, voluntarily and freely."[26] Apparently, Ghannouchi, like so many other Islamist figures, has an abiding faith in the wisdom of crowds. He writes that "the umma is guided in the path of God and granted protection from collective error," echoing the prophetic statement that "my umma will not agree on an error."[27]

In 1994, when Ghannouchi published *Public Liberties*, it sounded almost revolutionary, coming so soon after the Algerian debacle, when it seemed like the conflict between Islam and democracy might persist indefinitely. In the work of Ghannouchi and similar thinkers, one sometimes gets the sense that they are trying to solve a problem; that they are trying to reconcile two different worldviews, both of which they value for different reasons. But choosing to operate within the bounds of Islamic political theory has its inherent limitations. As the political theorist Andrew March points out in his excellent study of Rachid Ghannouchi's political thought, sharia remains, in Ghannouchi's own words, "the original, foundational authority for the community and the government."[28] March concludes that "for Ghannouchi, the doctrine of man's universal vicegerency is primarily a move internal to Islamism that is certainly in a democratizing direction but not with European parliamentary democracy as its unambivalent aim."[29] Understood this way, even the most moderate explication of Islamic political theory—as per Ghannouchi—falls well short of liberal democracy. Despite his best efforts, or perhaps because of them, Ghannouchi simply cannot move his political philosophy onto a secular plane.

During the 1990s and 2000s, Islamists avoided delving into political philosophy for precisely this reason. "Islamic democracy," for it to be Islamic in any meaningful sense of the word, rests on a fundamentally different philosophical basis than that of liberal democratic theory. It cannot be otherwise, because Islamic democracy is *supposed* to be different. But to discuss this publicly with skeptical liberals and Western interlocutors would be to distract from the immediate goal of unseating or at least undermining dictatorial regimes—something nearly everyone could agree on. Worrying about the divisive ideological issues could come later, perhaps much later.

Islamist Theory and Political Reality

When Ghannouchi published his book in 1994, few would have even dreamed that the man, who was by then in exile, would ever have the opportunity to put his beliefs into practice. Ghannouchi returned to Tunis on January 30, 2011, two weeks after Ben Ali's fall. He received a hero's welcome, with over one thousand Tunisians greeting him at the airport. After waiting for nearly 30 years, the Ennahda party was finally legalized on March 1. In his early interviews, Ghannouchi said all the right things, demonstrating a subtlety and sophistication that his fellow Islamists in Egypt and elsewhere often lacked.

After coming first in the October 2011 elections, Ennahda formed a governing coalition—known as the *troika*—with two secular parties.

Ennahda promised that it would not govern alone and that it intended to live up to its pledges of reaching out to the opposition (which, as in Egypt, had quickly grown fearful of Islamist domination). Anything less, the thinking went, would undermine trust in Ennahda and lead to polarization and instability. The second test for Ghannouchi and his supporters came during the drafting of the constitution. While some proposed clauses, such as those on blasphemous speech and women's "complementarity" with men, aroused the ire of the secular opposition, there was no real effort to Islamize the constitution. Even in some "secular" autocracies, such as Mubarak's Egypt, there would often be a stock clause on the principles of sharia being a source of legislation. But an Islamist-led government was either unable or unwilling to include such a clause in Tunisia's draft constitution.

Tunisia's post-revolution constitution, ratified in 2014, is a far cry from the sharia-centric model that Ghannouchi had begun outlining two decades before. There is nothing in the text that so much as hints at vicegerency, the philosophical and theological foundation of Ghannouchi's Islamic democratic model. Of course, Tunisia had a strong, influential minority which believed in an aggressive French-style secularism. In Tunisia, the time wasn't right. Islamization could still happen but at a slower, more measured pace. If Ghannouchi believed in the majority, then the majority would surely come around, and, eventually, their preferences would be more clearly reflected in public life. But none of these considerations changed the fundamental reality: to the extent that Tunisia provides a "model," it is *not* a model of reconciling Islamism and liberal democracy, at least not yet.

Unlike its counterparts in Tunisia, the Egyptian Muslim Brotherhood has not featured any major intellectuals for some time. While it has drawn inspiration from any number of thinkers across the region, there are no recent texts to turn to for the group's vision of the Islamic state. The group's last ideologue of any great stature was Sayyid Qutb, who advanced an increasingly radical vision that the Brotherhood distanced itself from after his death.

If we look at "Islamization" as something gradual and unfolding in stages, then the Brotherhood found itself much further along than Tunisia's Islamists. After decades of continuous Islamic revival, spreading across every sector of society, Egyptians had been primed. In five successive elections after the revolution, Egyptians handed Islamists a victory each time. The Brotherhood, however, struggled to translate this electoral support into a coherent vision of Islamic governance, for some of the reasons already discussed. Having discarded the insistent gradualism of the past, the Brotherhood and its Freedom and Justice Party seemed more in a rush, but unsure of where they wanted to go.

This led to considerable confusion, with some accusing them of being *too* Islamist and turning Egypt into a theocracy, while others from within the Islamist camp worried that the Brotherhood, corrupted by power, had lost sight of its original core mission. Ibrahim El-Houdaiby, despite being a liberal Islamist, found himself in the latter camp. The great-grandson of former General Guide Hassan al-Houdaiby, Ibrahim had by the mid-2000s become one of the Brotherhood's most promising young intellectuals. A onetime protégé of Khairat al-Shater, he grew disillusioned with the group's direction and left the organization in 2008.

Four years later, Houdaiby would write an intriguing article in *Ahram Online* that is worth looking at more closely.[30] He begins by recounting a Brotherhood leader telling him that he was "more worried about the Brotherhood being tainted by power than the state being tainted by the Brotherhood." Houdaiby criticizes the group for failing to detail anything resembling a coherent vision. "Maintaining the unity of the group," he writes, "has come at the expense of the political project's intellectual clarity and political maturity." Interestingly, he criticizes the Brotherhood from the right: "Talk about sharia is fading and there is no vision defining it or the purpose of applying it, while neo-liberal culture dominates all aspects of life."

Lacking any such vision, the Brotherhood descended into a cycle of reactive, ad-hoc policymaking. Facing what it saw to be existential threats, power became the most important currency and survival its own kind of victory. When the Brotherhood wrapped itself in religious rhetoric, which it increasingly did—particularly during the constitutional crisis of November and December 2012—it seemed to be much more about politics than a "project." It was guided not by an intellectual framework but by a vaguely defined majoritarianism. As Houdaiby himself had warned years before, "politics should serve your comprehensive project, not other way around."[31]

The resulting constitution did, in fact, suggest a shift to the right, a natural product of a constituent assembly dominated by Islamists (the assembly members, after all, were selected by a parliament with an Islamist supermajority). But the thrust to the right itself—like much of what the Brotherhood did—seemed ill considered. Several articles aroused the opposition of liberals, not necessarily because they spelled out Islamic rule (they didn't), but because they laid the groundwork for future Islamization. That, at least, was what many of the constitution's critics feared. Article 219 defined the principles of sharia as including "general evidence, foundational rules, rules of jurisprudence, and credible sources accepted in Sunni doctrines and by the larger community." While more specific than Article 2, which it was meant to clarify, the formulation still left a number of questions unanswered. In explaining their own view of the provisions, Islamists saw it as giving greater meaning to the "principles" of Islamic law, which, they pointed out, could be interpreted by anyone to mean just about anything.[32]

Article 4 was even more vague in its assertion that "al-Azhar's council of senior scholars is to be consulted in matters relating to Islamic Sharia." As any issue could technically be considered as falling under the domain of Islamic law, liberals worried that this would lead to an Iranian-style clerical body constantly interfering in the democratic process. While the body's opinions would be nonbinding, it would be difficult for an elected parliament to go against a formal al-Azhar ruling. Perhaps more problematic, al-Azhar rulings could give cover to Islamist parties—self-proclaimed defenders of the faith—to push through controversial legislation, thereby contributing to greater polarization, once again along religious lines. With much more at stake, Article 4 would effectively politicize al-Azhar, with the Muslim Brotherhood, Salafis, and liberals jockeying to gain more allies on the scholars' council.

Meanwhile, other articles in the constitution appeared to endow the state with a moral, religious mission, although the imprecise wording made it difficult to know for sure. Article 10 declared that "the state and society oversee the commitment to the genuine character of the Egyptian family, its cohesion and stability, and the consolidation and protection of its moral values," while Article 11 said that "the state safeguards ethics, public morality and public order, a high level of education and of religious and patriotic values." To be sure, these articles could be used to justify future Islamic legislation, but the clauses in question are notable for their seemingly tacked-on nature. Contrary to popular belief, there wasn't an Islamist master plan at work.

Egypt's first "democratic" constitution is best understood as a hastily put together compromise document, with all the flaws and incoherence that that entails. It was a compromise between two completely different visions of the state, the liberal vision and the Islamist vision. The Brotherhood, at least as far as the constitution was concerned, was initially in the center, trying to hammer out a consensus between the various groups—namely liberals and Salafis. They failed, with most non-Islamist members eventually walking out of the assembly, undermining the legitimacy of both the process and the substance. But was a consensus even possible in the first place? Liberals believe in rights and freedoms that are, by definition, nonnegotiable. Naturally, then, they would oppose any articles allowing the state, particularly an Islamist-led state, to interfere in the private affairs of citizens. More importantly, anything giving the state an explicit role in promoting religion or public morality would be a fundamental point of contention.

Salafis, on the other hand, felt that the constitution didn't go nearly far enough. For months, they had threatened to withdraw from the constituent assembly if their demands weren't met. They wanted to change Article 2 so that the "rulings," and not just the principles, would be enshrined as the main source of legislation. The Brotherhood hoped to avoid getting bogged down in a controversy that would almost certainly derail negotiations. So, instead, they added Article 219. For their part, the Brotherhood and the Salafis saw this as a concession. This was the middle ground, somewhere in between liberal and Islamist conceptions of the good. But this was precisely the problem: the liberal and Islamist conceptions of the good—and the state—were irreconcilable.

At times, it almost seemed that the Brotherhood and Salafi representatives viewed the very presence of "liberals" in the assembly as a gesture of goodwill and magnanimity. The Brotherhood's disdain for liberals was nothing new and was a product, at least in part, of the Mubarak years, when many liberals tolerated autocracy as the lesser of two evils. But it ran deeper than that: Islamists generally didn't see liberals as having any natural constituency. Moreover, they represented an ideology that was foreign to Egypt and, worse, morally subversive. In my interviews with Brotherhood officials both before and after the revolution, I usually got the sense that, despite occasionally trying, they simply couldn't bring themselves to take liberals seriously.

It is worth recalling that, in their earlier incarnations, Islamist groups had had doubts about the right of liberals to participate in political life in the first place. For example, in Chapter 3, I noted the harsh exchanges between the Brotherhood and the leftist Tagammu party in the 1980s. General Guide Hamed Abu Nasr argued that "the philosophy of Tagammu rests on a foundation of the denial of God."[33] In Jordan, during the early 1990s, Islamists spoke out against the participation of "atheistic" parties.[34] In a pamphlet released in 1990, the Brotherhood there explained its stance on political pluralism: "The nation has reached a high level of awareness toward the role of [Islam in] its life [and] we view with disdain and disgust anyone who underestimates this fundamental aspect. We classify such people as outside the circle of the nation and we reject their belonging to it."[35]

Although not everyone was aware of it, there was a philosophical basis to such claims. In more established democracies where the constitution enshrines some degree of secularism, all political actors must agree to work within the confines of liberal democracy, even if they are Islamists. This, for example, is what happened in Turkey, where successive Islamist parties had little choice but to de-Islamize their entire political platforms. The constitution, after all, was rather explicit about secularism. The preamble states that "there shall be no interference whatsoever by sacred feelings in state affairs and politics," while Article 2 enshrines the secular order "based on the fundamental tenets set forth in the preamble." Even if the vast majority of Turks and their elected representatives wished to amend Article 2, they wouldn't be able to: the first three articles of the constitution are among the so-called "irrevocable provisions," which cannot be amended under any circumstances.

Even without such supra-constitutional clauses, constitutions remain difficult to amend, requiring at least a supermajority. This is why the drafting of new constitutions in countries like Egypt and Tunisia is such a charged, polarizing event: it defines the contours of acceptable politics in countries torn between liberal democracy—and international human rights norms—and a more religiously based form of democracy.

In a country with an actual "Islamist" constitution, liberal parties would still be able to participate in politics, but only so long as they accepted the centrality of sharia. Several Arab countries still prohibit the formation of parties based on religion. In a hypothetical Islamic democracy, legislation could be expected to ban parties based on secularism or the separation of religion from politics. Just as in Turkey, where the judiciary can dissolve parties that violate the constitutional principles of secularism, in an Islamic democracy, the courts could be expected to do something similar, but just in reverse. This might seem repressive and unjust and, if considered from within the liberal democratic tradition, it certainly is.

No matter how you look at it, there is a real ideological gap, and the nature of this gap—its thorniness and seeming intractability—is, for now, unique to the Arab world. Even if we take Ghannouchi's mild Islamism as a starting point, popular sovereignty is possible but under one condition: that the people and, by extension, their elected representatives accept to act as vicegerents. By definition, a secular party would not be able to accept vicegerency, because the role of the state, from a liberal conception, is *not* to respect and reflect God's will and his law. As Andrew March explains, "the sovereign community in [Ghannouchi's] scheme is not 'the people' as such—any people that might find itself contracting or founding a new polis—but rather the umma."[36] This leads us to an important question. March asks: "Are secular co-citizens of countries like Tunisia and Egypt, in the sense of co-citizens who do not begin with the covenant of vicegerency and the obligation to execute the sharia (however this is understood) as the source of all political meaning, participants in this universal caliphate?"[37]

If there are in fact irreconcilable differences in the liberal and Islamist conceptions of the good, liberals would respond that their solution is the compromise solution since it provides a neutral public space, where each group—secular and Salafi alike—can express its religious preferences freely without government interference. But the notion that liberalism is "neutral" can be accepted only within a liberal framework. Political liberalism, as expounded by John Rawls in his numerous works, is based on the "veil of ignorance"—the notion that the founders of a new polity are free to construct their own society without any knowledge of their future position or power and without any distinctive set of preferences or values. As Lenn Goodman writes in a thoughtful critique that seems especially prescient today: "So even neutrality, in Rawls's scheme, is not neutral . . . Every one of Rawls's choosers is trapped in a liberal society."[38] "They are not free," he goes on, "to construct a value system for themselves."[39]

Certainly, Islamists wouldn't see a secular society as allowing them to express their deepest beliefs and convictions. Ghannouchi's recollections of his time in France as a graduate student are illustrative. "The one year I spent in Paris was the hardest and most trying in my entire life," he wrote in his diary.[40] It is not too difficult to imagine a secularist living in Iran or Saudi Arabia experiencing something similar. Salem Falahat, the former general overseer of the Jordanian Brotherhood, conveyed the challenges of living under a government where you are estranged from the law of the land: "In the context of the Islamic state, everyone is compelled to follow and respect the laws of the Islamic state. In America, a Muslim must respect the laws of the land even if they go against his belief."[41]

But it is not a just a matter of cultural alienation or personal comfort. If it was, it might be easier to address. For Islamists, it is a matter of religious obligation. For example, Ghannouchi argues that, if certain conditions are met, the establishment of an Islamic government is a legal obligation upon the entirety of the Muslim community.[42] Elsewhere he goes further, writing that the "resort to the [Islamic] fundamentals of governance and consenting to them is not just an obligation, but it is the dividing line between faith and disbelief."[43] And that is Ghannouchi— one of the more "liberal" Islamists—speaking.

In short, religion for Islamists is something that, at its very core, includes a conception of the good that goes well beyond the individual and extends to the very nature of the state. All of this might seem objectionable or even dangerous, but it is what they think and what they believe. So, from that standpoint, a strictly liberal democracy would violate *their* freedom of religion and freedom of belief. Liberalism cannot hold within it Islamism. One possible resolution to this is the Turkish model, where Islamists, over time, gradually give up on their larger project and make peace with secular democracy. Some supporters of the

Tunisian "model" hold out hope that Ghannouchi and his fellow travelers might opt to follow a similar path. The other "resolution" is that it be left to the ballot box as a final arbiter. If elected majorities decide that they want to try out an alternative ideological project, then they could. In essence, they would be deciding, through democratic means, that they do *not* want to be liberals.

8

A Tunisian Exception?

DURING THE QUESTION-AND-ANSWER SESSION of a lecture I gave in Tunis two years after the revolution, a well-known scholar in attendance called Tunisia a "laboratory" for political scientists. The country was small and homogenous and, considering its strategic remoteness, there was less foreign meddling to account for. Decades of forced secularization had come to an end. Now, Tunisians, for the first time in their modern history, could return to something resembling a natural equilibrium. But no one quite knew what that would look like.

There was a lot riding on the Tunisian experiment, particularly when it came to the role of religion. Just one day after the country's first post-revolution assassination of leftist politician Chokri Belaid and amid fears of civil strife, the prominent socialist parliamentarian Lobna Jribi told me that Tunisia offered perhaps "the last chance to show that Islam and democracy can work together."[1] This might have been going too far, but there is something to be said about Tunisian "exceptionalism." Tunisian Islamists aren't quite the Muslim equivalent of Christian Democrats that they sometimes make themselves out to be, but they are, along with Morocco's Justice and Development Party, as "moderate" as you can probably get in the Arab world and still call yourself Islamist.

Like most Brotherhood-inspired groups in the region, the Movement of the Islamic Tendency (MTI), as it was originally called, gained a following among university students in the 1970s and peaked in the 1980s, before a government crackdown effectively eliminated the movement.[2]

When MTI released its founding statement in 1981, it had already set itself apart. Although the statement avoids using the word "democracy" and is heavy on references to moral and cultural renewal, there is no explicit discussion of applying sharia law or establishing an Islamic state.[3] The rest of the decade saw MTI updating its discourse and displaying a growing comfort with the tenets of democratic life. As Rachid Ghannouchi would put it in his first interview after the revolution, "we drank the cup of democracy in one gulp back in the 1980s while other Islamists have taken it sip by sip."[4]

As we saw in the previous chapter, Ghannouchi, first in prison and then in exile, would push the boundaries of what was possible in Islamic political theory, embracing popular sovereignty and democratizing the notion of the umma. Sharia, rather than something preexisting or imposed, was whatever the people decided it would be.

For Ghannouchi and the rest of Ennahda's leaders, getting to that point wasn't easy. The extent of repression in Tunisia had few parallels in the Arab world. At first, religious associations, such as Society for the Preservation of the Quran, were allowed some degree of freedom in the 1970s. In a story that repeated itself throughout the region, Habib Bourguiba, an Ataturk-like secular modernizer, thought he could use Islam to counter the Marxist left. But Ghannouchi and his colleagues, initially content to focus on preaching and education, turned their attention to politics and soon formed the largest and best organized opposition group in the country. In the 1989 elections, an increasingly confident Ennahda party—it dropped the "Islamic" moniker of MTI in a show of good faith—won 14 percent of the vote (party officials claim they won as much as 60 percent in some areas). For the regime, this was both a shock and a provocation. In the subsequent years, Ben Ali—who upon assuming power in 1988 organized a "national pact" and promised a democratic transition—quickly changed course, systematically dismantling Ennahda's organizational structure and detaining tens of thousands of Islamists. The lucky ones, like Ghannouchi, fled into exile.

Ben Ali went much further than his Egyptian and Jordanian counterparts could ever hope to go. With the exception of Syria, Tunisia became the closest thing the region had to a full-on totalitarian state. While their husbands disappeared into Ben Ali's dungeons, the women of Ennahda led a steely existence, ostracized by their communities and monitored by the authorities. "Other than with my immediate family, I virtually had no contact with people," recalled Monia Brahim, who became a member of Ennahda's executive committee in 2011.[5] It is one thing to repress political opposition, a normal feature of Arab authoritarian politics, but it is quite another to try to erase an entire movement, anyone associated with it, and anything it might stand for.

For anyone who has spent much time in the "rest" of the Arab world, walking the streets of Tunis, the capital city, can be disorienting. Tunisia, today, is a product of more than five decades of forced secularization, imposed by first Bourguiba and then Ben Ali. After the revolution, Ennahda's Osama al-Saghir became one of the country's youngest members of parliament. Only 28 years old, he had spent the previous 17 years—his entire adult life—in Italy, where he became an Italian citizen and a founding member of the Democratic Party (which came first in the February 2013 elections). For those who had built new lives in exile, returning to Tunisia could be a confusing process. Many, like Saghir, found a country they didn't quite recognize. "After coming back," he told me, "I was surprised to notice that there wasn't one mosque on Bourguiba Avenue [the main avenue in the capital]." But even early on as a child growing up in Tunis, he knew something was amiss. "It was confusing," Saghir said, "when in Egyptian movies, they talked about having big social events on Thursday night. Why Thursday night? I realized later it was because we had a different weekend."[6]

Indeed, Tunisia is one of only three Arab countries that share their weekends with France (the other two, Morocco and Lebanon, are also former French colonies). It has some of the region's lowest levels of support for Islamic punishments: only 18 percent of Tunisians support the death penalty for apostasy, 28 percent favor cutting of the hands of thieves, while 28 percent think adulterers should be stoned (the comparable numbers for Egypt are 88, 70, and 80 percent).[7]

Bourguiba, the country's first post-independence leader, remains a towering figure in Tunisian life, casting a long shadow over the country's politics. He fashioned himself a secular modernizer who would bring Tunisia into European-style modernity no matter what it took. While Bourguiba was not beyond instrumentalizing Islam for his own purposes, he saw orthodox Islam—and particularly its Islamist incarnations—as a grave threat to his secularizing project. What flowed from this were a series of acts that, to many religiously minded Tunisians, were simply unforgivable, including, most famously, his purposeful breaking of the Ramadan fast with a glass of orange juice on national television. They were key to shaping the narrative of cultural alienation, which continues to be a major theme of Islamist discourse to this day.

The profound changes under way in Tunisia would shape Ghannouchi's thinking as a young man, even though a full embrace of political Islam would not come until later, after a period of near-atheism. Ghannouchi had grown up in a traditional religious family, where Islam was a natural, unquestioned part of everyday life. Yet, when he ventured off to Tunis to study at Zaytouna College, he was confronted with the rapid secularization of life under Bourguiba. Ghannouchi was one of the last cohorts of students to complete the religious education curriculum at Zaytouna, which had been, along with Egypt's al-Azhar, one of the region's preeminent centers of Sunni Islamic scholarship. But even at Zaytouna, only a few students—out of nearly three thousand—used the prayer room on campus.[8]

In his biography of Ghannouchi, Azzam Tamimi, himself a prominent Islamist figure associated with Hamas, writes that Ghannouchi and his fellow students felt as if they were "[touring] a history museum that had no relevance to the present. The tour failed to provide them with any guidance and failed to explain to them how to live Islam in a milieu that had already been westernized. To him, that was a somber tour."[9] Everywhere, there seemed to be an absence of Islam: "In the lecture hall, nothing was mentioned about an Islamic economy, an Islamic state, an Islamic art; and nothing was mentioned about the position of Islam on contemporary issues." Even the very manner in which Ghannouchi grew up—as part of a polygamous family, with two different women he called "mother"—would no longer possible under Bourguiba's banning of multiple marriages.

By the time Bourguiba's reign ended nearly three decades later, Tunisia had been transformed in a way that no other Arab country was. The once-controversial Code of Personal Status, which had liberalized laws on marriage, divorce, and inheritance, had taken hold and gained widespread acceptance. The headscarf, which Islamists considered a religious obligation, had been banned in public buildings, including institutions of higher education.

This unique history and cultural context is critical to understanding the meaning of the "Islamic project" in Tunisia. When Ghannouchi and the leaders of Ennahda returned from exile (or prison), they had no organizational presence in the country. A majority of Tunisians who had come of age after the movement was dismantled had no real memory of Ennahda beyond what they had heard in the state media. Elsewhere, the situation couldn't be any more different. In Egypt, for example, Islamists had already, in a sense, claimed victory. After being released from prison in the early 1970s, they returned to preaching their message of religious renewal across the country. They began the slow, difficult work of rebuilding an organization that had effectively disappeared from public life. By the time Mubarak fell nearly 40 years later, society had been Islamized to a large degree, with religion—and, increasingly, its more conservative strains—imbuing every aspect of public life. Where the personal status code in Tunisia had become "sacred," in Egypt, Article 2 of the constitution—which enshrined the principles of sharia as the primary source of legislation—had become similarly beyond reproach. Much of civil society was Islamist in nature, composed of religious charities and foundations that served hundreds of thousands of Egyptians throughout the country. And while the Brotherhood had been blocked from the national media, Salafis had risen to prominence on the airwaves.[10]

In short, after the 2011 revolution, the Brotherhood and Salafis were, in a sense, solidifying something that was already there and had been for decades. In Tunisia, Ennahda had a fundamentally different task at hand. Any process of "Islamization" in the Arab world's most secular nation would require a re-rendering of society, something that would prove both slow and challenging, not to mention a profound threat to the country's avowedly secular elites.

The Politics of Stages

They had risen to power within a year of Ben Ali's overthrow and within a year of returning to a country they thought they had lost forever. But perhaps they, like their Egyptian counterparts, had moved too quickly. If any Islamist group had appropriated the lessons of Algeria, it was

Ennahda. Where other Islamist parties had made a habit of "losing on purpose," Ennahda in 1989 opted, in a rushed decision, to contest the vast majority of seats, despite the objections of several leading figures in the movement.[11] Not only that, they performed well beyond anyone's expectations. Officially, they won 14 percent of the vote, although the actual figure was likely significantly higher. Altogether, secular parties garnered less than 5 percent. Like in Egypt and Jordan, the Tunisian regime finally realized the extent to which Islamists had become a threat to its hold on power. The crackdown that would decimate Tunisia's Islamic movement was not far behind. Ghannouchi himself would later acknowledge that he had employed a "provocative discourse."[12] And there was little doubt: the regime had been provoked.

In quick succession, Egypt, Algeria, and Jordan, after experiencing unprecedented democratic openings, reversed course and began the descent into unbridled authoritarianism. But it was Algeria that, for the region's Islamists, was the most tragic. Never before had they stood suspended between outright victory and total destruction. "Victory is more dangerous than defeat," Abdelkader Hachani said in the days before the Algerian military made its move in January 1992. After the coup and the subsequent crackdown, Islamists adopted an increasingly cautious posture, perhaps over-learning the lessons of the past.

But that caution was of little use after Ben Ali fell in an uprising that was a surprise to the ruling regime as much as it was to Ennahda. Party leaders returned triumphant to Tunisia, with the rare legitimacy acquired from decades of torture, imprisonment, and exile. No one had suffered more. Even if society hadn't yet been Islamized, Ennahda stood out from a crowded field of dozens of parties, many of whom employed an elitist discourse and lacked a coherent ideology. Others were tarred by their association with the old order.

Another explanation, however, was more controversial: even five decades of forced secularization weren't enough to limit the appeal of political Islam. Once the regime's totalizing repression was removed, Tunisians were able to make their own choices about religion for the first time. In the months after the revolution, the early signs of what was to come were impossible to ignore. Salafis, with their trademark thick beards, had become a visible if still small minority. The headscarf, along with the more conservative *abaya*, could also be seen in growing numbers. Women protested for the right to wear the *niqab*—showing only their eyes and nothing else—at universities. Religious charities and organizations proliferated. Mosques became centers of social change as well as a prize to be fought for between competing visions of Islamism.

Caught up in a groundswell of support and Islamic sentiment, and with Tunisians hoping for a fundamental break from the old, secular regime, Ennahda found itself by far the most popular, best organized political party in the country. Before the October 2011 elections, there was some debate within Ennahda over the dangers of winning by too much, too soon. Mere months after a revolution, it would have been difficult to lose on purpose—and explain that to an excited base. As Ennahda's Noureddin Bhiri, then minister of justice, put it to me: "We can't call on people not to vote for us. There is no party that does this."[13]

He had a point. But, as in Egypt, there were other fears shaping Islamist behavior—that democratic gains were far from secure; that the old regime was preparing its return. There were hardline secularists who would seek to limit the power of Islamists and even turn again to repression if they had the opportunity. Before the uprisings, losing was the best means of survival. Now it was winning. If anyone else found their way to power, then there was simply no guarantee of what might happen.

As they saw it, Islamists' fears were soon confirmed. They saw a secular opposition that would stop at nothing to destroy them. In the tense, difficult months of early 2013, Ennahda leaders were blamed for the assassination of Chokri Belaid. They were accused of being little more than Salafis in disguise, smarter and more cunning, perhaps, but with the same ultimate, obscurantist goals. Shortly after the shocking murder of Belaid, tens of thousands took to the streets, and the trade union UGTT announced its first general strike in 34 years. Beji Caid Essebsi, the former prime minister and leader of the opposition, suggested dissolving the country's first democratically elected parliament. Ennahda felt that this was all a bit much for an assassination that it had nothing to do with.

In July 2013, a second leftist politician, Mohamed al-Brahmi, was assassinated, sparking Tunisia's most serious political crisis yet. This time, the calls for dissolving either parliament or the government, or both, became the demand of most of the secular opposition. Meanwhile, drawing inspiration from the Tamarod movement, which helped topple Morsi, Tunisia's own "Tamarod" called for Egypt-style mass protests to bring down the government. The also similarly named Salvation Front announced the campaign "Irhal"—meaning "leave" in Arabic—with the goal of sacking local and national officials appointed by Ennahda.[14]

A Clash of Cultures

If there was anywhere that the Arab uprisings might be expected to succeed, it was in Tunisia, a country that had any number of things going for it. By the region's standards, it had relatively low levels of income inequality, high educational attainment and literacy, a sizable middle class, and a homogenous population.

The country could also claim what was arguably the most moderate Islamist party in the region, Ennahda. While the group had suffered untold persecution at the hands of the authorities, many of its leading figures—including Rachid Ghannouchi—had managed to escape and set up shop in Europe, allowing them the space and time to develop their ideas and strategy in a way their Egyptian counterparts never did.

Upon returning to Tunisia, Ghannouchi and other senior officials went out of their way to strike a note of conciliation and cooperation with secular parties. In an unprecedented move, Ennahda joined forces with Ettakatol and the Congress for the Republic (CPR) to form a coalition government of Islamists, liberals, and leftists. Despite the large gap between themselves and Ennahda, CPR and Ettakatol were given veto powers over major as well as lesser appointments (in one controversial instance, CPR insisted on blocking the appointment of Tunisian-American Radwan Masmoudi as ambassador to the United States).[15]

Ennahda also backed down on three controversial clauses in the draft constitution—on sharia, gender quality, and blasphemy—after encountering opposition from civil society and the secular opposition. Ennahda's parliamentary bloc had proposed including sharia as a "source among sources [of legislation]" in the constitution. By the standards of most Arab countries, this would be considered fairly innocuous. An Islamist party, by definition, is one that believes that sharia has an important role to play in public and political life, yet here was Ennahda accepting a constitution without even a mention of sharia, despite the fact that it was by far the largest party in the country. Conservatives in Ennahda as well as many Salafis had voted for the party because they hoped it would enact "Islamic" policies and stand up for sharia. Not surprisingly, then, Ennahda found itself doing a delicate balancing act, taking care to avoid overreach while trying to reassure impatient supporters that the Islamization they were hoping for would require time and patience.

But what Ennahda did in power mattered less than who and what it was. And there was little doubt: Ennahda, for all its moderation, was still an Islamist party. Its leaders, despite their otherwise impressive efforts to stay on message, would routinely say things that sounded alarming to secularists, such as when Prime Minister Hamadi Jebali called for a sixth caliphate[16] or when Ghannouchi, in a seeming fit of anger, said that a journalist who had accused an Ennahda cabinet minister of adultery should be flogged.[17]

In the most obvious respects, polarization in Tunisia wasn't as bad as it was in some other countries, including Egypt. Few thought civil war or a military coup against the Islamist-led government was likely. But, in some ways, it was worse, or at least more intractable. In Tunisia, there are hardline secularists—so-called *laïcistes*—who have no real corollary in the rest of the region. Inspired by French-style *laïcité*, they oppose even a hint of Islam in public life, believing instead that religion should be restricted to matters of personal belief and conscience. From their perspective, *laïcistes* are right to be concerned. Islamists in Tunisia may be more constrained, considering the country's secular traditions. However, that also means that there is greater room for society to change in fundamental ways. In this sense, Tunisia is indeed a "laboratory" of sorts. Some Tunisian secularists insist that the nature of Tunisians is inclined toward liberalism. Tunisian Islamists argue that their nature is inclined toward Islamism.

Despite seemingly lower levels of polarization, then, more— potentially much more—is at stake in Tunisia. In other transitions, the changes were considerable, of course, but they were of a fundamentally different nature. The 2003 German movie *Goodbye Lenin* amusingly dramatizes the plight of a mother who falls into a coma just before the fall of the Berlin Wall. When she awakes, the doctor tells her son that major shocks might destroy her health. The son dutifully recreates the old world and limits her exposure to a new, frightening reality of capitalism and Coca-Cola billboards. The shift from socialism to the free market, whether in Eastern Europe, Latin America, or Asia, was nothing short of a transformation, but the changes under way did not in any way limit personal freedom, but rather the opposite.

In Tunisia, moving from the quasi-totalitarianism of Ben Ali to something resembling democracy meant more freedom, but there was the open question of what Tunisians would choose to do with that freedom. As we saw in previous chapters, during the repression of the 1990s and 2000s, Islamists in Egypt and Jordan made political freedom and democratization their main focus. The gradual Islamization of society—one of the primary objectives of any Islamist movement—could be made possible only if there was, first, a sufficient degree of freedom to operate, to preach, and to practice politics.

A Future of Islamization?

The fact that Islamization hadn't happened yet meant that Islamists in Tunisia would have a different focus than their counterparts elsewhere. It made little sense to prioritize Islamic law when the population wasn't "ready." Islamist movements like the Brotherhood and Ennahda believed in gradualism, that before changes happened at the level of the state, they needed first to take hold in the hearts of individuals. This is why in Egypt and Jordan, Islamists had spent decades focusing on religious education and preaching: before calling for the implementation of sharia, you needed a large enough constituency willing to support and advocate for it.

In Tunisia, Ennahda quickly found that, despite their dominant electoral position, secular parties and a vibrant civil society would push back at any perceived attempts at Islamization, particularly when it came to the constitution. The three draft clauses in question, although mild by the region's standards, provoked a firestorm of opposition, and Ennahda was forced to backtrack. Yet, despite its care to avoid overreaching, the party was accused, all the same, of harboring a radical agenda. As the prominent secular intellectual Neila Sellini told me, "we know them. We live with them. You don't really know what they're about. You fall for the double discourse!" By "you," she meant Western researchers and policymakers, and she had a point: the West wanted Ghannouchi to be more moderate than he actually was.

Ghannouchi and the leaders of Ennahda were being pragmatic. They knew full well the domestic and international constraints that were waiting for them every step of the way.[18] Ennahda officials would point out that the issue of "sharia" had simply become too divisive. Putting it in the constitution would only serve to politicize something that they hoped would, in time, become the heritage of all Tunisians. To what extent, then, was Ennahda's much remarked-on moderation a product of a genuine ideological shift, or was it a tactical accommodation with reality? Was it both? Did it even matter?

The ideological concessions, the public reassurances, the watered-down declarations of intent did not seem to have their intended effect. To his enemies, Ghannouchi was demonized as a sort of Manchurian candidate. It was his pretensions to moderation that made him so dangerous. And, increasingly, his supporters wondered if "moderation" was worth all the trouble. Many Tunisians voted for Ennahda because it was an Islamist party, not in spite of it. Wanting sharia to play a larger role in politics, they grew disappointed each time Ennahda backed down.

It was this frustration that Sheikh Habib Ellouze—one of the leaders of Ennahda's "conservative" wing—hoped to channel. In the late 1980s, he had opposed MTI's decision to drop the word "Islamic" from its name and become Ennahda. More than 20 years later, he saw little use in more dilution. When I sat down with him on the margins of a tense parliamentary session after the Belaid assassination, he insisted that everyone in the party shared the same commitment to sharia. "There aren't any of us who do not believe in the rulings of sharia (*ahkam al-sharia*). This much should be clear. All of us believe in banning alcohol one day," he told me. "What we disagree on is how best to present and express our Islamic ideas."[19] As Ellouze saw it, the liberals and moderates of Ennahda were too concerned with appeasing everyone else—secularists, the old regime, the international community—but their own supporters.

In various internal debates—such as whether sharia should be enshrined in the constitution—Ellouze and the conservatives lost by a wide margin (with about 80 percent voting "no" in an internal Shura Council vote). For Ellouze, this only offered more evidence that the party leadership was out of touch with popular sentiment. If Tunisians could choose, he argued, at least 80 percent would vote to include sharia in the constitution.[20] Despite his disagreement with the party's decision, he respected the outcome. It was Ennahda's internal democracy that allowed it to encompass these seemingly contradictory trends—a "liberal" wing represented by Sheikh Abdel Fattah Morou and a conservative one, with Ghannouchi holding forth in the center. When I met with Ellouze, he was calm and confident, despite being attacked and labeled in the press as an extremist. "If we look at the rank-and-file of the movement," he said, "you will see them calling for sharia." The future was theirs. And, because Ennahda had a higher degree of internal democracy than most parties, the sentiments of the masses would inevitably trickle up to the leadership.

Pressure was also coming from outside the movement, from Salafis on Ennahda's right flank. As Mohamed Khouja, president of Tunisia's first legal Salafi party, explained, "Ennahda supporters are leaving. They are coming to us now because they know we won't concede our project."[21] In the 2011 elections, Khouja's party—the Reform Front—ran candidates in a limited number of districts and told its supporters to vote for Ennahda everywhere else. The Salafis of the Reform Front had their differences with Ennahda, but they shared, at least in its vague outlines, a similar project. But a year and a half later, Khouja suggested it was unlikely Ennahda would receive their support a second time; Ennahda has been "too eager to please the secular parties," he told me.

In Rachid Ghannouchi, Ennahda had a towering figure, an intellectual, a strategist, and a symbol, all wrapped into one. But what held the party together more than an individual was an ideology. This—along with a commitment to internal democracy—is what allowed Ennahda, unlike some of its counterparts, to remain a truly big-tent party.

The liberals of Ennahda either didn't feel particularly strongly about applying sharia or opposed such talk altogether. Some, like Sheikh Morou, believed that Tunisia, in any case, was already an Islamic state. "Sharia is already implemented in Tunisia," he explained. "There is freedom of religious practice, the mosques are there, no one denies anyone the right to pray or proselytize."[22]

In a country as secular as Tunisia once was, this could be enough to make one an Islamist (Morou probably wouldn't feel comfortable in the Egyptian Brotherhood). It was all relative. There were the *laïcistes* who wished to privatize Islam, keeping it out of public view. Not only did some oppose any mention of sharia in the constitution, but they also objected to the milder compromise clause stating that Islam was the religion of the state.[23] If you believed, on the other hand, that Islamic values should in some way be reflected in public life, there was nowhere really to go except Ennahda. For some of the liberals in the party, like Zied Ladhari, Islam was "a source of inspiration," and that was sufficiently distinctive in a society where other parties saw Islam as a "source of social regression, underdevelopment, and a non-democratic culture."[24] Nearly all of Ennahda's leaders are practicing Muslims. Before and after major meetings, they join together for prayer as a group. Islam is their starting point, even if the end point—the specific positions they advocate—may differ. In a political party, particularly a mass organization like Ennahda, this sense of solidarity and shared purpose is critical to maintaining internal cohesion.

The Problem of Polarization

During democratic transitions, it is generally better for the stronger parties to emphasize inclusion and to share power. Ideological parties should postpone divisive battles over identity and instead build consensus around the requirements of state-building and institutional reform. Exclusionary politics runs the risk of pushing weaker parties outside the democratic process, providing them ample incentive to play "spoiler" and threaten the transition.[25]

However, in environments of intense polarization, even the more well-intentioned attempts at consensus-building can fall short and even backfire. For many if not most secularists, it is not only about what Islamists do; it is about who they are. As we saw in the previous chapter, even at their most conciliatory, Islamists do not operate within the confines of liberal democracy. In countries with a secular tradition like Tunisia, the gulf can be especially wide.

Tunisia, for all its troubles, was generally seen as the closest thing the Arab Spring had to a success story, or even a "model," at least compared to Egypt, which often appeared on the brink of state collapse. When some in the Muslim Brotherhood looked to Tunisia, though, they begged to differ—at least before the 2013 military coup turned things upside down. As they saw it, Ennahda's eagerness for compromise came at a price. As one senior Brotherhood official remarked, "Ghannouchi tried to please everyone so no one is pleased. He would say things that even [Egyptian liberal leader] Mohamed ElBaradei wouldn't say, like how Tunisia's personal status code was part of the overall framework of sharia." "But did it help him get more popularity?" He asked. "Every time he makes concessions, they're not happy. They want more, and it angers his own supporters."[26]

The argument here was that moderation—if by that one meant Ennahda's willingness to soften its Islamist edges—simply did not pay. Ennahda was giving up some of what it stood for while receiving little in return. If anything, the secular opposition pointed to Ghannouchi's statements as evidence of insincerity and bad faith. He was speaking the language of compromise now because he needed to. But once Ennahda solidified its hold on power, they reasoned, it would gradually seek to alter the nature of society and perhaps even that of the state. They had a point.

When Ennahda first rose to power in October 2011, it was operating within a particular set of constraints. There was a real secular opposition. And there was a real secular tradition that couldn't simply be undone overnight. Meanwhile, the international community—and international donors—were watching, and they had little patience for excessive displays of ideological fervor.

In any case, Ennahda officials, even the conservatives among them, understood which priorities took precedence during a difficult transition. "Freedom" remained the number-one concern. Without it—or if it was taken away from them again—then nothing else would matter. "If we don't realize our freedoms," Sheikh Morou told me in January 2013, "we will not be able to realize any gains, whether Islamic, democratic, or whatever."[27] There was still a fear that the old regime was reconstituting itself in the form of Nidaa Tounes, a coalition of parties and politicians sharing little besides an animus toward the governing Islamists. In addition to assorted liberals and leftists, it included a significant number of old regime officials, including its leader, former Prime Minister Beji

Caid Essebsi. They tended to view Ennahda not just as an opponent to be challenged in elections but as an existential threat to be defeated. "They [Ennahda] exist outside of Tunisian history," as Mohsen Marzouk memorably put it.[28]

As long as politics remained so raw and existential, it was unlikely Ennahda would venture into more divisive territory. Now wasn't the time to get distracted with banning alcohol or putting sharia in the constitution. What was needed now—before anything else—was ensuring the party's survival and completing the transition period. They needed to win the upcoming parliamentary elections, which would allow the party to appoint more of its members to senior government posts. Once democracy was accepted as "the only game in town," then Islamists could begin to use their electoral mandate to push more controversial initiatives. This, again, was a testament to Ennahda's caution and pragmatism. Others, though, saw it less positively: this, they said, was the "politics of stages."

At the start of Tunisia's transition, it seemed like an "Islamic state," or anything resembling it, was as far away as ever. Politics was the art of the possible, and so little of what Islamists wanted—and have wanted for decades—seemed possible considering the constraints. This is why the majority of Salafis refused to enter the electoral process. As a leading Salafi preacher in the town of Bizerte explained it to me: "In politics, we would be required to make concessions on the fundamental principles we believe in. You can't be who you are. But it's the very fact that we haven't changed, regardless of the circumstances, that has led people to embrace us."[29] Indeed, nothing about the constitution or the country's institutions suggested a bright future for the Islamization of the state or its constituent bodies. But that it wasn't possible now was precisely what worried secularists: what if it became possible *later*?

It was here that the far left and the far right converged, one in despair and the other in hope. They both saw the possibility that Tunisian society could be reordered. The former feared it; Salafis, meanwhile, anticipated it with a sense of assuredness. They could wait. "Ennahda believe in sharia even if they don't always admit it. What the secularists say is right!" joked the Salafi preacher. Of course, it was difficult to know for sure. There were too many variables to predict how an entire society might evolve. But Islamization, to varying degrees, had taken hold nearly everywhere else in the region. Why should Tunisia be any different?

In this respect, ideological and, by extension, political polarization was embedded within Tunisian society. Attitudes were "inelastic," meaning that what Islamists did or didn't do would have little effect on how their staunchest opponents viewed them. What frightened secularists most wasn't what Ennahda had already done, but what it might do.

Understood this way, the deep polarization that emerged early on in Tunisia's transition was inevitable. Even if Ennahda did all the right things, it wouldn't be enough: the problem wasn't just a matter of politics but of irreconcilable worldviews. The ideological divides of the Arab world are unique for precisely this reason. Illiberal democracies exist all over the world, but, whether of the leftist or right-wing varieties, their illiberalism is usually negotiable. Restricting personal rights or freedoms is a product of the desire to consolidate power, rather than stemming from any particular ideological conviction. Yet, illiberalism is central to the Islamist raison d'être: they're *supposed* to be illiberal.

9

The Past and Future of Political Islam

I BEGAN WRITING THIS book before the start of the Arab uprisings. It made little sense, then, to focus on the doctrine and ideology of Islamist parties. Of course, what Islamists believed mattered, but it mattered less than their political context—the repression they faced from their own regimes and the constraints imposed by an international community wary of their rise. The earlier idealism of Islamist groups—when they, naïvely in retrospect, made sharia law a call to arms—gave way to the daily grind of survival. The fear that the secret police could come at dawn, at any time unannounced, had a way of concentrating the mind on what really mattered. There was little time for long-term planning and strategy. Survival became a means as well as an end.

Even the self-conscious efforts of Islamist groups to moderate and modernize their political programs were essentially reactive exercises. They were, in effect, *forced* to moderate by their circumstances. Little thought was expended on the implications of so publicly diluting the Islamist contents of their message. Whether in Egypt, Tunisia, Jordan, or any number of other countries, they simply could not envision a world in which they might govern. And if power remained elusive, there was little reason to think about what "Islamic democracy" was or what it could be. Their ideal, whatever it was, ceased to exist except as a vague desire far off into the future.

When in power, all of this changes. The constraints on Islamist ambition—whether from within or without—are gradually removed. Repeated electoral contests offer them a mandate to take power and wield it. But, at least at the beginning, the imperative of survival—this time in the guise of acquiring and securing state power—continues to dominate. That the Morsi government did not survive, succumbing to the military's machinations, suggests that the fixation on survival, if not necessarily the resulting policies, was appropriate.

When trying to understand Islamist parties, it is easy to get caught up in the power plays, in the cynical electoral maneuvers, in the messy, everyday political battles. But that shouldn't obscure the fact that, in today's Arab world, belief and ideology matter more than ever before. In the decades before the Arab Spring, the gulf between rulers and the ruled grew wider and more intractable. To be sure, Arab regimes weren't truly "secular." Islam was instrumentalized by the state to advance political objectives and consolidate power. Religious institutions were controlled by government appointees, with clerics becoming just another arm of the state. But Arab leaders' vision of the role of religion in political life differed, sometimes dramatically, from that of their populations. They sought to constrain and, at times, eliminate explicitly political expressions of religion.

These pseudo-secular regimes that portrayed themselves as progressive, liberal, and pro-women's rights were growing increasingly detached from a public mood that sought more, rather than less, mixing of religion and politics. In those rare occasions where meaningful elections were held, citizens made those preferences all too clear. With democratization, what voters think and believe matters more than ever. This needs to be factored in to our understanding of how Islamist parties are likely to evolve in countries experiencing political openings. Just as the ideological inclinations of ordinary voters becomes more important, so too do those of Islamist politicians themselves. They may be pragmatic and all too willing to compromise, but this should not obscure the fact that Islamists have a distinctive worldview. That it may not be clear or well defined does not mean it should be cast aside as irrelevant. In this book, I have tried to document how Islamist groups in Egypt and Jordan moderated not because of democracy, but *before* it. There was never any reason to believe that this process of moderation would continue indefinitely under an entirely different set of circumstances. Some Islamist parties, as in Tunisia, are more willing to come to terms with liberal democracy than others. But all Islamist parties, by definition, are at least *somewhat* illiberal. That illiberalism will inevitably find expression in their positions and policies, to varying degrees.

Islamists' commitment to pragmatism and their commitment to a distinctive, if vague, ideological project make the move to the right both more tempting and more likely. They may, for example, come under pressure from Salafi parties to demonstrate their Islamic *bona fides*. Similarly, a leader in the Brotherhood or Ennahda may feel a need to push for "Islamic" legislation on a given issue because that's what his conservative base demands. The politicization of religion can be used to bolster support among the rank-and-file. It is a way to consolidate, justify, and legitimate political power. This becomes more useful the more unpopular Islamists become. If Islamists cannot point to tangible economic gains—if they can't, in other words, fix the potholes—then the temptation to cloak themselves in religion becomes all the more irresistible.

Religion, particularly the more it is politicized, becomes a marker of difference. Here, the underlying patterns of political competition become critical. Party systems are products of a country's particular history. In their seminal 1967 study *Party Systems and Voter Alignments*, Seymour Martin Lipset and Stein Rokkan argue that the process of state formation as well as fundamental shifts in economic structures— the Industrial Revolution and accompanying urbanization—gave rise to differences among citizens that provoked lasting cleavages.[1] That economic cleavages are paramount in most Western democracies, then, is no accident, given the particular sequencing of events in the modernization process. Similarly, it was in Catholic-majority coun- tries that clericalism and anticlericalism became a major dimension of conflict. On the other hand, where the Reformation succeeded in displacing the Catholic Church and its role in economic and politi- cal life, religious divides, while still relevant, tended to fade into the background.[2]

Parties decide what issues to prioritize in order to distinguish them- selves from the competition. It is this process of parties interacting with the electorate and each other that, over time, produces the party system. "Class is salient in any society," Przeworski and Sprague note, "if, when, and only to the extent to which it is important to political parties which mobilize workers."[3] This is how "outbidding" occurs. Parties inject cleavages into politics. Those cleavages, in turn, become more salient, forcing other parties to respond to and address them in the public arena.

By the time Egypt and Tunisia experienced their revolutions, the Islamist–secular divide was already well entrenched. Many hoped that democratic transitions would allow Arab societies to put the ideological polarization of the past behind them. For a brief moment, it seemed like they might. When the myriad parties of the Muslim Brotherhood-led Democratic Alliance sat down to plan their electoral strategy in the lead-up to the 2011 elections, they found that they agreed on most things, at least in the abstract. Shadi Taha, a leader in the al-Ghad party, amusingly described it this way: "With all the parties, we [met and] said what is our program. Let's see, who's against the fact that we need reform in the police department? Nobody? Okay. Who's against the fact that the judicial system in Egypt should be independent? Okay, nobody."[4]

After the uprising, Egypt's economic situation deteriorated considerably. For most ordinary Egyptians, this was the abiding concern. Egypt as well as Tunisia would have seemed particularly ripe for economic, class-based appeals. For their part, candidates routinely promised more jobs, better wages, and campaigns to root out poverty, corruption, and any number of other social ills. But they were, in the end, promising much the same things. In societies where most parties seem to have similar—and similarly vague—economic programs, Islamists distinguish themselves by underscoring their Islamism. (Liberals distinguish themselves by underscoring their anti-Islamism.) Doing so becomes even more attractive if Islamist leaders themselves are driven by long-held convictions about promoting the role of religion in society. This is what the coming together of pragmatism, expediency, and ideology looks like.

The key in all of this is the extent to which Islamist parties are constrained by politics. Democratization removes at least some of those constraints, allowing Islamists to more faithfully express their original core mission of Islamization. This is what the academic literature on "post-Islamism"—the notion that some groups have, over time, shed their ideological commitments to the extent that they outgrow the original label—seems to miss. Cavatorta writes, for instance, that "post-Islamism is truly alive in Ennahda, a political party with virtually no Islamic agenda."[5] But some of the factors that have transformed Ennahda—the experience of exile and repression and its remoteness from power—are no longer there. To be sure, there are limits to how far Islamists can go in a country like Tunisia, with its organized minority of French-style secularists who advocate the privatization of religion. But they will test those limits, pulling back and pushing forward over time.

In Egypt and much of the rest of the region, even liberals express their commitment to Islamic law as a source of legislation. The more conservative nature of society means that the Muslim Brotherhood—as well as Salafis—face less obvious ideological constraints in a democratic setting. They can go further because society has already been Islamized to a significant degree. In one particularly interesting example, the anti-Islamist National Salvation Front (NSF), at the height of its conflict with President Morsi, accepted an invitation to meet with a group of Salafi clerics. Not only did the front seek to reassure its interlocutors that it had nothing against Islam or Islamists, but one NSF leader insisted that Egyptians were all effectively Islamists anyway.[6] (This echoed former liberal darling Abul Futouh's claim during his presidential campaign that Egyptians were all Salafis because they were loyal to the Salaf, the earliest generations of Muslims.) Of course, this rightward thrust would come to an end with the July 3, 2013 military coup.

Far from unique, this rightward ideological thrust in Arab politics confirms a pattern common to transitioning countries. While mature democracies rarely fight each other, young democracies—especially those in the throes of economic crisis—are particularly susceptible to ideological appeals, whether Islamism or hyper-nationalism.[7] In Egypt, the old regime never went away and the army retained the ability to intervene if it felt Islamists were going too far. It was this part that Islamists underestimated. In the aftermath of the coup, a large section of the population embraced a different kind of far-right politics, which included army worship and authoritarianism, xenophobic nationalism, and a desire for revenge against the Brotherhood.

In one excellent study, the political scientists Edward Mansfield and Jack Snyder argue that "incomplete democratic transitions . . . increase the chance of involvement in international war in countries where government institutions are weak at the outset of the transition."[8] What results are what they aptly call "wars of democratization." They focus on interstate wars, but the same can be said for wars within. When Morsi and the Brotherhood were at their weakest, they beat the war drums, organizing a mass rally calling for "jihad" in Syria. After Morsi was overthrown, the military-backed government called for a war on "terrorists," by which they meant not just militants in Sinai but also the Muslim Brotherhood.

The fundamental problem is one that Samuel Huntington pointed to decades ago in his seminal work *Political Order in Changing Societies.* In modernizing countries, the process of urbanization and a rapid surge in educational attainment produce increasingly mobilized populations. Institutions, however, are too weak to meet rising popular demands and expectations. Ideology can fill the gap, providing meaning and purpose where accountability is weak. It is no accident that civil strife and political violence are regular features of post-revolutionary situations from the French Revolution onwards. In Britain, for example, the move to universal suffrage coincided with the British Empire's growing imperial ambitions, including launching the Crimean War.[9]

Politicians use ideology—whether populist nationalism or Islamism, or some combination of both—to channel the energies of a restless, frustrated citizenry in the hope of diverting attention away from their own record of governance. Politicians and popular movements feed off each other's nationalism, while politicians try to outbid each other in their displays of ideological fervor. Foreign adventurism and domestic populism are linked together. Nationalism needs enemies abroad as well as at home. These are the dangers of mass politics. In other regions, such as the Balkans and the former Soviet Union, the targets were often ethnic and religious minorities. In Africa, democratization has often fueled and entrenched ethnic divisions (with political parties forming along ethnic lines).

Seen in such a light, the ideological polarization that has plagued post-revolutionary Egypt and Tunisia is not so surprising. But it is also worth emphasizing that the divisions between Islamists and liberals are not manufactured; they are based around fundamental differences on questions of nationhood and national identity. Arab societies will need to work them out through an uneven, painful, and sometimes bloody process of democratic bargaining and institution building. The divide can be better managed, but it is unlikely to disappear as a major and per-haps defining point of contention. Just as economic cleavages became entrenched in Western democracies, ideological cleavages around the role of religion in public life are solidifying themselves across the Middle East. Once entrenched, such cleavages are difficult to undo. It might be dispir-iting to say so, but the unity on display in Tahrir Square during 18 days of revolt was not a promise of something to come, but an aberration.

In this sense, the very existence of sizable Islamist parties helps to explain both the durability of authoritarianism and the profound diffi-culty of establishing democracy even after autocrats fall. The possibility that Islamist parties will win in free elections provokes anti-democratic actions on the part of an array of domestic and international actors. This was long the case before the Arab Spring and it was confirmed—again—by the military coup in Egypt, which enjoyed near-unanimous support from the country's liberals. In Tunisia, where Ennahda ruled in coalition with secular parties and made major concessions on the constitution, the opposition, made up of liberals, leftists, and old regime elements, sought to dissolve both the democratically elected parliament and government. Even in the best of circumstances, then, ideological cleavages—amplified by widespread economic discontent—threatened to derail a democratic transition.

As Robert Dahl argued in his classic *Polyarchy*: "Tolerance and mutual security are more likely to develop among a small elite sharing similar perspectives."[10] This is what the Arab world always seemed to lack, both before and after the Arab uprisings.

The Role of the International Community

As we saw earlier, Islamist parties developed something of an obsession with the role of Western powers in supporting democracy—or, more likely, not supporting it. They were fighting on two fronts, not just against repressive regimes but their international backers as well. This made Arab regimes seem more durable than they actually were and the task of unseating them more daunting. Coupled with their characteristic cau-tion and seeming aversion to power, this prevented Islamists from play-ing the role that opposition parties are generally expected to play. They could wait, and so they did. None of the Arab uprisings were launched by the Islamist opposition.

The Tunisian revolution—and then the revolts that followed—seemed to shatter the illusion that Arabs had to wait. Even if America was not with them—and, at least at first, it wasn't—they could defy expectations, bringing about their own revolutions. Even in Tunisia, where little was at stake for the United States, the Obama administration failed to side with the revolution until the very end. As late as two days before Ben Ali's fall, Secretary of State Hillary Clinton was still saying that the United States was "not taking sides."[11] But it was easy to argue that Tunisia was exceptional. The United States could live without the Tunisian regime, but could it live without a staunch ally like Hosni Mubarak, a dogged opponent of Iran and stalwart supporter of the peace treaty with Israel? But, here too, Mubarak's longtime ties with Western governments would prove insufficient.

There was a temptation, then, from the very start, to discount the importance of external powers both during and after the Arab Spring. It became commonplace to hear some variation of the following: that the Arab uprisings were a truly indigenous movement and that Arabs, themselves, did not want foreign powers to "interfere." That would, the thinking went, go against the very spirit of the revolutions. President Obama and other senior officials repeatedly insisted that this was not about America. As Clinton remarked, "these revolutions are not ours. They are not by us, for us, or against us."[12] In reality, it *was* partly about America, not just because of the past U.S. role in backing Arab dictatorships but because of the critical role it would continue to play.

For both better and worse, international actors not only influenced the first phase of the Arab Spring but, in several countries, defined it. In Libya, Yemen, and Syria, Western and regional powers in the Gulf played significant, even decisive roles. In the one stalled revolution—Bahrain—it was Saudi Arabia's military intervention that quelled the uprising and kept the ruling family afloat. Even in Egypt, the 2011 uprising was effectively internationalized, with foreign media devoting countless hours to covering every turn and, in the process, putting the issue at the top of the Western policy agenda. The United States also exerted considerable pressure on the Egyptian military to refrain from using force against protesters.

When the uprisings first broke, Western officials were heartened that the protests focused primarily on domestic issues. While protesters were no doubt angry over the lack of "bread and freedom," the third element—the demand for dignity—was more difficult to characterize. Here, Egypt's pro-Western policies and perceived subservience to the United States figured prominently, including in the defining chant that echoed throughout Tahrir Square the night Mubarak fell: "You're Egyptian; raise your head up high." Over the 18 days of protest, numerous chants attacked Mubarak for being a lackey of the United States and Israel (one such chant claimed that Mubarak understood only one language—Hebrew).

In Egypt and Tunisia, what the United States did—and did not do— continued to matter well after the initial uprisings. Newly elected governments facing deteriorating economic conditions at home needed as much outside support as they could get, in the form of direct financial assistance, loans, trade, asset recovery, and private investment. Even during its own recession, the United States, with its vested interest in regional stability, important convening role, and influence within international financial institutions, would be critical in supporting economic growth.

A growing academic literature has pointed to the role of international actors in bringing down autocrats. In their recent book, Steven Levitsky and Lucan Way provide extensive empirical support to what many have long argued. They write: "It was an externally driven shift in the cost of suppression, not changes in domestic conditions, that contributed most centrally to the demise of authoritarianism in the 1980s and 1990s." Levitsky and Way find that "states' vulnerability to Western democratization pressure . . . was often decisive."[13]

The outsized role of external actors was confirmed, once again, during the July 2013 military coup and its tragic aftermath. In the two-and-a-half years leading up to the coup, the United States had several opportunities, particularly during 2012, to exert pressure on the Supreme Council of the Armed Forces but was unwilling to do so, sending the message that the army could get away with nearly anything (including, apparently, a military coup). After the coup and subsequent crackdown against the Brotherhood and supporters of Mohamed Morsi, the U.S.

response was muted. Despite a legal obligation to suspend aid in the event of a coup, the Obama administration, along with most of Congress, insisted on the importance of maintaining the flow of military aid. A month after the military's intervention, Secretary of State John Kerry appeared to endorse the coup, saying that the army was "in effect, restoring democracy" and averting civil war.[14]

While the United States would remain a critical player, the Obama administration was making a concerted effort to reduce its footprint in the Middle East. The phrase "leading from behind" may have been pejorative, but it captured a very real shift in American policy. Nina Hachigian and David Shorr called it the "Responsibility Doctrine," a strategy of "prodding other influential nations to help shoulder the burdens of fostering a stable, peaceful world order."[15] But in stepping back, the United States left a power vacuum, with many hoping to project their influence. During Morsi's tenure, Qatar became the single largest contributor of financial assistance to Egypt, providing about $8 billion in loans and grants (with Turkey offering another $2 billion).[16] Just days after the military made its move, it was Saudi Arabia, the United Arab Emirates, and Kuwait which pledged $12 billion to the new army-appointed government, providing a crucial economic lifeline. It was transparently political, but it also made perfect sense.

The new Middle East was seeing the birth of a contentious, polarized mass politics with Egyptian and Tunisian parties and politicians mobilizing supporters like never before. But it wasn't and couldn't be that simple. The region was becoming a center of proxy struggle with a seemingly endless number of players jockeying for influence. For Islamists, this presented a number of challenges. They may have enjoyed popular support at home, but, in the conservative Gulf monarchies and the broader international community, Islamist parties have been treated with considerable suspicion, if not outright hostility.

Islamist groups often find themselves in an odd position, doing a delicate dance between two audiences that want two completely different things. They have a long history of vehemently anti-Western and anti-Israel positions, including refusing to accept the Jewish state's right to exist. From the very beginning, the Muslim Brotherhood had a strong anticolonial bent and even sent volunteers to Palestine to fight against Jewish rebels in 1948. Mohamed Morsi, in particular, could claim a long history of inflammatory remarks. While some Brotherhood leaders, particularly lead strategist Khairat al-Shater, were less strident in their condemnations in public and with their conspiracy theories in private, Morsi was not. In a conversation a few months after the revolution, Morsi volunteered his views on the 9/11 terrorist attacks without prompting. "When you come and tell me that the plane hit the tower like a knife in butter," he told me, shifting to English, "then you are insulting us. How did the plane cut through the steel like this? Something must have happened from the inside. It's impossible."[17]

Echoing anti-Semitic tropes, Morsi, before he had any inkling of becoming president, called Zionists "descendants of apes and pigs" on a television program in 2010. But what Morsi himself believes in his heart and what he actually did in power were two different things. In power, groups like the Brotherhood have little choice but to dial down the rhetoric and avoid alienating the United States and other powerful allies. As long as Islamists in government are dependent on the international community for economic survival, their freedom of movement on foreign policy—and to a lesser extent on domestic policy—will remain constrained. When repression returns, as it did in Egypt, Islamists revert to a more schizophrenic posture, calling on the United States and other international actors to back their democratic struggle while, almost in the same breath, attacking the United States for betraying those same values and siding with autocrats as it always has.

While President Morsi's foreign policy departed from Mubarak's in significant ways, it was far from the wholesale shift that some of his supporters were hoping for. In his year in office, Morsi forged a positive working relationship with the Obama administration and played a critical role in brokering a resolution to the Gaza crisis of November 2012. The plaudits for responsible, mature foreign policymaking were quick to follow. To be sure, Morsi brought Egypt closer to Hamas, but he did so in a way that fell well short of fundamentally challenging the U.S.-led regional order. The model for Morsi was Turkey or Qatar, countries that were tied to the United States militarily and strategically but were both able and willing to establish themselves as independent, assertive regional powers, despite intermittent American grumbling.

The red lines were clear enough, and they included respecting the Camp David peace treaty and cooperating with Israel on security. At times, Morsi seemed uncomfortable with his new, rather constrained role. In one instance, Morsi's address to the United Nations in September 2012 had included a line endorsing the Arab Peace Initiative, which would pave the way for the recognition of Israel. The line was circulated to the press in Morsi's prepared remarks, but in his actual speech as delivered, he skipped the line.[18] Apparently, this was one step too far.

Islamists' Israel Problem

There was a time when Islamists would speak of liberating "every inch" of Palestinian land. In mass rallies, Hamas was hailed, suicide bombing supported, and Israel's destruction pledged. Islamists had long staked their credibility on the refusal to compromise and recognize the "Zionist entity." When I first started conducting research for this book—before the thought of Islamists coming to power was even a possibility—I would prod Brotherhood leaders in Egypt and Jordan on questions of Israel and foreign policy. To me, this always seemed to be the fundamental obstacle to U.S.-Islamist engagement. The United States could bear, as it had for decades, domestic repression, rigged elections, and discrimination against women and minorities. To be sure, Washington always questioned whether Islamists' religious commitments could coexist with respect for pluralism and basic freedoms. But what the United States really feared were the kinds of foreign policies Islamists were likely to pursue if they ever assumed power.

The international community realized that it could learn to live with Islamists, whose willingness, when in power, to compromise and eschew ideology often shows itself more in foreign than domestic policy. When they were in opposition, it was nearly the reverse. Islamists ceaselessly attacked existing regimes for their subservience to the United States and Israel. They would often tie foreign policy to the domestic, arguing that it was Arab regimes' very closeness to the United States that required them to silence domestic opposition. In some countries, like Jordan, these arguments were convincing because they happened to be true. In 1989, Jordan held free elections for the first time in decades, with Islamists and nationalists winning the majority of seats. But with peace with Israel on the horizon, King Hussein grew increasingly autocratic, dismissing the parliament and enacting a new electoral law to limit Islamist power at the polls. It worked, and a parliament—dominated by regime loyalists—ratified the peace treaty in 1994.

Islamist critiques had broad resonance in most Arab countries, where popular opinion had long been implacably hostile to U.S. policy and to Israel's very existence. Islamist groups did not create the anti-Israel sentiment that exists in Arab societies; they simply reflected and amplified it, and were more than comfortable using it for political gain. In a 2005 Pew Global Attitudes survey, 99 percent of Jordanians polled were found to hold a "very unfavorable" opinion of Jews.[19] The other 1 percent held "somewhat unfavorable" views. Even in Morocco, home to the Arab world's largest Jewish community, the figure was 88 percent.

What Islamists, or really anyone else for that matter, believe in their hearts and what they do in power can sometimes seem like the province of alternate universes. When I asked Islamist leaders over the course of the 2000s how they would deal with Israel—if they were ever given the opportunity to govern—their replies could be strident. When he was general guide of the Brotherhood, Mahdi Akef told me angrily that "of course" they would cancel the peace treaty.[20] The more pragmatic among them adopted a different tone, usually one of resignation. They were aware of the constraints, they insisted; they were "realistic" and would deal with such issues "when the time came." One senior IAF official in Jordan put it this way: "If we must, we will always, at the very least, believe and long for the liberation of Palestine in our own hearts."

The United States and International Pressure

It is in the realm of foreign policy that the dissonance between ideology and practice is the most striking but also the least surprising. Islamist parties in government simply cannot do the things they might like to do in an ideal world; the structure of the regional and international order cannot allow it. As long as countries like Egypt and Tunisia are dependent on Western powers for economic survival, there will be limits to how far elected governments, Islamist or otherwise, can go. However, if that dependency for whatever reason weakens, then Islamist parties will have greater freedom of movement on foreign policy. And it is then that we might expect to see a more ideological, assertive foreign policy on their part. Ideology, to express itself, needs to be freed of its various constraints.

Some of these same constraints are present in the domestic realm as well. In their desire to be perceived as mature, responsible actors, Islamist groups are, again, limited. That said, these constraints have less force. As long as Islamists are willing to "behave" on the regional stage, they are likely to be given considerable latitude at home, as was the case during Morsi's stint in power. In its broad outlines, this is not too dissimilar to the bargain that had been struck for decades. Arab governments would do America's bidding in the region; in return, the United States would turn a blind eye to the suppression of domestic dissent. The Arab Spring demonstrated the shortsightedness of the "stability paradigm" that had animated U.S. and European policy for a half-century. Regimes that once seemed resilient crumbled more quickly than anyone could have imagined. If any lesson was to be learned, it was that human rights and democratization would need to be prioritized after the Obama administration had—hoping to distinguish itself from its predecessors—deemphasized their importance. But the reorientation that many in both the region and within the foreign policy community had hoped for did not come to pass. In most Arab countries, with the exception of Libya, the Obama administration was content to tinker around the margins of existing policies. This *laissez-faire* approach produced its own set of consequences.

In Egypt, the United States failed to put any significant pressure on the Supreme Council of the Armed Forces, which dominated—and mismanaged and corrupted—Egypt's transition in those early, critical days after the revolution. The United States wagered that a military-led transition would facilitate (and manage) the democratization process while safeguarding American interests. SCAF, though, grew increasingly autocratic, culminating in one very bad week in June 2012, when SCAF and its allies dissolved parliament, reinstated martial law, and decreed a constitutional addendum stripping the presidency of many of its powers.

The precedent had been set: even the most egregious violations of the democratic process would receive little more than the usual, bland expressions of concern and disapproval. America's unwillingness to pressure SCAF would make it all the more difficult for the United States to hold future Islamist-led governments to democratic standards. SCAF wasn't elected. How, then, could the United States justify exerting more pressure, say by freezing bilateral assistance to the country's first democratically elected government?

While President Obama, in particular, had little interest in a proactive policy in Egypt or elsewhere in the region, there were limits on how much any U.S. administration could involve itself in Egypt's internal affairs. Members of Congress had little reason to push the administration to change course, given the scant domestic support for more robust engagement. Within Egypt, anti-Americanism, already quite high under Mubarak, continued to get worse. It reached a fever pitch during and after the July 2013 coup. (On August 8, for example, the state-owned daily *al-Akhbar* ran with the front-page headline "Egypt refuses advice of the American Satan"[21]). The rise of ultra-nationalist sentiment meant that the international community would have to tread carefully.

The unwillingness or inability to use American leverage to pressure Arab governments, including those with Islamist leanings, comes at a cost. The early chapters in this book considered how repression, or the threat of it, shapes and constrains the behavior of Islamist parties. Where Western governments are actively engaged, international pressure can potentially serve as a substitute for the threat of regime repression. The United States, in particular, can provide a credible threat of sanction by suspending or canceling much-needed financial assistance. Such a punitive approach can backfire, of course, considering the understandable sensitivities over outside interference. A better alternative is "positive conditionality"—providing economic and political incentives for governments to meet explicit, measurable benchmarks on democratic reform.[22]

A model for what this might look like is Turkey. After coming to power in 2002, the Islamist-rooted AKP passed a series of far-reaching reforms that moved Turkey further along the democratic path. The prospect of EU membership played a crucial role in providing incentives for the AKP to pursue difficult but necessary changes, including revising the penal code, easing restrictions on freedom of expression, reining in the power of the military, and expanding rights for the Kurdish minority. After the negotiations with the EU faltered, the AKP government seemed to lose interest in democratization, increasingly adopting illiberal and authoritarian practices.

The EU has the ability to "embed" countries within a thick regional order. No comparable mechanism exists in the Arab world. Yet the template is relevant for understanding how the United States might bind struggling democracies within a mutually beneficial regional order. That the United States appears unwilling to play such a role means that Islamist parties—pushed by their Salafi competitors and empowered by conservative electorates—are likely to veer rightward and overreach if and when they reach power, alienating old and new allies in the process. As we saw in Egypt during Morsi's tenure, the governance failures of Islamist parties can have devastating effects on the course of a country's democratic transition.

Faith and the Islamist Project

When Rachid Ghannouchi wrote *Public Liberties in the Islamic State*, he was writing about an idea. It was an exercise in political theory—in other words, the sort of thing you did in a room outside the glare of politics. There are two questions then: what do Islamists want? And, is it possible? The answer to the latter question will vary widely from country to country. In Tunisia, at least at the time of writing, the state that Ghannouchi envisioned when he was in prison and later in exile was simply not within the realm of possibility.

Ghannouchi's state had sharia at its center. In that hypothetical state, elected representatives pledged to uphold the ideal of sharia and, in the process, became more than just parliamentarians. They were, in effect, God's vicegerents. But Tunisia, unlike most Arab countries, had a significant minority that refused to begin from that starting point. In Egypt, by comparison, even the most ostensibly "secular" parties went out of their way to affirm their commitment to the principles of sharia being the primary source of law.

In Tunisia, the "Islamic project" had only just begun. Speed is less of an issue because the groundwork for a more explicitly Islamic democracy hadn't been laid. Tunisia experienced a long period of forced seculari- zation, and that cannot be done away with overnight. Islamists were nearly nonexistent for 20 years. This may help explain Ennahda's gradu- alism and greater willingness to work with leftist and liberal parties. The movement seems to realize that its time simply has not come yet.

Despite regime repression, Egypt, first under Sadat and then Mubarak, witnessed a slow but striking Islamization of the social, cultural, and religious spheres. When the Brotherhood came to power in 2012, their longer-term time horizon had been cut. If not now, when? There simply wasn't much more to do on the grassroots level. And if anything, the longer the democratic transition went on, they reasoned, the more time liberals would have to organize and make their case to the Egyptian people (and perhaps to the army).[23] Ultimately, however, the experiment came to a premature end. Morsi's brief stint in power was inconclusive, with both sides wondering—or asserting—what would have been.

With the economy deteriorating and polarization worsening—par- ticularly after the presidential palace clashes of December 2012—the Morsi government, had, in the words of one Brotherhood official, "re- turned to the mentality of the mihna," referring to the period of per- secution under the Nasser regime.[24] For liberals too, December 5, 2012 was, in some ways, the point of no return.[25] In the pitched battles of that day, each side would claim its own martyrs. For the first time, it was Egyptians against other Egyptians, fanning fears of civil war.

Believing more than ever that the opposition was out to destroy it, the Brotherhood was once again focused on one thing—survival and self-preservation. Like Ennahda in Tunisia, the Brotherhood was tech- nically in power. They had won five consecutive elections—one presi- dential election, two parliamentary elections (lower and upper house), and two referendums—but that wasn't enough. They had assumed the presidency with FJP members at the helm of at least a quarter of the ministries. But the institutional constraints were as constraining as ever. There were new Islamist elites at the top rung of the state, but the ma- chinery of the state—bloated and corrupt to the core—remained much the same. "Suppose you are a cabinet minister and everyone underneath you is resisting you," was how the FJP's Amr Darrag, the secretary- general of the constituent assembly and later minister of international cooperation, put it to me just months before the coup.[26]

Increasingly, over the course of Egypt's troubled transition, the Muslim Brotherhood allowed itself to be driven by paranoia. When Morsi was sworn in as Egypt's head of state, Brotherhood members were buoyed by what seemed like redemption, but they also saw their fears confirmed. As one senior Morsi advisor explained, "when we first got in [the presidential palace], they gave us handwritten notes rather than proper permits [for entry]. What does that tell you? We walked into the presidency and realized there wasn't a presidency."[27]

President Morsi—described by those close to him as "doing things by the book"—decided to work within the state apparatus rather than adopting a more revolutionary posture. Perhaps he had no other choice, but it was a decision with consequences. The goal was to slowly solidify his and the Brotherhood's authority and to gradually wrest some control of the state bureaucracy. The longer Morsi stayed in power—convincing skeptics that he was not simply passing through—the more the state would accept and respect him, or so the thinking went.

With survival taking precedence in power—as in opposition—the Brotherhood would, again, need to put its ideological project to the side. Pushing Islamic legislation—particularly in the absence of a real parliament—made little sense until Islamists had first secured their position in power. "Islamization" would have to wait. The Brotherhood was still playing the politics of stages. Where others accused them of rushing and losing their cool, many of their own supporters wanted them to move more aggressively. Why, they were asking, wasn't there a prime minister from the FJP instead of a hapless bureaucrat?

In any case, politics had consumed Islamists, distorting their original core mission. The balance had moved, decisively, from preaching, education, and charity work to partisan politics (despite the vastly different social and political environment after the revolution, the Brotherhood's educational curriculum had stayed much the same). The organization's resources and energy were focused on one thing—Morsi not failing. If Morsi failed, or if he fell, there would be no Islamic project to begin with. Morsi's survival was the starting point.

But did the Brotherhood's gradualism mean liberals, and the international community, had nothing to fear? Not necessarily. Liberals believed, rightly, that Islamists had different discourses for different audiences at different times. They did not trust Islamists. Even if they were moderate now, there was simply no guarantee they would be in the future. The Islamists' response was that they would respect the democratic process. They would not act against the will of the people. Islamist groups, in this sense, tended to reflect popular opinion rather than lead it. This, though, tended to worry liberals more than reassure them.

Some Brotherhood leaders occasionally had the tendency to see government as a mere receptacle for whatever it was that the people wanted, at any given time. One senior Brotherhood official offered a hypothetical: "A secular government would be fine if it implemented the people's will . . . if the people wanted to ban wine, for example, the government would oblige."[28] If there were ever a pure expression of majoritarianism, this would probably be it.

There was another, related problem for opponents of Islamism: Islamists had a built-in advantage that distorted the playing field. Shadi Taha, the liberal al-Ghad leader who ran for parliament under the FJP's list in 2011, saw how the Brotherhood campaigned up close. He was in awe—the Brotherhood's get-out-the-vote operation was simply unparalleled—but he was also worried. "To them, it's faith," he told me. "You tell me how you can add faith to liberalism and I'll build you an organization like [the Brotherhood's]." But, of course, you can't. "That's why religion always beats politics in any match," Taha concluded.[29] Faith helped Islamist movements maintain internal cohesion and organizational discipline. Faith is why Brotherhood members willingly gave the organization a percentage of their salary (usually 7 to 10 percent).

Faith is an inspiration and a motivation. It makes you do things you otherwise might not. That much is clear. But what did faith-based politics end up looking like in a modern era of nation-states, interconnected economies, and American power? It was ironic that the advent of Arab democracy had made this new experiment possible. Through democracy—that supposed Western construct—Islamists, drawing on populism, majoritarianism, and of course faith, would try to give shape and meaning to what had long been a lofty but improbable aspiration. Their opponents sensed that latent ambition. On this, and little else, they could agree. It is a sobering thought: the real ideological battles were only just beginning.

NOTES

Chapter 1

1. "Egypt: Proposed Constitutional Amendments Greatest Erosion of Human Rights in 26 Years," Amnesty International, March 18, 2007, http://www.amnesty.org/en/library/info/MDE12/008/2007
2. Interview with author, Mohamed Morsi, May 8, 2010.
3. Interview with author, Gehad al-Haddad, August 4, 2013.
4. This phenomenon will be discussed in greater detail in Chapter 5. See also Shadi Hamid, "Arab Islamist Parties: Losing on Purpose?" *Journal of Democracy* 22 (January 2011): pp. 68–80.
5. The General Guide is the highest-ranking figure in the Egyptian Muslim Brotherhood.
6. Barbara Zollner, *The Muslim Brotherhood: Hasan al-Hudaybi and Ideology* (New York: Routledge, 2008), p. 117.
7. Francis Fukuyama, "The End of History," *The National Interest*, Summer 1989
8. Lia Brynjar, *The Society of the Muslim Brothers in Egypt: The Rise of an Islamic Mass Movement, 1928–1942* (Reading, UK: Ithaca, 1998), p. 68.
9. Ali Abdul Kazem, "The Muslim Brotherhood: The Historic Background and the Ideological Origins," in *The Islamic Movement in Jordan*, ed. Jillian Schwedler (Amman: Al-Urdun Al-Jadid Research Center, 1997), p. 20.
10. Hasanayn Tawfiq Ibrahim and Hoda Raghib Awad, *al-Dawr al-Siyasi li Jama'a al-Ikhwan al-Muslimin fi Dhil al-Ta'adudiya al-Siyasiya al-Muqayada fi Misr* [The Political Role of the Muslim Brotherhood under Limited Political Pluralism in Egypt] (Cairo: Markaz al-Mahrusa, 1996), p. 99.
11. Michael Willis, *Power and Politics in the Maghreb: Algeria, Tunisia and Morocco from Independence to the Arab Spring Brothers* (New York: Columbia University Press, 2012), p. 172.
12. For an account of the crackdown on FIS and other Islamist groups in Algeria, see Michael Willis, *The Islamist Challenge in Algeria* (New York: NYU Press, 1999) and Emad Eldin Shahin, *Political Ascent: Contemporary Islamic*

Movements in North Africa (Boulder, CO: Westview Press, 1997). For paral-
llels between the Algerian and Egyptian military coups, see Hicham Yezza,
"What Algeria 1992 can, and cannot, teach us about Egypt 2013," Open-
Democracy, July 9, 2013, http://www.opendemocracy.net/hicham-yezza/
what-algeria-1992-can-and-cannot-teach-us-about-egypt-2013.

13. Interview with author, Abdel Moneim Abul Futouh, May 4, 2010.

14. Interview with author, Ennahda member, January 30, 2013.

15. Interview with author, Muslim Brotherhood official, August 9, 2010.

16. Interview with author, Adnan Hassouneh, May 17, 2008.

17. Interview with author, Ibrahim El-Houdaiby, July 23, 2008.

18. Interview with author, Hamdi Hassan, November 26, 2010.

19. Graham Fuller, *The Future of Political Islam* (New York: Palgrave MacMillan, 2004), p. 136.

20. Interview with author, Mohamed Khouja, January 31, 2013.

21. John O. Voll, foreword in Richard P. Mitchell, *The Society of the Muslim Brothers* (New York: Oxford University Press, 1993), p. x.

22. Ibid.

23. Noah Feldman turns the modernization paradigm on its head, pointing out that "if one notices that, for thirteen hundred years, Islam provided the dominant language of politics in the Middle East, and if one treats the twen-tieth century as a brief aberration . . . then the reemergence of Islam looks like a return to the norm, and the rise of a secular nationalism looks like the historical phenomenon in need of special explanation" (Feldman, *The Fall and Rise of the Islamic State*, Princeton, NJ: Princeton University Press, 2008, p. 20).

24. For an argument on why the call for an "Islamic state" and the establishment of Islamic law have had such durable appeal see Feldman, *The Fall and Rise of the Islamic State*, p. 20.

25. For example, in a 2006 Gallup survey, 66 percent of Egyptians said that "sharia must be the *only* source of legislation" while another 24 percent said "sharia must be a source of legislation, but not the only source" (Gallup World Poll, "Islam and Democracy," 2006, http://www.gallup.com/press/109693/ Islam-Democracy.aspx). More recently, in a 2012 Pew poll, 60 percent of Egyptians said "laws should strictly follow the teachings of the Quran," while 32 percent said "laws should follow the principles of Islam but not strictly follow the teachings of the Quran" (Pew Global Attitudes Project, "Most Muslims Want Democracy, Personal Freedoms, and Islam in Political Life," July 10, 2012, http://www.pewglobal.org/2012/07/10/most-muslims-want-democracy-personal-freedoms-and-islam-in-political-life/). In a 2011 Pew survey, 74 percent said that sharia should be "the official law of the land." Of those, 55 percent believe sharia should be applied to both Muslims and Christians. 44 percent said their views on compulsory veiling were closer to the following statement "women should *not* have the right to decide whether to wear a veil." 73 percent said their views on the right to divorce are closer

to the statement "a wife should *not* have the right to divorce her husband." Meanwhile, only 8 percent think polygamy is "morally wrong" (Pew Research Center, "The World's Muslims: Religion, Politics and Society," April 30, 2013, http://www.pewforum.org/files/2013/04/worlds-muslims-religion-politics-society-full-report.pdf). Older polls show the same basic trends. For example, in a 2006 Gallup survey, 66 percent of Egyptians said that "sharia must be the *only* source of legislation," while another 24 percent said "sharia must be a source of legislation, but not the only source" (Gallup World Poll, "Islam and Democracy," 2006, http://www.gallup.com/press/109693/Islam-Democracy.aspx).

26. In the 2011 Pew survey, 70 percent favor whipping and cutting off the hands for theft, 80 percent support stoning for adultery, and 88 percent support the death penalty for apostasy. Pew Research Center, "The World's Muslims: Religion, Politics and Society," April 30, 2013, http://www.pewforum.org/files/2013/04/worlds-muslims-religion-politics-society-full-report.pdf

27. Ibid.

28. Interview with author, Mustafa al-Naggar, October 15, 2011.

29. "The Beginnings of Transition: Politics and Polarization in Egypt and Tunisia," Brookings Doha Center, April 2012, p. 2, http://www.brookings.edu/research/reports/2012/04/19-democratic-transitions

30. Interview with author, Shadi Taha, November 20, 2011.

31. The Egyptian Constitution, 2012. Translation by International IDEA, http://www.constitutionnet.org/files/final_constitution_30_nov_2012_-english-_-idea.pdf. All subsequent citations of the 2012 constitution use this translation.

32. Stephane Lacroix, "Sheikhs and Politicians: Inside the New Egyptian Salafism," Brookings Doha Center, June 2012, p. 1, http://www.brookings.edu/research/papers/2012/06/07-egyptian-salafism-lacroix

33. Nathan Field and Ahmed Hammam, "Salafi Satellite Television in Egypt," *Arab Media & Society*, 8 (Spring 2009), http://www.arabmediasociety.com/?article=712

34. Voll, foreword in Richard P. Mitchell, *The Society of the Muslim Brothers* (New York: Oxford University Press, 1993), p. xiii.

35. Frances Hagopian, "Democracy by Undemocratic Means? Elites, Political Pacts, and Regime Transition in Brazil," *Comparative Political Studies* 23 (July 1990), p. 148.

36. For a variation of the path dependence argument in the context of political competition in Mexico, see Alberto Diaz-Cayeros and Beatriz Magaloni, "Party Dominance and the Logic of Electoral Design in Mexico's Transition to Democracy," *Journal of Theoretical Politics* 13 (2001), pp. 271–293.

37. Eva Bellin, "The Robustness of Authoritarianism in the Middle East: Exceptionalism in Comparative Perspective," *Comparative Politics* 36 (January 2004), p. 148.

38. Jason Brownlee, *Democracy Prevention: The Politics of the U.S.-Egyptian Alliance* (Cambridge, UK: Cambridge University Press, 2012), p. 10, Kindle edition. See also Amaney Jamal, who makes similar points in her 2013 book

Of Empires and Citizens: Pro-American Democracy or No Democracy at All? (Princeton: Princeton University Press, 2012).

39. For more on the role of external actors in supporting democratic transitions, see Shadi Hamid and Peter Mandaville, "Bringing the United States Back into the Middle East," *The Washington Quarterly*, Fall 2013, https://csis.org/files/publication/TWQ_13Winter_Hamid-Mandaville.pdf

40. Richard Rose and Doh Chull Shin, "Democratization Backwards: The Problem of Third-Wave Democracies," *British Journal of Political Science* 31 (April 2011), p. 332.

41. Fareed Zakaria, *The Future of Freedom: Illiberal Democracy at Home and Abroad* (New York: W.W. Norton, 2003), p. 124.

42. Ibid., p. 15.

43. Michael Signer, *Demagogue: The Fight to Save Democracy from its Worst Enemies* (New York: Palgrave Macmillan), Kindle edition, p. 31.

44. Ibid., p. 32.

45. Gregory Wilpert, "Venezuela: Participatory Democracy or Government As Usual?" *Socialism and Democracy* 19 (2005), p. 24.

46. Fareed Zakaria, "Islam, Democracy, and Constitutional Liberalism," *Political Science Quarterly* 119 (Spring 2004), p. 18.

47. Ibid., p. 19.

48. Diana Ayton-Shenker, "The Challenge of Human Rights and Cultural Diversity," United Nations Background Note, http://www.un.org/rights/dpi1627e.htm

49. See Bradley Hope, "Morsi Battles to Prove He Can Revive Egypt's Economy," *The National*, October 19, 2012, http://www.thenational.ae/news/world/africa/morsi-battles-to-prove-he-can-revive-egypts-economy

50. Fukuyama, "End of History".

51. See Abdel Moneim Abul Futouh, Interview, February 5, 2012, http://www.youtube.com/watch?v=hgWJRuVOyDc&list=UUQpLmeoGRIoL8MRC_d2aSrA&index=9&feature=plcp&fb_source=message

52. Interview with author, Abdel Moneim Abul Futouh, August 4, 2006. For more on Abul Futouh's political and religious thought, see Shadi Hamid, "A Man For All Seasons," *Foreign Policy*, May 9, 2012, http://www.foreignpolicy.com/articles/2012/05/09/man_for_all_seasons_fotouh_egypt

53. General Overseer is the highest-ranking position in the Jordanian Muslim Brotherhood. The title General Guide is reserved only for the leader of the Egyptian organization, which is seen as the mother movement.

54. Interview with author, Salem Falahat, August 16, 2008.

55. For more on the controversy over this proposed clause, see Monica Marks, "'Complementary' Status for Women," *Foreign Policy*, August 20, 2012, http://mideast.foreignpolicy.com/posts/2012/08/20/complementary_status_for_tunisian_women

56. For more on different types of secularism, see Ahmet Kuru, *Secularism and State Policies toward Religion: The United States, France, and Turkey* (Cambridge, UK: Cambridge University Press, 2009) and Ahmet Kuru, "Muslim Politics

Without an 'Islamic' State: Can Turkey's Justice and Development Party Be a Model for Arab Islamists?" Brookings Doha Center, February 2013, http://www.brookings.edu/research/papers/2013/02/21-akp-model-kuru

57. Azzam Tamimi, *Rachid Ghannouchi: A Democrat within Islamism* (New York: Oxford University Press, 2001), p. 5.

58. Ibid., p. 58.

59. Interview with author, Meherzia Laabidi, January 31, 2013.

60. Richard P. Mitchell, *The Society of the Muslim Brothers* (London: Oxford University Press, 1969), p. 328.

61. For a variation on this argument, see Mansour Moaddel, *Jordanian Exceptionalism: A Comparative Analysis of State-Religion Relationships in Egypt, Iran, Jordan, and Syria* (New York: Palgrave, 2002). Moaddel argues that the authoritarianism of Gamal Abdel Nasser produced the radicalism of Sayyid Qutb and that the moderation of the Jordanian monarchy contributed to the moderation of the Jordanian Muslim Brotherhood.

62. The hawks-doves distinction has been popularized by the Jordanian press, and even some leaders in the Brotherhood and the IAF use the terms themselves. Briefly, doves are seen as loyalists—even monarchists—and prefer to avoid overt confrontation with the authorities. They advocate the prioritization of domestic issues, while the more confrontational hawks put more of an emphasis on support for Hamas and the Palestinian cause. There are notable exceptions, but most doves are indigenous Jordanians, while hawks tend to be of Palestinian origin.

63. Such works include Mohamed Abu Faris, *Safahat min al-Tarikh al-Siyasi li al-Ikhwan al-Muslimin fi al-Urdun* [Pages from the Political History of the Muslim Brotherhood in Jordan] (Amman: Dar al-Furqan, 1997) and Ibrahim al-Gharaibeh's *Jama'a al-Ikhwan al-Muslimin fi al-Urdun, 1946–1996* [The Society of the Muslim Brothers in Jordan] (Amman: Al-Urdun Al-Jadid Research Center, 1997).

64. Bassam al-Emoush, *Mahatat fi Tarikh al-Ikhwan al-Muslimin* [Stations in the History of the Muslim Brotherhood] (Amman: Academics for Publishing and Distribution, 2008).

65. Since the cases in question do not satisfy the necessary criteria for a "most similar" research design, I employ for Jordan and to a lesser extent Egypt a before–after design, which can be done by "dividing a single longitudinal case into two—the 'before' case and an 'after' case that follows a discontinuous change in an important variable." (Alexander L. George and Andrew Bennett, *Case Studies and Theory Development in the Social Sciences*, Cambridge, MA: MIT Press, 2004, p. 81). What this requires is a "turning point," where the independent variable of interest undergoes a qualitative shift. As will be discussed in Chapters 3 and 4, Egypt and Jordan experienced significant shifts in the early 1990s, moving from democratic openings to varying levels of political exclusion and repression.

Chapter 2

1. Quinn Mecham, "The Rise of Islamist Actors: Formulating a Strategy for Sustained Engagement," Project on Middle East Democracy, April 2012, p. 5.

2. For more on the "pothole theory of democracy," see Sheri Berman, "Taming Extremist Parties: Lessons from Europe," *Journal of Democracy* 19 (January 2008), p. 6.

3. "Transcript: Bush News Conference," *Washington Post*, March 16, 2005, http://www.washingtonpost.com/wp-dyn/articles/A40191-2005Mar16_4.html

4. U.S. State Department, Daily Press Briefing, May 11, 2012.

5. Islamists, too, may have been drawing from an emerging body of Western scholarship. When I interviewed Mohamed Morsi in May 2011, he mentioned in passing that a 2006 MERIP article by Samer Shehata and Joshua Stacher on the Muslim Brotherhood's experience in parliament was a "breakthrough."

6. Samuel P. Huntington, *The Third Wave: Democratization in the Late Twentieth Century* (Norman, OK: University of Oklahoma Press, 1991), p. 169.

7. Adam Przeworski and John Sprague, *Paper Stones: A History of Electoral Socialism* (Chicago, IL: University of Chicago Press, 1986), p. 50.

8. Ibid.

9. Stathis N. Kalyvas, "Unsecular Politics and Religious Mobilization: Beyond Christian Democracy," in *European Christian Democracy: Historical Legacies and Comparative Perspectives*, eds. Thomas Kselman and Joseph A. Buttigieg (Notre Dame: University of Notre Dame Press, 2004), p. 309. See also Kalyvas, *The Rise of Christian Democracy in Europe* (Ithaca, NY: Cornell University Press, 1996).

10. Vali Nasr, "The Rise of Muslim Democracy," *Journal of Democracy* 16 (April 2005), p. 15.

11. Muriel Asseburg, "The Challenge of Islamists: Elements of a Shared US–EU Agenda Towards the Muslim World," in *The Challenge of Islamists for EU and US Policies: Conflict, Stability and Reform*, eds. Muriel Asseburg and Daniel Brumberg (Berlin, Germany: German Institute for International and Security Affairs, 2007), p. 75.

12. In an influential article, Mona el-Ghobashy writes that if Egypt's Muslim Brotherhood has "responded with such flexibility to the threats and opportunities of their authoritarian environment, one can speculate how much more they would acclimate themselves to the rigors of free and open electoral politics undistorted by repression" (Mona el-Ghobashy, "The Metamorphosis of the Egyptian Muslim Brothers," *International Journal of Middle East Studies* August 37, 2005, p. 391).

13. Daniel Brumberg, "Islam is Not the Solution (or the Problem)," *The Washington Quarterly* 29 (Winter 2005–2006), p. 99.

14. Graham Fuller, *The Future of Political Islam* (New York: Palgrave Macmillan, 2003), p. 125.

15. Bruce W. Jentleson et al, "Strategic Adaptation: Toward a New U.S. Strategy in the Middle East," Center for a New American Security, June 2012, http://www.cnas.org/strategicadaptation

16. Jonathan Brown, "Salafis and Sufis in Egypt," Carnegie Endowment Papers, December 2011, p. 2, http://carnegieendowment.org/2011/12/20/salafis-and-sufis-in-egypt/8kfk

17. Jillian Schwedler, *Faith in Moderation: Islamist Parties in Jordan and Yemen* (Cambridge, UK: Cambridge University Press, 2006), p. 195.

18. Ibid., p. 213.

19. M. Hakun Yavuz, *Secularism and Muslim Democracy in Turkey* (Cambridge, UK: Cambridge University Press, 2009), p. 68.

20. Alan B. Krueger and Jitka Maleckova, "Seeking the Roots of Terrorism," *The Chronicle of Higher Education*, June 2003.

21. Shadi Hamid and Steven Brooke, "Promoting Democracy to Stop Terror, Revisited," *Policy Review*, February/March 2010, http://www.hoover.org/publications/policy-review/article/5285

22. Christian Davenport uses a nine-point scale that combines measures of civil liberties and political terror to create an aggregate metric for repression, ranging from "low violence, low restriction" to "high violence, high restriction." This upper bound of repression is only one among nine possible categories of repression (Davenport, *State Repression and the Domestic Democratic Peace*, Cambridge: Cambridge University Press, 2010, pp. 95–100).

23. Muriel Asseburg, "Conclusions and Recommendations," in *Moderate Islamists as Reform Actors: Conditions and Programmatic Change*, ed. Muriel Asseburg (Berlin, Germany: German Institute for International and Security Affairs, 2007), p. 76.

24. Janine A. Clark, "The Conditions of Islamist Moderation: Unpacking Cross-Ideological Cooperation in Jordan," *International Journal of Middle East Studies* 38 (November 2006), p. 541.

25. Niche parties, according to Bonnie Meguid, "eschew the comprehensive policy platforms common to their mainstream party peers, instead adopting positions only on a restricted set of issues . . . [They] rely on the salience and attractiveness of their *one* policy stance for voter support" (Bonnie M. Meguid, "Competition Between Unequals: The Role of Mainstream Party Strategy in Niche Party Success," *American Political Science Review* August 9, 2005, p. 348). See also Avital Livni, "When Niche Parties Go Mainstream: The Case of the Islamist AKP in Turkey," unpublished paper, November 2008, pp. 1–3.

26. Mona el-Ghobashy, "The Metamorphosis of the Egyptian Muslim Brothers," *International Journal of Middle East Studies* 37 (August 2005).

27. Conway W. Henderson, "Conditions Affecting the Use of Political Repression," *The Journal of Conflict Resolution* 35 (March 1991), p. 121.

28. See for example "Egypt's Muslim Brothers: Confrontation or Integration?" International Crisis Group, June 18, 2008, p. 9.

29. Quintan Wiktorowicz, *The Management of Islamic Activism* (Albany, NY: State University of New York Press, 2001), p. 20.

30. Robert Michels, *A Sociological Study of the Oligarchical Tendencies of Modern Democracy* (New York: The Free Press, 1962), p. 335.

31. Ibid., p. 336.

32. Bassam al-Emoush, "Awluwiyat al-'Amal al-Siyasi li al-Haraka al-Islamiya fi al-Urdun fi 'Aqd al-Tis'eenat" [Priorities of Political Action for the Islamic Movement in Jordan in the Period of the 1990s], internal working paper, in *Mahatat fi Tarikh al-Ikhwan al-Muslimin* (Amman: Academics for Publishing and Distribution, 2008), pp. 291–292.

33. Emoush, "Ru'iya Tahleeliya li Awluwiyat Istiqrar al-Urdun wa Ta'ayush al-Haraka al-Islamiya ma' al-Nidham" [An Analytical View of the Principles of Jordan's Stability and Coexistence of the Islamic Movement with the Regime], internal working paper, in *Mahatat*, p. 299.

34. Janine A. Clark, *Islam, Charity, and Activism* (Bloomington, IN: Indiana University Press, 2004), p. 93.

35. Emoush, "Ru'iya Tahleeliya li Awluwiyat Istiqrar al-Urdun," p. 299.

36. *Jordan Times*, July 6, 2006.

37. Nancy Bermeo, "Democracy and the Lessons of Dictatorship," *Comparative Politics* 22 (April 1992), p. 273.

38. Ibid., p. 278.

39. Interview with the author, Jameel Abu Bakr, February 7, 2005. Abu Bakr has held a variety of leadership posts in the IAF, including deputy secretary-general.

40. Interview with author, Nael Masalha, April 10, 2005.

41. Ibid.

42. Mohamed Mamoun al-Houdaiby, *A Quiet Discussion on Heated Issues* (Cairo: al-Falah, 2000).

43. Bermeo, "Democracy and the Lessons of Dictatorship," p. 284.

44. Houdaiby, *A Quiet Discussion on Heated Issues*.

45. Khalil al-Anani, *al-Ikhwan al-Muslimun fi Misr: Shaikhoukha Tassaru' al-Zaman* [The Muslim Brotherhood in Egypt: Gerontocracy Fighting the Clock] (Cairo: Maktaba al-Shorouq al-Dawliya, 2007), p. 74.

46. Interview with author, Abdel Moneim Mahmoud, July 14, 2008.

47. Ibid.

48. Ibid.

49. Interview with author, Khaled Hamza, September 7, 2009.

50. Schwedler, *Faith in Moderation*, p. 92.

51. Anani, *al-Ikhwan al-Muslimun fi Misr*, p. 82.

52. *Al-Manhaj al-Thaqafi li al-Akh al-'Amil* [Educational Curriculum for the Active Brother], internal document, 2008. *Akh 'Amil*, or active brother, is the highest level of membership in the organization.

53. Interview with author, Muslim Brotherhood official, September 9, 2009.

54. Anani, *al-Ikhwan al-Muslimun fi Misr*, p. 83.

55. Pew Global Attitudes Project, "Most Muslims Want Democracy, Personal Freedoms, and Islam in Political Life," July 10, 2012, http://www.pewglobal. org/2012/07/10/most-muslims-want-democracy-personal-freedoms-and-islam-in-political-life/

56. Arab Barometer: Jordan Country Report (August 2011), p. 23, http://www. arabbarometer.org/sites/default/files/countyreportjordan2_0.pdf.

57. Pew Global Attitudes Project, "Most Muslims Want Democracy, Personal Freedoms, and Islam in Political Life," July 10, 2012.

58. Pew Research Center, "The World's Muslims: Religion, Politics and Society," April 30, 2013, http://www.pewforum.org/files/2013/04/worlds-muslims-religion-politics-society-full-report.pdf

59. Interview with author, Mahdi Akef, August 10, 2006.

60. Interview with author, Abdel Moneim Abul Futouh, August 4, 2006.

61. Interview with author, Jihad Abu Eis, May 27, 2005.

62. See Robert Satloff, "Assessing the Bush Administration's Policy of 'Constructive Instability' (Part II): Regional Dynamics," Washington Institute for Near East Policy, March 16, 2005, http://www.washingtoninstitute.org/policy-analysis/view/assessing-the-bush-administrations-policy-of-constructive-instability-part-

Chapter 3

1. The Freedom House index is the most widely used measure of human rights and democracy. Each country receives two scores on annual basis. As the organization explains in the methodology section of its annual world report, *Freedom in the World*, the "political rights" score includes measures on "electoral process," "political pluralism and participation," and "functioning of government." The "civil liberties" score includes measures of "freedom of expression and belief," "associational and organizational rights," and "rule of law." For more on the methodology used, see Raymond D. Gastil, "The Comparative Survey of Freedom: Experiences and Suggestions," in *On Measuring Democracy: Its Consequences and Concomitants*, ed. Alex Inkeles (New Brunswick, NJ: Transaction), pp. 21–46.

2. Noha el-Mikawy, *Building Consensus in Egypt's Transition Process* (Cairo: American University in Cairo Press, 1999), p. 42.

3. Anthony McDermott, *From Nasser to Mubarak: A Flawed Revolution* (New York: Croom Helm, 1988), p. 76.

4. Khaled Mohieddin, a key figure in the Free Officers movement, recounts the moment he and Nasser formally joined the Brotherhood's "secret apparatus": "We were taken into a totally darkened room where we heard a voice, and, placing our hand on the Quran and a gun and repeating after the voice, we took an oath of obedience and total allegiance for better or worse to the Grand Master [Hassan al-Banna], swearing by the Book of God and the sunna of the Prophet. Though those rites were meant to stir the

emotions, they had very little impact on Nasser and myself" (Moheiddin, *Memories of a Revolution: Egypt 1952*, The American University in Cairo Press: Cairo, 1995, p. 22). Interestingly, President Sadat, Nasser's successor, was the primary liaison between the Brotherhood and the group of discontented military officers that included Nasser. In his memoirs, Sadat recalls being overwhelmed after meeting Banna for the first time, his admiration for the man "unbounded" (Anwar el-Sadat, *In Search of Identity*, New York: Harper & Row, 1977, p. 22). He was "like a saint," Sadat said (Sadat, *Revolt on the Nile*. New York: John Day, 1957, p. 29).

5.   Robert Satloff, *Troubles on the East Bank: Challenges to the Domestic Stability of Jordan* (New York: Praeger, 1986), p. 7.

6.   See Carrie Rosefsky Wickham, *Mobilizing Islam: Religion, Activism and Political Change in Egypt* (New York: Columbia University Press, 2002), p. 97.

7.   Eugene L. Rogan, "Physical Islamization in Amman," *The Muslim World* 76 (January 1986), p. 36.

8.   Ibid.

9.   Satloff, *Troubles on the East Bank*, p. 40.

10. Marion Boulby, *The Muslim Brotherhood and the Kings of Jordan, 1945–1993* (Atlanta, GA: Scholars Press, 1999).

11. Several Brotherhood members and supporters won seats in the 1976 parliament but did so in their personal capacities.

12. Fauzi M. Najjar, "The Application of Sharia Laws in Egypt," *Middle East Policy* 1 (2002): p. 64.

13. Mohamed al-Taweel, *al-Ikhwan fi al-Parliman* [The Muslim Brotherhood in Parliament] (Cairo: al-Maktab al-Masri al-Hadith, 1992), p. 66.

14. Ibid., p. 70.

15. Ibid.

16. Ibid., p. 72. For more on the efforts of the maritime code committee, see p. 76.

17. Ibid.

18. Ibid., p. 74.

19. Robert Springborg, *Mubarak's Egypt: Fragmentation of Political Order* (Boulder, CO: Westview, 1989), p. 159.

20. Richard P. Mitchell, *The Society of the Muslim Brothers* (London: Oxford University Press, 1969), p. 261.

21. Hasanayn Tawfiq Ibrahim and Hoda Raghib Awad, *al-Dawr al-Siyasi li Jama'a al-Ikhwan al-Muslimin fi Dhil al-Ta'adudiya al-Siyasiya al-Muqayada fi Misr* [The Political Role of the Muslim Brotherhood under Limited Political Pluralism in Egypt] (Cairo: Markaz al-Mahrusa, 1996), p. 97.

22. Ibid., p. 99.

23. Ibid., pp. 88, 134.

24. Ibid., p. 137.

25. Ibid.

26. Ibid., p. 176.
27. Taweel, *al-Ikhwan fi al-Parliman*, p. 82.
28. Ibrahim and Awad, *al-Dawr al-Siyasi li Jama'a al-Ikhwan al-Muslimin*, p. 157.
29. Ibid., p. 255.
30. Ibid., pp. 293–294.
31. Ibid., p. 296.
32. *Al-Barnamaj al-Intikhabi li al-Tahaluf al-Islami* [The Electoral Program of the Islamic Alliance], as reproduced in Mohamed Muru, *al-Haraka al-Islamiya fi Misr min 1928 ila 1993* [The Islamic Movement in Egypt from 1928 to 1993] (Cairo: Dar al-Misriya li al-Nashr wa al-Tawzi, 1994), p. 211.
33. Ibid., p. 212.
34. Ibid.
35. Ibid., p. 216.
36. Ibid.
37. Ibid.
38. Ibrahim and Awad, *al-Dawr al-Siyasi li Jama'a al-Ikhwan al-Muslimin*, p. 333.
39. Ibid., p. 328.
40. Ibid., p. 337.
41. Ibid., p. 364.
42. Ibid., p. 365.
43. Ibid., pp. 377–397. Due to the dominance of the executive branch, parliamentary activity focused less on drafting legislation and more on government oversight. Opposition deputies had three main tools of monitoring—*as'ila* (questions), *talabat al-ahata* ("for your information"), and *istijwabat* (interpellations). A deputy could address *as'ila* to any cabinet minister. The "for your information" was little more than a means to notify ministers of information relevant to their office. Through an interpellation—addressed to the prime minister or other members of the cabinet—a deputy could initiate debate on a particular issue of concern.
44. "Zaki Badr, 71, Egyptian Official Who Opposed Islamic Militants," *New York Times*, April 4, 1997.
45. Ibrahim and Awad, *al-Dawr al-Siyasi li Jama'a al-Ikhwan al-Muslimin*, p. 338.
46. Ibid., p. 285.
47. Ibid., p. 286.
48. *Jordan Times*, November 9, 1989.
49. The Brotherhood ran 26 candidates out of a total of at least 640.
50. Fahed Fanek, "Election Campaign and the Economic Crisis," *Jordan Times*, October 22, 1989.
51. *Jordan Times*, November 5, 1989.
52. *Jordan Times*, November 16–17, 1989.
53. *Jordan Times*, November 2–3, 1989.
54. Ali Abdul Kazem, "The Muslim Brotherhood: The Historic Background and the Ideological Origins," in *The Islamic Movement in Jordan*, ed. Jillian Schwedler (Amman: Al-Urdun Al-Jadid Research Center, 1997), p. 31.

55. Sabah el-Said, *Between Pragmatism and Ideology: The Muslim Brotherhood in Jordan, 1989–1994* (Washington, DC: Washington Institute for Near East Policy, 1995), p. 6.

56. Interview with author, Mudar Badran, February 23, 2005.

57. 9 of 80 seats were reserved for Christians, so the 31 percent figure derives from 22/71 rather than 22/80.

58. Interview with author, Mudar Badran, February 23, 2005.

59. *Al-Islam howa al-Hal: Al-Barnamaj al-Intakhabi li-Murashahi al-Ikhwan al-Muslimin, 1989–1993* [Islam is the Solution: The Electoral Program of the Muslim Brotherhood Candidates], pp. 4–5.

60. *Jordan Times*, February 18, 1990.

61. *Jordan Times*, May 19, 1990.

62. *Jordan Times*, May 23–24, 1991.

63. Ibid.

64. Ibid.

65. *Jordan Times*, May 11, 1991.

66. *Jordan Times*, May 23–24, 1991.

67. *Jordan Times*, April 2, 1991.

68. *Jordan Times*, March 23, 1991.

69. Russell E. Lucas, *Institutions and the Politics of Survival in Jordan: Domestic Responses to External Challenges: 1988–2001* (Albany: State University of New York Press, 2005), p. 37.

70. National Charter, December 1990, see http://www.kinghussein.gov.jo/charter-national.html

71. Lucas, *Institutions and the Politics of Survival in Jordan*, p. 38.

72. Ibid., p. 37.

73. *Jordan Times*, March 7, 1990.

74. Musa al-Kilani, *al-Harakat al-Islamiya fi al-Urdun wa Falastine* [Islamic Movements in Jordan and Palestine] (Amman: Dar al-Bashir, 1994), p. 98.

75. Article 21, Political Parties Law of 1992, see http://www.kinghussein.gov.jo/pol-parties.html

76. *Nidham al-Assasi*, Islamic Action Front, Amman, 1992, p. 1.

77. Ibid., p. 2.

Chapter 4

1. For more on the tensions between President Mubarak and Zaki Badr, see Robert Springborg, *Mubarak's Egypt: Fragmentation of Political Order* (Boulder, CO: Westview, 1989), pp. 148–151.

2. Ibrahim and Awad, *al-Dawr al-Siyasi li Jama'a al-Ikhwan al-Muslimin*, p. 411.

3. Hesham al-Awadi, *In Pursuit of Legitimacy: The Muslim Brothers and Mubarak, 1982–2000* (London: Tauris Academic Studies, 2004), p. 193.

4. Mona el-Ghobashy, "The Metamorphosis of the Egyptian Muslim Brothers," *International Journal of Middle East Studies* 37 (August 2005), p. 381.

5. Eberhard Kienle, "More than a Response to Islamism: The Political Deliberalization of Egypt in the 1990s," *Middle East Journal* 52 (Spring 1998): p. 287.

6. Carrie Rosefsky Wickham, *Mobilizing Islam: Religion, Activism and Political Change in Egypt* (New York: Columbia University Press, 2002), p. 178.

7. Ibid., p. 117.

8. Joel Campagna, "From Accommodation to Confrontation: The Muslim Brotherhood in the Mubarak Years," *Journal of International Affairs* 50 (Summer 1996), p. 293.

9. Interview with author, Khaled Hamza, October 4, 2009.

10. Ibid.

11. Campagna, "From Accommodation to Confrontation," p. 299.

12. Eberhard Kienle, *A Grand Delusion: Democracy and Economic Reform in Egypt* (London: IB Tauris, 2001), p. 93.

13. Kienle, "More Than a Response to Islamism," p. 222.

14. Wickham, *Mobilizing Islam*, p. 107.

15. Ibid., p. 110.

16. Ibid., pp. 110–111.

17. Ghobashy, "The Metamorphosis of the Muslim Brothers," p. 384.

18. Kienle, "More Than a Response to Islamism," p. 226.

19. These can be found in the appendix of Hesham al-Awadi's *In Pursuit of Legitimacy*.

20. Awadi, *In Pursuit of Legitimacy*, p. 213.

21. Mohammed M. Hafez, *Why Muslims Rebel: Repression and Resistance in the Islamic World* (Boulder, CO: Lynne Rienner, 2003), p. 34.

22. Hamed Abu Nasr, Public Statement, December 18, 1992, in Muru, *al-Haraka al-Islamiya fi Misr*, p. 200.

23. Hamed Abu Nasr, Public Statement, November 26, 1993, in Muru, p. 201.

24. Fawaz A. Gerges, "The End of the Islamist Insurgency in Egypt?: Costs and Prospects," *Middle East Journal* 54 (Autumn 2000), p. 594.

25. Campagna, "From Accommodation to Confrontation," p. 11.

26. Interview with author, Khalil al-Anani, October 7, 2009.

27. Mary Anne Weaver, "The Novelist and the Sheikh," *New Yorker*, January 30, 1995.

28. Interview with Khalil al-Anani, October 7, 2009.

29. "Our Testimony," Muslim Brotherhood document, 1994, see http://www.ikhwanweb.com/article.php?id=4185.

30. Interview with author, Muslim Brotherhood official, September 9, 2009. While in prison, Sayyid Qutb advanced radical ideas, particularly in his book *Milestones*, which would provide an intellectual and theological framework for the many extremist groups that emerged in the 1970s and 1980s. For an intellectual biography of Qutb, see John Calvert, *Sayyid Qutb and the Origins of Radical Islamism* (New York: Columbia University Press, 2010). For more on the Brotherhood's disavowal of Qutb's most controversial ideas,

see Barbara Zollner, *The Muslim Brotherhood: Hasan al-Hudaybi and Ideology* (New York: Routledge, 2008). For the relevance of Sayyid Qutb to splits within political Islam, see Shadi Hamid, "Demoting Democracy in Egypt," *New York Times*, July 4, 2013, http://www.nytimes.com/2013/07/05/opinion/demoting-democracy-in-egypt.html

31. Ghobashy, "The Metamorphosis of the Muslim Brotherhood," p. 382.

32. Interview with author, Khaled Hamza, September 7, 2009.

33. "Al-Mar'a al-Muslima fi al-Mujtama' al-Muslim" [The Muslim Woman in Muslim Society] and "Moujiz min al-Shura fi al-Islam wa Ta'adud al-Ahzab fi al-Mujtama' al-Muslim" [Overview of Shura in Islam and Political Party Pluralism in Muslim Society], Muslim Brotherhood, pamphlet (Cairo: Al-Markaz al-Islami li al-Darasat wa al-Buhuth, March 1994), p. 3. The pamphlet includes both statements.

34. Ibid., pp. 37–38.

35. Ibid., p. 39.

36. Ibid., p. 40.

37. Ibid., p. 6.

38. Ibid., p. 23.

39. Interview with author, Essam al-Erian, July 16, 2008.

40. Interview with author, Mahmoud Ghozlan, July 14, 2008.

41. Mamoun al-Houdaiby, *Nuqat Liqa' wa Wifaq 'Am li Mashrou' al-Mithaq al-Watani* [Points of General Agreement on the National Charter Initiative], 1995, p. 11.

42. Ghobashy, "The Metamorphosis of the Muslim Brothers," p. 384.

43. Talaat Rumayh, *al-Wasat wa al-Ikhwan* [The Wasat and the Brotherhood] (Cairo: Markaz Yaffa li al-Darasat wa al-Abhath, 1997), p. 41.

44. Interview with author, Khaled Hamza, October 4, 2009.

45. Ibid.

46. Ibid.

47. Interview with author, Muslim Brotherhood official, September 9, 2009.

48. Interview with author, Khalil al-Anani, October 7, 2009.

49. Ibid.

50. Khaled Dawoud, "Islamism in crisis," *Al-Ahram Weekly*, December 31, 1998–January 6, 1999.

51. Carrie Rosefsky Wickham, "The Path to Moderation: Strategy and Learning in the Formation of Egypt's Wasat Party," *Comparative Politics* 36 (2004), p. 207.

52. Amira Howeidy, "A Major Split in the Brotherhood," *Al-Ahram Weekly*, July 30–August 5, 1998.

53. Wickham, "The Path to Moderation," p. 213.

54. Joshua Stacher, "Post-Islamist Rumblings in Egypt: The Emergence of the Wasat Party," *Middle East Journal* 56 (Summer 2002), see http://arabist.net/post-islamist-rumblings-in-egypt-the-emergence-of-the-wasat-party/

55. Wickham, "The Path to Moderation," p. 213.

56. Rumayh, *al-Wasat wa al-Ikhwan*, p. 51.

57. Ibid., p. 37.

58. Ibid., p. 43.

59. Ibid., p. 37.

60. Ghobashy, "The Metamorphosis of the Muslim Brothers," p. 387.

61. Stacher, "Post-Islamist Rumblings in Egypt".

62. Markus Bouillon, "Walking the Tightrope: Jordanian Foreign Policy from the Gulf Crisis to the Peace Process and Beyond," in *Jordan in Transition: 1990–2000*, ed. George Joffe (New York: Palgrave, 2002), p. 10.

63. Ibid.

64. Russell E. Lucas, "De-liberalization in Jordan," *Journal of Democracy* 14 (January 2003), p. 138.

65. For example, a Brotherhood supporter could vote for the two Brotherhood candidates running in his or her district, vote for one Christian, one leftist, and still have one vote to spare. Similarly, a Christian, with a vote to spare, could vote for two Christian candidates as well as the two Brotherhood candidates. By being selective about which districts to contest and by forming alliances with a variety of groups and individuals, the Brotherhood could effectively guarantee the victory of nearly all its candidates.

66. See "Assessment of the Electoral Framework: The Hashemite Kingdom of Jordan," Democracy Reporting International and New Jordan Research Center (Berlin, Germany: Democracy Reporting International, 2007), p. 16.

67. The 1993 election law, which would serve as the basis for all subsequent electoral legislation, provides no criteria for apportionment or districting. Instead, the government has had full discretion to determine the number and size of electoral districts. Ibid., p. 18.

68. Ibrahim al-Gharaibeh, *Jama'a al-Ikhwan al-Muslimin fi al-Urdun, 1946–1996* [The Society of Muslim Brothers in Jordan] (Amman: Al-Urdun Al-Jadid Research Center, 1997), p. 129.

69. Gharaibeh writes that the Brotherhood's percentage of the vote went from 12 percent in 1989 to 17 percent in 1993 (Ibid., p. 133). However, it is difficult to compare results because the electoral systems were extremely different (plurality block voting versus single non-transferable vote). In addition, the number of candidates the Brotherhood ran increased from 26 in 1989 to 35 in 1993. So even if the Islamist share of the vote increased, it may be attributable not to increased popularity but to increased coverage of districts.

70. Gharaibeh, *Jama'a al-Ikhwan al-Muslimin*, p. 133.

71. Malik Mufti, "Elite Bargains and the Onset of Political Liberalization in Jordan," *Comparative Political Studies* 32 (February 1999), p. 120.

72. *Freedom in the World 1994–1995: The Annual Survey of Political Rights and Civil Liberties* (Washington, DC: Freedom House, 1995), p. 329.

73. Ibid., p. 330.

74. Laurie Brand, *Jordan's Inter-Arab Relations: The Political Economy of Alliance Making* (New York: Columbia University Press, 1995), p. 61.

75. Ibid., p. 62.

76. Glenn E. Robinson, "Can Islamists be Democrats? The Case of Jordan," *Middle East Journal* 51 (Summer 1997), p. 406.

77. Jillian Schwedler, *Faith in Moderation: Islamist Parties in Jordan and Yemen* (Cambridge, UK: Cambridge University Press, 2006), p. 110.

78. Janine A. Clark, "The Conditions of Islamist Moderation: Unpacking Cross-Ideological Cooperation in Jordan," *International Journal of Middle East Studies* 38 (November 2006), p. 547.

79. Letter to Prime Minister. IAF Parliamentary Bloc, March 25, 1995, as reproduced in Emoush, *Mahatat fi Tarikh al-Ikhwan al-Muslimin* (Amman: Academics for Publishing and Distribution, 2008), pp. 114–116.

80. Letter to Speaker of the House. Opposition Deputies, March 5, 1997, in *Mahatat*, p. 139.

81. Nathan J. Brown, "Jordan and Its Islamic Movement," Carnegie Endowment, November 2006, p. 3.

82. Interview with author, Bassam al-Emoush, May 29, 2005.

83. Interview with author, Azmi Mansour, May 29, 2005.

84. Emoush, *Mahatat fi Tarikh al-Ikhwan al-Muslimin*, pp. 164–165.

85. "Li Matha Yuqati' al-Ikhwan al-Muslimun al-Intakhabat al-Niyabiya li 'Am 1997, Hatha Bayan li al-Nas" [Why is the Muslim Brotherhood Boycotting the Parliamentary Elections in 1997? A Statement to the People], Amman, July 13, 1997.

86. Ibid.

87. Schwedler, *Faith in Moderation*, p. 111.

88. Ibid., p. 112.

89. Freedom House. *Annual Survey of Freedom Country Scores, 1972 to 2008*. See http://www.freedomhouse.org/template.cfm?page=15.

90. Lucas, *Institutions and the Politics of Survival*, p. 99.

91. Emoush, *Mahatat fi Tarikh al-Ikhwan al-Muslimin*, p. 268.

92. Ibid., p. 269.

93. Ibid.

94. Lucas, "De-liberalization in Jordan," p. 143.

95. Suleiman al-Khalidi, "Jordan Breaks Up Pro-Palestinian Rally," Reuters, May 11, 2001.

96. Ibid.

97. Interview with author, Nael Masalha, April 20, 2005.

98. *Jordan Times*, December 9, 1997.

Chapter 5

1. Marc Morje Howard and Philip G. Roessler, "Liberalizing Electoral Outcomes in Competitive Authoritarian Regimes," *American Journal of Political Science* 50 (April 2006), pp. 365–381.

2. How political parties respond to and interpret electoral losses is an important, albeit undertheorized, facet of electoral competition. "From a theoretical

perspective," Laurence Whitehead writes, "the theme of 'learning to lose' can hardly be isolated from a broader specification of the relevant political structures and processes. What is the nature of the 'game' in which the possibility of 'loss' is embedded? How severe are the likely consequences of accepting such a loss?" Whitehead has in mind cases where a dominant party comes to terms with electoral loss, but mass parties, in this case Islamists, also "learn to lose" in their own particular way in the context of semi-authoritarian rule (Laurence Whitehead, "Dominant Parties and Democratization: Theory and Comparative Experience," in *Political Transitions in Dominant Party Systems: Learning to Lose*, eds. Edward Friedman and Joseph Wong, New York: vRoutledge, 2008, p. 2).

3. Charles Kurzman and Ijlal Naqi, "Do Muslims Vote Islamic?" *Journal of Democracy* 21 (April 2010), p. 52.

4. Ibid., p. 53.

5. Azzam Tamimi, *Rachid Ghannouchi: A Democrat within Islamism* (New York: Oxford University Press, 2001), p. 70.

6. This figure does not include Morocco since, due to the particularities of the country's electoral system, it is possible to measure only districts contested, not seats contested. Once a party decides to contest a district, it is required by law to contest each seat in the district (through a party list). For example, in a three-member district, each party needs to put forward a list of three candidates.

7. Interview with author, Ziad Abu Ghanimeh, May 28, 2005.

8. This issue is contested by IAF leaders and has been a source of considerable controversy within the organization. Some officials I spoke to vigorously denied the existence of any "deal" between the government and the IAF. However, there is ample evidence that there was at least an understanding, although it is unclear how explicit it was or to what extent it was the initiative of individual leaders acting without official authorization from the party. In any case, several senior IAF leaders and former members confirmed the existence of such an "understanding," while others suggested there was some degree of "coordination."

9. Interview with author, Tayseer Fityani, May 19, 2008; interview with author, Ruheil al-Gharaibeh, June 8, 2008; interview with author, Mohamed Bzour, May 15, 2008; interview with author, Abdul Latif Arabiyat, June 11, 2008.

10. Michael Willis, "Morocco's Islamists and the Legislative Elections of 2002: The Strange Case of the Party That Did Not Want to Win," *Mediterranean Politics* (Spring 2004), p. 60.

11. See Ibid., pp. 69–70 for more on the allegations.

12. Geneive Abdo, *No God but God: Egypt and the Triumph of Islam* (New York: Oxford University Press, 2000), p. 93.

13. Ibid., p. 94.

14. Holger Albrecht and Eva Wegner, "Autocrats and Islamists: Contenders and Containment in Egypt and Morocco," *Journal of North African Studies* 11 (June 2006), pp. 132–133.

15. Willis, "Morocco's Islamists and the Legislative Elections of 2002," p. 63.

16. Giovanni Sartori, "Political Development and Political Engineering," *Public Policy* 17, 1968, p. 273.

17. Malik Mufti, "Elite Bargains and the Onset of Political Liberalization in Jordan," *Comparative Political Studies* 32 (February 1999), p. 116.

18. "Ra'is kutla al-ikhwan al-parlamaniya fi al-urdun: musta'idun li tasallum al-sulta wa zaman al-tahmish wala" [Head of the Brotherhood parliamentary bloc in Jordan: We are ready to take power, the time of marginalization has passed], *Al-Hayat*, January 30, 2006.

19. Rana Sabbagh-Gargour, "Of Hawks and Doves." *Jordan Business Magazine*, http://www.jordan-business.net/magazine/index.php?option=com_content&task=view&id=246

20. Interview with author, Essam al-Erian, July 16, 2008.

21. As Gunes Tezcur notes: "Moderation at the behavioral level implies that risk-aversive strategies and electoral tactics are given priority over bold strategies and non-violent but contentious tactics such as grassroots mobilization and civic disobedience" (Tezcur, *Muslim Reformers in Iran and Turkey: The Paradox of Moderation*, Austin, TX: University of Texas Press, 2011, pp. 19–20).

22. *Freedom in the World 2001–2002: The Annual Survey of Political Rights and Civil Liberties*, eds. Adrian Karatnycky et al. (Washington, DC: Freedom House, 2002), p. 216.

23. Ibid.

24. "Egypt: Margins of Repression: State Limits on Nongovernmental Organization Activism," *Human Rights Watch*, July 2005, p. 6.

25. Law No. 84 of the Year 2002 on Non-Governmental Organizations, p. 9, http://www.icnl.org/research/library/files/Egypt/law84-2002-En.pdf

26. "Country Report—Egypt," Freedom House, 2005, see http://www.freedomhouse.org/modules/mod_call_dsp_country-fiw.cfm?year=2005&country=6730

27. See Khalil al-Anani, *al-Ikhwan al-Muslimun fi Misr: Shaikhoukha Tassaru' al-Zaman* [The Muslim Brotherhood in Egypt: Gerontocracy Fighting the Clock] (Cairo: Maktaba al-Shorouq al-Dawliya, 2007), pp. 222–223.

28. Ibid., p. 170.

29. Ibid.

30. "Egypt's Muslim Brothers: Confrontation or Integration?" International Crisis Group, June 18, 2008, p. 9.

31. *Mubadira al-Ikhwan al-Muslimin hawl Mabadi' al-Islah fi Misr* [The Initiative of the Muslim Brotherhood regarding Principles of Reform in Egypt], March 2004.

32. Interview with author, Khaled Hamza, October 4, 2009.

33. Ibid.

34. Each *shu'ba*, or branch, is made up of around five *usras*, or families.

35. Interview with author, Khaled Hamza, October 4, 2009.

36. *Al-Barnamaj al-Intikhabi li al-Ikhwan al-Muslimin fi al-Intakhabat al-Tashri'iya* [The Electoral Program of the Muslim Brotherhood in the Legislative Elections], Cairo, November 2005.

37. Zakat is one of the five pillars of Islam. Muslims are expected to contribute a portion of their wealth to charity, on an annual basis.

38. Salah Nasrawi, "Group Launches Campaign to Oust Mubarak," Associated Press, June 30, 2005.

39. Ibid.

40. Anani, *al-Ikhwan al-Muslimun fi Misr*, p. 238.

41. Mansour Moaddel, *Jordanian Exceptionalism: A Comparative Analysis of State-Religion Relationships in Egypt, Iran, Jordan, and Syria* (New York: Palgrave, 2002).

42. Interview with author, Nael Masalha, April 10, 2005.

43. Julia Choucair, "Illusive Reform: Jordan's Stubborn Stability," Carnegie Endowment, p. 9.

44. Michelle Burgis, "Judicial Reform and the Possibility of Democratic Rule in Jordan: A Policy Perspective on Judicial Independence," *Arab Law Quarterly* Vol. 21, No. 2 (2007), pp. 135–169.

45. *Na'am al-Islam howa al-Hal: Al-Barnamaj al-Intakhabi li Murashahi Hizb Jabha al-'Amal al-Islami, 1993–1997* [Yes, Islam is the Solution: The Electoral Program of the Islamic Action Front Candidates], Amman, October 1993, p. 1.

46. Ibid., p. 1.

47. *Na'am wa ila al-Abad al-Islam howa al-Hal: Al-Barnamaj al-Intakhabi li Murashi Hizb Jabha al-'Amal al-Islami, 2003–2007* [Yes and Forever, Islam is the Solution: The Electoral Program of the Islamic Action Front Candidates], Amman, October 2003, p. 5.

48. Ibid.

49. Ibid., pp. 6–8.

50. *Ru'iya al-Haraka al-Islamiya li al-Islah fi al-Urdun* [Vision of the Islamic Movement Toward Reform in Jordan], the Islamic Action Front and the Muslim Brotherhood, Amman, 2005, p. 17.

51. Ibid., p. 18.

52. Ibid., p. 20.

53. Ibid., p. 27.

54. Ibid., p. 27.

55. Ibid., p. 28.

56. Ibid., p. 33.

57. Ibid., p. 19.

58. Ibid., p. 33.

59. *Jordan Times*, January 18, 2005.

60. *Jordan Times*, March 2, 2005.

61. *Jordan Times*, March 7, 2005.

62. Speech, Amman, August 16, 2005.

63. "Country Report—Jordan," Freedom House, 2007.

64. *Jordan Times*, June 17, 2006.

65. *Jordan Times*, July 6, 2006.

66. Nathan J. Brown, "Jordan and Its Islamic Movement," Carnegie Endowment, November 2006, p. 20.

67. Stathis N. Kalyvas, "Commitment Problems in Emerging Democracy: The Case of Religious Parties" *Comparative Politics* 32 (2000), pp. 379–398.

68. Noah Feldman, *After Jihad: America and the Struggle for Islamic Democracy* (New York: Farrar, Straus and Giroux, 2003), p. 23.

69. Jason Brownlee, "Unrequited Moderation: Credible Commitments and State Repression in Egypt," *Studies in Comparative International Development* 45 (2010), p. 480.

70. Personal attendance, Cairo, February 9, 2011.

71. Nathan Brown makes a similar point, arguing that "the real assurance that Islamists can give regimes—and they generally do give far too easily for would-be democratizers—is to lose elections. That hardly seems like a promising start for a democratic transition" (Nathan J. Brown, *When Victory is Not An Option: Islamists Movements in Arab Politics*, Ithaca, NY: Cornell University Press, 2012, p. 213).

72. Maria J. Stephan and Erica Chenoweth, "Why Civil Resistance Works: The Strategic Logic of Nonviolent Conflict," *International Security* 33 (Summer 2008), p. 12.

73. I explore these arguments in more detail in Shadi Hamid, "Islamists and the Failure of Nonviolent Action," *Civilian Jihad: Popular Struggle, Democratization, and Governance in the Middle East*, edited by Maria J. Stephan (New York: Palgrave, 2009).

74. For more on the Arab "democratic deficit," see Larry Diamond, "Why Are There No Arab Democracies?" *Journal of Democracy* 21 (January 2010).

75. Amr Hamzawy and Michele Dunne, "Brotherhood Enters Elections in a Weakened State," Carnegie Endowment Guide to Egypt's Elections, http://egyptelections.carnegieendowment.org/2010/11/15/brotherhood-enters-elections-in-a-weakened-state

76. See Shadi Hamid, "Arab Elections: Free, Sort of Fair . . . and Meaningless," *Foreign Policy*, October 27, 2010, http://mideast.foreignpolicy.com/posts/2010/10/27/arab_elections_free_sort_of_fair_and_meaningless

Chapter 6

1. Interview with author, Abdel Rahman Ayyash, February 9, 2011.

2. For more on the Brotherhood's role in the 2011 uprising, see Carrie Rosefsky Wickham, *The Muslim Brotherhood: Evolution of an Islamist Movement* (Princeton, NJ: Princeton University Press, 2013), p. 166–9.

3. Abdel Moneim Abul Futouh, "Democracy Supporters Should Not Fear the Muslim Brotherhood," *Washington Post*, February 9, 2011.

4. "Competing Muslim Brotherhood Visions for Egypt," BBC, March 3, 2011.

5. Marwa Awad, "Egypt's Brotherhood Backs Vote on Constitution," Reuters, March 12, 2011.

6. "Egypt Brotherhood to Join Wider Election List," Agence France Presse, March 16, 2011.

7. "Muslim Brotherhood Won't Cap Ambitions Forever," Reuters, March 23, 2011.

8. Interview with author, Essam al-Erian, May 8, 2011.

9. "Rise of the Brothers: Interview with Essam al-Erian," *Cairo Review of Global Affairs*, February 21, 2013, http://www.aucegypt.edu/gapp/cairoreview/pages/articleDetails.aspx?aid=31

10. Matt Negrin and Reem Abdellatif, "US Ambassador to Egypt Won't Sit Down with Muslim Brotherhood . . . Yet," *Global Post*, October 18, 2011, http://www.globalpost.com/dispatches/globalpost-blogs/tahrir-square/us-ambassador-egypt-won%E2%80%99t-sit-down-muslim-brotherhoodyet

11. "13 Parties Unite to Form 'National Coalition for Egypt'," *Ahram Online*, June 15, 2011, http://english.ahram.org.eg/NewsContent/1/64/14330/Egypt/Politics-/-Parties-unite-to-form-National-Coalition-for-Egyp.aspx

12. Interview with author, Muslim Brotherhood official, August 9, 2010.

13. See p. 14 for more on the importance of the usra.

14. Mohamed ElBaradei, CNN interview, January 30, 2011, http://www.youtube.com/watch?feature=player_embedded&v=lSVjv3hz3cY

15. Dina Mustafa, "Al-taswit bi na'm wajib shara'i fi ra'iy al-jama'a al-salafiya bi al-menoufiya" [Voting 'yes' is a religious duty in the opinion of the Salafi group in Menoufiya], *al-Ahram*, March 19, 2011.

16. "MB Opinion on Last Week's Events," Ikhwanweb, July 21, 2011, http://www.ikhwanweb.com/article.php?id=28857

17. "Tahadiyat tuwaji' al-thawra" [Challenges facing the revolution], Ikhwanonline, July 27, 2011, http://www.ikhwanonline.com/Article.aspx?ArtID=88480&SecID=118

18. "Bayan min al-ikhwan hawl fa'aliyat al-juma'a 7/29/2011" [Brotherhood statement on the events of Friday 7/29/2011], Ikhwanonline, July 30, 2011, http://www.ikhwanonline.com/Article.aspx?ArtID=88621&SecID=212

19. "FJP endorses constitutional principles of freedom, human rights," Ikhwanweb, August 16, 2011, http://www.ikhwanweb.com/article.php?id=28942

20. "Bayan min al-ikhwan hawl ma sadar 'an al-'askar wa na'ib ra'is al-wuzara' bi isdar a'lan dusturi bi mawad hakima li al-dustur" [Brotherhood statement on the comments by SCAF and the deputy prime minister regarding the issuing of a constitutional declaration with supraconstitutional articles], Ikhwanonline, August 13, 2011, http://www.ikhwanonline.com/Article.aspx?ArtID=89395&SecID=212

21. Interview with author, Dina Zakaria, November 22, 2011.

22. Interview with author, Mohamed al-Beltagy, November 27, 2011.

23. Noha el-Hennawy, "Brotherhood contests over 50 percent of parliamentary seats," *Egypt Independent*, October 25, 2011, http://www.egyptindependent. com/news/brotherhood-contests-over-50-percent-parliamentary-seats

24. "MP causes uproar in Parliament by calling to prayer during session," *al-Masry al-Youm*, February 7, 2012, http://www.egyptindependent.com/ news/mp-causes-uproar-parliament-calling-prayer-during-session

25. Interviews with author, Brotherhood parliamentary candidates, Dumyat, November 23, 2011.

26. David D. Kirkpatrick, "Military Flexes its Muscles as Islamists Gain in Egypt," *New York Times*, December 7, 2011, http://www.nytimes.com/2011/12/08/ world/middleeast/egyptian-general-mukhtar-al-mulla-asserts-continuing-control-despite-elections.html

27. "Brotherhood inclined to nominate deputy guide for premiership," *al-Masry al-Youm*, January 10, 2012, http://www.egyptindependent.com/news/ brotherhood-inclined-nominate-deputy-guide-premiership

28. "Dr. el-Erian: No special status for constitution nor immunity for military," Ikhwanweb, January 3, 2012, http://www.ikhwanweb.com/article.php?id= 29506

29. "Bayan min al-ikhwan al-muslimin bi khusus ahdath majlis al-sha'b" [Muslim Brotherhood statement regarding the People's Assembly incidents of January 31, 2012], Ikhwanonline, February 1, 2012, http://www.ikhwanonline.com/ Article.aspx?ArtID=100478&SecID=212

30. Heba Afify, "Parliament review: A week of laws," *Egypt Independent*, May 11, 2012, http://www.egyptindependent.com/news/parliament-review-week-laws

31. Sarah Carr, "Parliament review: Scuffles and laws," *Egypt Independent*, June 8, 2012, http://www.egyptindependent.com/news/parliament-review-scuffles-and-laws

32. Interview with author, Essam al-Erian, May 8, 2011.

33. See David D. Kirkpatrick, "In Egyptian Hard-Liner's Surge, New Worries for the Muslim Brotherhood," *New York Times*, April 1, 2012, http://www. nytimes.com/2012/04/02/world/middleeast/attacking-the-west-islamist-gains-in-egypt-presidential-bid.html

34. Stephane Lacroix, "Sheikhs and Politicians: Inside the New Egyptian Salafism," Brookings Doha Center, June 2012, p. 7.

35. Interview with author, Muslim Brotherhood activist, May 20, 2012.

36. Relevant parts are translated in Shadi Hamid, "Egypt's Uncomfortable Challenge: Balancing Security and Civil Liberties," *The Atlantic*, August 20, 2013, http:// www.theatlantic.com/international/archive/2012/08/egypts-uncomfortable-challenge-balancing-security-and-civil-liberties/261260/

37. Hesham Sallam, "Morsy, the coup and the revolution: Reading between the red lines," *Jadaliyya*, August 15, 2012, http://www.jadaliyya.com/pages/ index/6870/morsy-the-coup-and-the-revolution_reading-between

38. Interview with author, Amr Darrag, November 28, 2012.

39. Interview with author, Muslim Brotherhood official, November 28, 2012.

40. The flip side of strong bonds of loyalty and friendship between Brotherhood members is the high social cost of leaving the organization. Ex-members sometimes find themselves shunned and ostracized. Since being a Brotherhood member is a way of life—with a strict educational curriculum, moral guidelines, as well as considerable religious and political commitments—opting to leave can be a difficult and disorienting process. For more on this, see Wickham, *The Muslim Brotherhood*, p. 184.

41. Interview with author, Mustafa Kamshish, May 22, 2012. Kamshish was a member of the Muslim Brotherhood's Shura Council in Giza governorate.

42. Interview with author, Abdel Moneim Abul Futouh, August 4, 2006.

43. Interview with author, Ali Abdel Fattah, August 8, 2006.

44. Gareth Jenkins, "Erbakan on a razor's edge," *Al-Ahram Weekly*, March 16–22, 2000, http://weekly.ahram.org.eg/2000/473/re5.htm

45. *Halal* and *haram* are religious terms meaning "permissible" and "forbidden." To "make halal what is haram" is considered a major transgression for observant Muslims since it suggests actively changing or undoing God's law. The rejoinder to Abu Faris's argument here is that the ministers of education, health, and justice do not need to directly execute "un-Islamic" laws, such as permitting alcohol consumption. Abu Faris's objection, however, becomes more relevant at the local level. The Brotherhood's Yasser Omari, who served as mayor of Zarqa in the 1990s, faced opposition from fellow Islamists who argued that he would have no choice but to grant liquor licenses and allow for interest on loans and deposits (see for example *Jordan Times*, May 16, 1990).

46. Omar al-Ashqar, an Islamist academic associated with the doves, authored a rebuttal of Abu Faris's arguments in his book *Hukm al-Musharika fi al-Wazara wa al-Majalis al-Niyabiya* [Rulings on Participation in the Executive Branch and Parliament] (Amman: Dar al-Nafa'is, 1992).

47. Abu Faris, *al-Musharika fi al-Wazara*, pp. 26–27.

48. Interview with author, Mustafa al-Naggar, July 21, 2008.

49. Interview with author, Sondos Asem, November 15, 2011.

50. Nathan Brown, "Just Because Mohamed Morsi is Paranoid Doesn't Mean he Doesn't Have Enemies," *New Republic*, December 3, 2012, http://www.newrepublic.com/blog/plank/110625/just-because-egypts-president-paranoid-doesnt-mean-he-doesnt-have-enemies#

51. David D. Kirkpatrick, "Judge Helped Egypt's Military to Cement Power," *New York Times*, July 3, 2012, http://www.nytimes.com/2012/07/04/world/middleeast/judge-helped-egypts-military-to-cement-power.html

52. David D. Kirkpatrick, "Egyptian Judge Speaks Against Islamist Victory Before Presidential Runoff," *New York Times*, June 7, 2012, http://www.nytimes.com/2012/06/08/world/middleeast/egyptian-judge-speaks-against-islamist-victory-before-presidential-runoff.html

53. Ibid.

54. "Official page of Member of Parliament Emad Gad," Facebook, July 17, 2012, https://www.facebook.com/emadgad2012/posts/269345346499754

Chapter 7

1. Stephane Lacroix, "Sheikhs and Politicians: Inside the New Egyptian Salafism," Brookings Doha Center, June 2012, p. 1.

2. Nathan Field and Ahmed Hammam, "Salafi Satellite Television in Egypt," *Arab Media & Society*, 8 (Spring 2009), http://www.arabmediasociety.com/?article=712

3. Ibid.

4. Hamdi Dabash and Hany ElWeziery, "Brotherhood leader: Media highlights mistakes to disparage group," *al-Masry al-Youm*, May 28, 2011, http://www.almasryalyoum.com/en/node/454611

5. Lacroix, "Sheikhs and Politicians," p. 4.

6. Ibid.

7. Joseph Chinyong Liow, *Piety and Politics: Islamism in Contemporary Malaysia* (New York: Oxford University Press, 2009), p. 222.

8. Ibid., p. 13.

9. Khalil al-Anani, *al-Ikhwan al-Muslimun fi Misr: Shaikhoukha Tassaru' al-Zaman* [The Muslim Brotherhood in Egypt: Gerontocracy Fighting the Clock] (Cairo: Maktaba al-Shorouq al-Dawliya, 2007), p. 93.

10. Pew Research Center, "The World's Muslims: Religion, Politics and Society," April 30, 2013, http://www.pewforum.org/files/2013/04/worlds-muslims-religion-politics-society-full-report.pdf

11. YouGov Siraj Survey Results: Egypt Poll, April 2011, http://today.yougov.co.uk/sites/today.yougov.co.uk/files/ygs-archives-yougovsiraj-egypt-200411.pdf

12. Abu Dhabi Gallup Center, "Egypt: From Tahrir to Transition," June 2011, p. 4.

13. Pew Global Attitudes Project, "Most Muslims Want Democracy, Personal Freedoms, and Islam in Political Life," July 10, 2012, p. 64, http://www.pewglobal.org/files/2012/07/Pew-Global-Attitudes-Project-Arab-Spring-Report-FINAL-Tuesday-July-10-2012.pdf

14. Dankwart A. Rustow, "Transitions to Democracy: Toward a Dynamic Model," *Comparative Politics* 2 (April 1970), p. 359.

15. "Al-Shater fi awal ijtima' lahu ba'd tarashuhihi li al-ri'asa li al-hay'a al-shara'iya: al-sharia kanat wa satudhal mashrou'i wa hadafi al-awal wa al-akhir" [Shater to the Islamic Legitimate Body in his first meeting as a candidate for the presidency: sharia has been and will remain my ultimate project and goal], Islamic Legitimate Body for Rights and Reform, April 4, 2012.

16. David D. Kirkpatrick, "In Egypt Race, Battle is Joined on Islam's Role," *New York Times*, April 23, 2012, http://www.nytimes.com/2012/04/24/world/middleeast/in-egypt-morsi-escalates-battle-over-islams-role.html

17. Ibid.

18. "Dr. Morsi: We Have a great deal of faith in the people," Ikhwanweb.com, April 20, 2012, http://www.ikhwanweb.com/article.php?id=29910

19. "Brotherhood and Salafis Exchange Rebukes Again," *Egypt Independent*, May 12, 2012, http://www.egyptindependent.com/news/brotherhood-and-salafis-exchange-rebukes-again

20. "Dr. Mahmoud Ghozlan yaktub: risala ila ikhwanina fi al-da'wa al-salafiya (1)" [Dr. Mahmoud Ghozlan writes: a message to our brothers in the Salafi Call], Ikhwanonline, May 6, 2012, http://www.ikhwanonline.com/Article.aspx?ArtID=107902&SecID=391

21. Ghada Mohamed al-Sherif, "Brotherhood draws on Salafi and al-Azhar preachers to support Morsy," *Egypt Independent*, May 16, 2012, http://www.egyptindependent.com/news/brotherhood-draws-salafi-and-al-azhar-preachers-support-morsy

22. Ibid.

23. Interview with author, Mustafa al-Naggar, July 21, 2008.

24. Interview with author, Essam al-Erian, May 8, 2011.

25. Interview with author, Abdel Moneim Abul Futouh, August 4, 2006.

26. Rachid Ghannouchi, *al-Hurayat al-'Amma fi al-Dawla al-Islamiya* [Public Liberties in the Islamic State] (Tunis: Dar al-Mujtahid, 2011), p. 190.

27. Ibid., p. 134.

28. Andrew March, "Genealogies of Sovereignty in Islamic Political Thought," working paper, p. 14.

29. Ibid., p. 16.

30. Ibrahim El-Houdaiby, "The Brotherhood in power: Governance kills the project," *Ahram Online*, October 31, 2012, http://english.ahram.org.eg/News/56842.aspx

31. Interview with author, Ibrahim El-Houdaiby, July 23, 2008.

32. According to a Brotherhood statement which sought to clarify Article 219: "What is meant by 'general evidence' is everything mentioned from the Quran and the authentic Sunna [prophetic example]. 'Foundational and jurisprudential rules' are those derived from general evidence upon which there is scholarly consensus and which realize the objectives of sharia. 'Credible sources' refers to the Quran, Sunna, consensus, and analogical deduction. With this article, the debate over the meaning of 'principles of sharia' has been resolved" ("Bayan min al-ikhwan al-muslimin hawl al-sharia al-islamiya wa huwiya al-umma" [Statement from the Muslim Brotherhood on Islamic sharia and the umma's identity], Ikhwanonline, October 31, 2012, http://www.ikhwanonline.com/Article.aspx?ArtID=127040&SecID=212).

33. Hasanayn Tawfiq Ibrahim and Hoda Raghib Awad, *al-Dawr al-Siyasi li Jama'a al-Ikhwan al-Muslimin fi Dhil al-Ta'adudiya al-Siyasiya al-Muqayada fi Misr* (Cairo: Markaz al-Mahrusa, 1996), p. 328.

34. Russell E. Lucas, *Institutions and the Politics of Survival in Jordan: Domestic Responses to External Challenges: 1988–2001* (Albany: State University of New York Press, 2005), p. 37.

35. *Jordan Times*, March 7, 1990.

36. March, "Genealogies of Sovereignty in Islamic Political Thought," p. 17.

37. Ibid.

38. Lenn Goodman, "The Road to Kazanistan," *American Philosophical Quarterly* 45 (April 2008), p. 85.

39. Ibid.

40. Azzam Tamimi, *Rachid Ghannouchi: A Democrat within Islamism* (New York: Oxford University Press, 2001), p. 26.

41. Interview with author, Salem Falahat, August 16, 2008.

42. Ghannouchi, *al-Hurayat al-'Amma*, p. 100.

43. Ibid., p. 110.

Chapter 8

1. Interview with author, Lobna Jribi, February 7, 2013.

2. For discussion of MTI's origins and rise, see Emad Shahin, *Political Ascent: Contemporary Islamic Movements in North Africa* (Boulder, CO: Westview Press, 1997) and Marion Boulby, "The Islamic Challenge: Tunisia since Independence," *Third World Quarterly* 10 (April 1988), pp. 590–614.

3. "Al-bayyan al-tassisi li haraka al-itigaa al-islami" [The Founding Declaration of the Movement of the Islamic Tendency] in Rachid Ghannouchi, *al-Hurayat al-'Amma fi al-Dawla al-Islamiya* (Tunis: Dar al-Mujtahid, 2011), p. 377.

4. "Interview transcript: Rachid Ghannouchi," *Financial Times*, January 18, 2011, http://www.ft.com/intl/cms/s/0/24d710a6-22ee-11e0-ad0b-00144feab49a. html#axzz2R0gD5th6

5. Doris H. Gray, "Tunisia after the Uprising: Islamist and Secular Quests for Women's Rights," *Mediterranean Politics* 17 (2012), p. 298.

6. Interview with author, Osama al-Saghir, February 15, 2013.

7. Pew Research Center, "The World's Muslims: Religion, Politics and Society," April 30, 2013, http://www.pewforum.org/files/2013/04/worlds-muslims-religion-politics-society-full-report.pdf

8. Tamimi, *Rachid Ghannouchi*, p. 11.

9. Ibid.

10. See Nathan Field and Ahmed Hammam, "Salafi Satellite Television in Egypt," *Arab Media & Society*, 8 (Spring 2009), http://www.arabmediasociety. com/?article=712

11. Rory McCarthy, *The Return of Ennahda: The Paradox of an Islamist Election Victory in Secular Tunisia*, unpublished MPhil thesis, University of Oxford, 2012, p. 58.

12. Ibid.

13. Interview with author, Noureddin Bhiri, February 5, 2013.

14. Nissaf Slama, "'Irhal' Campaign Attempts to Oust Ennahda Officials," *Tunisia Live*, August 14, 2013, http://www.tunisia-live.net/2013/08/14/erhal-campaign-attempts-to-oust-enahdha-officials/

15. "Mokhtar Chaouachi Appointed Tunisia's New Ambassador to U.S.," *Tunisia Live*, January 26, 2013, http://www.tunisia-live.net/2013/01/26/mokhtar-chaouachi-appointed-tunisias-new-ambassador-to-the-u-s/#sthash.ntznbRqI.dpuf

16. Jonathan Mitchell, "Tunisia's Islamists hail arrival of the 'sixth caliphate'," *The Telegraph*, November 16, 2011, http://www.telegraph.co.uk/news/worldnews/africaandindianocean/tunisia/8894858/Tunisias-Islamists-hail-arrival-of-the-sixth-caliphate.html

17. "Tunis: fadiha wazir al-kharijiya Rafiq Abd al-Salam tatafaʻal wa al-Ghannouchi yadʻou li al-jald marwaji al-ishaʻat wa riʼasa al-hukuma tatadaman did hamla al-tashwiʼ" [Tunis: the 'scandal' of Foreign Minister Rafiq Abdessalem plays out; Ghannouchi calls for the flogging of rumor-mongers; the head of government stands firm against the smear campaign], *al-Quds al-Arabi*, December 30, 2012, http://www.alqudsalarabi.info/index.asp?fname=today/30qpt963.htm&arc=data/2012/12/12-30/30qpt963.htm

18. Jeffry A. Frieden's distinction between *preferences* and observable *outcomes* is also useful here. Frieden writes that "in any given setting, an actor *prefers* some outcomes to others and pursues a *strategy* to achieve its most preferred possible outcome" and that "the actor's preferences lead to its behavior but in ways that are contingent on the environment" (Frieden, "Actors and Preferences in International Relations," in *Strategic Choice and International Relations*, eds. David A. Lake and Robert Powell, Princeton: Princeton University Press, 1999).

19. Interview with author, Habib Ellouze, February 14, 2003.

20. See http://francais.islammessage.com/Article.aspx?i=1578

21. Interview with author, Mohamed Khouja, January 31, 2013.

22. Interview with author, Abdelfattah Morou, January 30, 2013.

23. As Doris Gray points out, "More radical liberals such as Sonja Hajri, also a history professor, insisted that discussions about a new constitution should include the possibility of removing the stipulation that Islam is the religion of the state thus making Tunisia a genuine secular state that guarantees religious freedom to all its citizens" (Doris H. Gray, "Tunisia after the Uprising: Islamist and Secular Quests for Women's Rights," *Mediterranean Politics* 17 (2012): 290).

24. Interview with author, Zied Ladhari, February 12, 2013.

25. For more on the "spoiler" problem, see Omar Ashour, "Egypt's 'Spoilers' Threaten Democracy," *Al-Monitor*, February 25, 2013, http://www.al-monitor.com/pulse/originals/2013/02/egypt-street-violence-opposition-muslim-brotherhood-salafist.html

26. Interview with author, senior FJP official, April 4, 2013.

27. Interview with author, Abdelfattah Morou, January 30, 2013.

28. Monica Marks and Omar Belhaj Salah, "Uniting for Tunisia?" *Sada*, March 28, 2013, http://carnegieendowment.org/sada/2013/03/28/uniting-for-tunisia/fu3g

29. Interview with author, Salafi preacher, February 2, 2013.

Chapter 9

1. Seymour Martin Lipset and Stein Rokkan, *Party Systems and Voter Alignments: Cross-National Perspectives* (London: The Free Press, 1967).

2. Carles Boix, "The Emergence of Parties and Party Systems," in *The Oxford Handbook of Comparative Politics*, eds. Carles Boix and Susan C. Stokes (Oxford: Oxford University Press, 2006), pp. 502–3.

3. Adam Przeworski and John Sprague, *Paper Stones: A History of Electoral Socialism* (Chicago, IL: University of Chicago Press, 1986), pp. 10–11.

4. Interview with author, Shadi Taha, November 20, 2011.

5. Francesco Cavatorta, "The Success of 'Renaissance' in Tunisia and the Complexity of Tunisian Islamism," Paper prepared for the International Political Science Association Conference, July 2012, p. 19.

6. "Kuwalis Liqa' Jabha al-Inqadh bi Shiyoukh al-Salafiya" [Scenes of the meeting between the Salvation Front and Salafi sheikhs], Islamion.com, http://www.islamion.com/post.php?post=4065&buffer_share=7240b&utm_source=buffer

7. Bennett and Nordstrom, for example, find that states are more likely to initiate conflicts with their neighbors during periods of low economic growth and less likely to do so in periods of high growth. (Scott Bennett and Timothy Nordstrom, "Foreign Policy Substitutability and Internal Economic Problems in Enduring Rivalries," *Journal of Conflict Resolution* 44, no. 1 February 2000, pp. 33–61).

8. Edward D. Mansfield and Jack Snyder, Electing to Fight: Why Emerging Democracies go to War (Cambridge, MA: The MIT Press, 2007), Kindle edition.

9. Ibid.

10. Robert A. Dahl, *Polyarchy: Participation and Opposition* (New Haven: Yale University Press, 1972), p. 36.

11. For full transcript of Clinton's interview, see "Clinton tackles Tunisia, Iran, Lebanon & Mideast Talks," *al-Arabiya*, January 12, 2011.

12. Hillary Clinton, "Keynote Address at the National Democratic Institute's 2011 Democracy Awards Dinner" Washington, DC November 7, 2011. http://www.state.gov/secretary/rm/2011/11/176750.htm

13. Steven Levitsky and Lucan A. Way, *Competitive Authoritarianism: Hybrid Regimes After the Cold War* (Cambridge University Press, 2010), p. 24.

14. John Kerry, "Interview with Hamid Mir of Geo TV," August 1, 2013, http://m.state.gov/md212626.htm

15. Nina Hachigian and David Shorr, "The Responsibility Doctrine," *The Washington Quarterly*, Winter 2013, p. 73, http://csis.org/files/publication/TWQ_13Winter_HachigianShorr.pdf.

16. Robert F. Worth, "Egypt is Arena for Influence of Arab Rivals," *New York Times*, July 9, 2013, http://www.nytimes.com/2013/07/10/world/middleeast/aid-to-egypt-from-saudis-and-emiratis-is-part-of-struggle-with-qatar-for-influence.html?pagewanted=all; "Turkey to Give Egypt Rest of $2bln Loan

Within 2 Months—Sources," Reuters, April 17, 2013, http://www.reuters.com/article/2013/04/17/egypt-turkey-loan-idUSL5N0D41QX20130417.

17. Interview with author, Mohamed Morsi, May 8, 2011.

18. "Morsi Removed Arab Peace Plan from UN Speech," *Jerusalem Post*, November 1, 2012, http://www.jpost.com/Middle-East/Morsi-removed-Arab-peace-plan-from-UN-speech

19. Pew Global Attitudes Project, "Islamic Extremism: Common Concern for Muslim and Western Publics," July 14, 2005, http://www.pewglobal.org/2005/07/14/i-how-muslims-and-westerners-see-each-other/

20. Interview with author, Mahdi Akef, August 10, 2006.

21. "*Masr tarfud maw'idhat al-shaytan al-Amreeki* [Egypt refuses advice of the American Satan]," *al-Akhbar*, August 8, 2013, see https://twitter.com/shadihamid/status/365875460602736642

22. One example of positive conditionality is our proposed "Multilateral Endowment for Reform" for the Middle East. See Shadi Hamid and Peter Mandaville, "Bringing the United States Back into the Middle East," *The Washington Quarterly*, Fall 2013. For a discussion of what positive conditionality might look like in the case of post-coup Egypt, see Shadi Hamid and Peter Mandaville, "A Coup Too Far: The Case for Re-ordering U.S. Priorities in Egypt," Brookings Doha Center, September 2013.

23. Interviews with author, Muslim Brotherhood and FJP officials, April 2013.

24. Interview with author, Muslim Brotherhood official, April 3, 2013.

25. For more on the circumstances surrounding the events of December 5, see Evan Hill, "'This is Just the Beginning': A Bloody Night with Egypt's Protesters," *The Atlantic*, December 7, 2012.

26. Interview with author, Amr Darrag, April 5, 2013.

27. Interview with author, senior advisor to President Morsi, April 8, 2013.

28. Interview with author, senior Muslim Brotherhood official, April 6, 2013.

29. Interview with author, Shadi Taha, November 20, 2011.

INDEX

255